Cultural Compass

Ethnographic Explorations of Asian America

In the series

Asian American History and Culture,

edited by Sucheng Chan, David Palumbo-Liu, and Michael Omi

Cultural Compass

Ethnographic Explorations of Asian America

EDITED BY

Martin F. Manalansan IV

TEMPLE UNIVERSITY PRESS

PHILADELPHIA

Temple University Press, Philadelphia 19122

⊛The paper used in this publication meets the requirements of the American National Standard for Information Sciences—Permanence of Paper for Printed Library Materials, ANSI Z39.48–1984

Library of Congress Cataloging-in-Publication Data

Cultural compass : ethnographic explorations of Asian America / edited by Martin F. Manalansan IV.
    p. cm.—(Asian American history and culture)
   Includes bibliographical references.
   ISBN 1-56639-772-3 (cloth : alk. paper)—ISBN 1-56639-773-1 (pbk. : alk. paper)
   1. Asian Americans—Ethnic identity. 2. Ethnology—United States—Methodology. 3. Ethnology—Philosophy. I. Manalansan, Martin F., 1960- .
  II. Series.

E184.O6 M25 2000
305.895073—dc21

           99-087506

To my parents,

Martin R. Manalansan, Jr.

and

Francisca Fajardo Manalansan

Contents

Part III: Beyond Asian America and Back

Acknowledgments

Editing an anthology, as many people have told me, is a thankless job. Many contend that it is held in low esteem by people in tenure committees and by many scholarly institutions. However, the work I have done on this collection enabled me to renew my excitement about ethnographic fieldwork in a manner I have not felt since I was a tyro ethnographer trying out my first interview with an informant. It has also allowed me to witness and be the beneficiary of the great generosity of many people. Editing an anthology may be an unforgiving project, but it is not without its gifts and benefits.

I acknowledge my debt to the anthropology faculties at the University of the Philippines, Syracuse University, and the University of Rochester who provided me the professional training to help me to think more critically about the ethnographic project. Special thanks go to my mentors—Ponciano Bennagen, Susan Wadley, and Tom Gibson.

My former colleagues in Asian American service organizations such as APICHA (the Asian and Pacific Islander Coalition on HIV/AIDS, Inc.) have been responsible for keeping me from being complacent in merely deploying au courant theory, instilling a sober approach to fieldwork, and directing me to various immediate and pressing realities.

Asian American Studies was the perfect combination of the "field" and the "home." The comradeship of Lisa Lowe, Yen Espiritu, Karen Su, Oscar Campomanes, Jack Tchen, Gary Okihiro, Peter Kwong, and many others were especially vital in helping me navigate the interdisciplinary borders of the terrain. I wish to recognize the support of the Asian American Studies staff at both Hunter College and New York University, especially Lily Ng and Lisa Morimoto.

My friends and family have weathered the trials of my protracted academic career. Deb Amory, Rick Bonus, the "gang of four" in Manila, and numerous others scattered around the world (talk about transnational filiation) have remained faithful comrades. My parents are, to my mind, the quintessential figures if not embodiments of "home"—to them I owe everything.

Acknowledgments

Cultural Compass

Ethnographic Explorations of Asian America

Martin F. Manalansan IV

Introduction

The Ethnography of Asian America:
Notes toward a Thick Description

The title "Cultural Compass" is indicative of the cartographic impulse in ethnography. Ethnography can be likened to a cartographic project, mapping out and opening up spaces, relationships, and meanings for possible interventions and resistance. Among these spaces are that of Asian America and the cultures of Asian Americans.[1]

The emerging presence of Asian Americans in the U.S. imaginary has precipitated a windfall of critical inquiries into centuries of invisibility, exclusion, and erasure (Lowe 1996). This collection aims to confront the challenges of these historical and social vicissitudes through essays that nuance and trace the various trajectories of Asian American cultural journeys in the late twentieth century.

This project is situated at a time when specters of U.S. imperial exploits in Asia haunt popular discourses and the American public is witnessing the increasing participation of Asian Americans in national politics. Alongside these developments, Asian Americans are increasingly implicated in contemporary Orientalist rhetoric especially resonant in the recent debacle about their alleged role in the intrusion of "foreign interests" in Democratic Party fund raising. In the middle of a surge of anti-immigrant sentiment in the 1990s, Asian Americans are rendered in the media and political arenas as spies and illegal "aliens."[2] Therefore, this collection is part of an emerging body of interventionist works that seizes the opportunity of this historical moment by reading and configuring intersections of race, gender, class, and sexuality within constructions of an Asian America against the grain of the American nation and a globalizing world (Palumbo-Liu 1999). The notion of Asian America is not an already-made static reality. In fact, the ethnographic essays contained within this collection attempt to build, question, and contest the idea of Asian America as a space as well as a moment within the (trans)national imaginary. The essays point to various directions, paths, and journeys to and beyond Asian America in its various constructions and temporalities.

Why Ethnography?

Ethnography has not always enjoyed a privileged place in the study of Asian American communities. In the early 1990s, after I presented a lecture on my ethnographic project to an Asian American Studies audience in a major West Coast university, one student asked me, "What does ethnography have to do with the [Asian American] community?"

This seemingly innocent inquiry brings to light the gap in the Asian American Studies scholars' knowledge about the use and possible contributions of ethnography in the study of Asian American communities. This gap is in part due to the popular and prevalent modes of intellectual inquiries in the field of Asian American Studies. Scholarly productions about Asian American contexts have primarily concentrated on literary and popular media textual analyses in the humanities, and on historical/archival analyses and demographic and community surveys in the social sciences. Asian American ethnography, however, has remained largely unacknowledged in Asian American Studies despite some very impressive works (e.g., Wong 1982; Almirol 1985; Yanagisako 1985).

While literary, quantitative, and historical analyses enable sweeping views of social life, they are unable to go beyond an abstract and distant vantage point. Even the so-called "new" cultural studies that valorizes a kind of intricate hermeneutics of television shows, film, and other spectacular cultural expressions fails in many instances to privilege the "lived experiences" of "common" people and instead centers the voices of artistic producers and scholars. The aforementioned gap in and anxiety over ethnography in Asian American scholarship are in large part due to the contentious nature and turbulent history of the ethnographic enterprise in recent years.

Ethnography, as Clifford Geertz (1973) once said, allows readers a sense of "being there." Such a statement is predicated on the classical fixed points of the Western cultural compass of the world that mark "over here" as the West and "over there" as the field and/or the non-West. In recent years, views such as this have subjected ethnography to the most rabid and persistent criticisms, particularly from postmodernist camps. The postmodernist turn in ethnography, marked by several works but most notably by the book *Writing Culture* (Clifford and Marcus 1986), was a major turning point in refiguring the landscape of ethnographic method and text.

Postmodernism was shaped by and developed within the historical events that constituted the breaking down of Western empires and the reconfiguration of colonial worlds. As part of the decolonizing process in the Third World, ethnography was singled out to be a pivotal node of colonial rule. This trenchant criticism triggered a series of repercussions in relation to other aspects of ethnography. Among these resultant reactions is the critique of the modernist impulse toward universal rationality within traditional ethnography—that is, the creation and figuration of monolithic, homogeneous, self-contained societies. Ethnography has long been held to be a method for searching and analyzing encompassing patterns, symmetry, and logical social order. Traditional ethnographic texts have been narrated by an omniscient all-knowing author, who then systematically revealed the "reality" of the people in question (see Manganaro 1990). Arguing for the centrality of partial, ambiguous, and particular dimensions, contemporary theorists have suggested possible ways of reconfiguring ethnography and pointed to the "messy nature of fieldwork and the text" (Marcus 1998, 182). One of these ways include the critical use of the authorial voice. Instead of a God-like omniscience, the postmodernist call was for a polyphonic or coming together of divergent voices including that of the "native."

Postmodernist temper transformed the ethnographic enterprise by breaking the unproblematic link between "representation" and "reality" in traditional texts. In the critical moment that Marcus and Fischer (1986) called the "crisis of representation" in the ethnographic enterprise, problems of ethnographic authorship and authority, reception and interpretation increasingly gained much-needed scrutiny. George Marcus (1998, 186) suggests that postmodern effects on the rethinking of ethnography include the notion that ethnography "never fully assimilates difference"—that is, ethnographic objects and subjects of inquiry cannot be fully consumed or pinned down by "cracking" some cultural code or "better translation." This is related to the fact, Marcus continues, that there can be "no possibility of a fixed, final or monologically authoritative meaning." No longer the embodiment if not a faithful record of the observed reality, the ideal goals of postmodernist ethnographic projects[3] center the power of nuance and textual experimentation, and of partial and particular knowledge.

The postmodern trajectory in ethnography has also been induced by global changes in the economic, cultural, and political realms. Arjun Appadurai (1992) proposes that in a world where natives have relocated and settled in other places, usually in the metropolitan centers, the tasks of ethnographers, the mission of ethnography, and the very nature of "natives" themselves are no longer "incarcerated" to specific spatial and temporal dimensions. Immigrants, tourists, international entrepreneurs, and many other mobile people have forever changed the notion of "locality" and the "ethnographic site." Ethnography in the late twentieth century "remakes" the observer and the observed (Marcus 1992, 309–30) in ways that create new directions and new points of departure for discussion, understanding, and possible solution of social issues.

In many instances, the "researchers" are themselves "natives" or members of the community in which they are conducting research. This situation complicates relationships in the field and transforms the ethnographic enterprise. Ethnographers are no longer the distant omniscient strangers that they have traditionally been constructed to be. They have acquired a new role in viewing and representing communities and peoples. Subjects of ethnographies are no longer the ignorant natives who passively accept intrusion but are continuously asking "Why?" and "What for?" These subjects are now apprehended as producers as well as products of history, and shapers and builders of culture.

The essays in this volume rearticulate what Kamala Visweswaran (1994, 101–2) has perceptively pointed out: the coming together of the "field" and "home" through ethnographic "homework." Visweswaran constructs the notion of "homework" as opposed to "fieldwork" in an attempt to decolonize anthropology and to dislodge the hegemony of the "white West and the study of it as a field site" (Lavie and Swedenburg 1996, 20). Gupta and Ferguson (1997), echoing Visweswaran, suggest the collapsing of the field-home binary by considering the fact that in many new ethnographic situations, the notion of home as the site of similarity and affinity and the field as the site of estrangement and displacement have become untenable. "Homework," therefore, as the essays in this volume suggest, destabilizes the notions of "home" and field," "West" and "East," "other" and "self." As such, ethnographic "homework" among other things defamiliarizes home and its comfortable bounded area. Instead, this kind of ethnography documents what Lavie and Swedenburg (1996, 17) call "third time-spaces" that "refuse closure and are fluid, constantly shifting practices that create fault lines in both institutions and counterinstitutions." Such spaces are part of the global and transnational circulation of people, ideas, and images that increasingly confound easy demarcations of time and space.

Recent theoretical writings on ethnography suggest that identities and positions of researcher and subject are increasingly linked in complicated ways. Feminist anthropologists such as Abu Lughod (1991), Narayan (1992), and Visweswaran (1994) argue for the kinds of shifting conjunctures of identities or positionalities by so-called "halfies" or subjects who because of migration, overseas education, or parentage create "multiplex identities" that necessarily trouble if not remake traditional notions of the field and fieldwork. Furthermore, the postmodern influence in ethnography has been subjected to trenchant critiques by feminists, minority discourse theorists (including ethnic studies scholars), and Third World scholars, particularly around the ethical dangers of meaning deferral and play. Visweswaran (1994, 140) cautions that in attempting to establish a critical ethnography, or what she termed "identifying ethnography," the shifts and flux of identities are not mere products of "postmodern play" or aesthetic abandon but rather are products of power arrangements and processes. In others words, the positions the ethnographer/subject assumes are not always by choice and that positioning and maintaining oneself in opposition to the dominant "order of things" are vital to the reshaping and rethinking of the radical and critical potential of ethnography.

Gupta and Ferguson (1997) further suggest that the changing contours of the "field" also imply the necessary changes in the closely intertwined processes of "fieldwork" and globalization. The field is increasingly focused on not only the implications of "local" occurrences to various communities in the "area" but also on the continuous and discontinuous threads between the "local" and the "transnational." This is especially true in the case of Asian American communities. Immigrant and second- and third-generation Asian Americans have strengthened their ties with various homelands through modern communication and transportation technologies. These ties are made possible through circuits of contacts and exchanges with other countries of settlement. For example, Indian immigrants' networks in New York City imply not only relationships with people in India, but also with other Indian immigrant communities in Britain, South Africa, and other countries that form part of the Indian diaspora.

The emergence of these transnational realities has prompted George Marcus (1998) to suggest an innovative ethnographic form in the late twentieth century—that of multisited or multilocale ethnography. Multisited ethnography is part of social scientists' efforts to engage and critically connect specific localities with globalizing forces and structures through a sustained analysis of several field sites as points in a transnational cultural circuit of a particular group or groups of people. As Marcus (1998, 52) states:

> The idea [of a multisite/multilocale ethnography] is that any cultural identity or activity is constructed by multiple agents in varying contexts, or places, and that ethnography must be strategically conceived to represent this sort of multiplicity, and to specify intended and unintended consequences in the network of complex connections within a system of places.

At first glance, multisited ethnography appears to open up possibilities for the design, execution, writing, and understanding of Asian American communities. However, I submit that the ethnography of Asian America is always and already a multisited process. By multisited, I move beyond Marcus's conception[4] that centralizes multiple places or locales to a valorization of the conjunction of spaces within one specific physical location such as Chinatown (which I discuss below). The bifocal outlook involved in diasporic contexts and the forms of mobility of marginalized peoples, communities, and technologies necessitate this kind of ethnographic perspective. Furthermore, despite the insistence of the new ethnographic projects on a simplistic notion of "movement" as the fuel of multisitedness, I argue that especially among Asian Americans and other marginalized people, mobility is not always about trekking from one place to another in the classic "immigration" form of travel. Rather, movement for many of these people involves the careful and sometimes fearful navigation of various locations ascribed and prescribed by hegemonic forces. The mobility of oppressed peoples (including immigrants and migrant laborers of color, political refugees, and sexual marginals) needs to be paired with the dynamic of "immobility" or "nonmovement."[5] Even for those people who have physically traversed geographic borders, the reality of "nonmovement" is a glaring one when, due to skin color or the lack of legal identity papers or language and work skills, there are specific moments of immobility that must be examined.

Borderlands, as Anzaldúa (1987) has rightly argued, are not always about physical places but also about psychological, cultural, and other forms of boundaries and exclusions. It is imperative to view not only the crossings that occur in these spaces but those that are curtailed, hampered, or even marooned, and how people navigate their abject status not only *across* but also *within* such spaces. Travel, mobility, and the romance of multiple physical locales may be enticing and yet, in the final analysis, they render an incomplete and inadequate portrait of people in the margins.

The Ethnographic Refiguration of Chinatown

To amplify and illustrate my contentions about Asian American ethnography, let us take the space of Chinatown. Chinatown has always been the quintessential site of Asian otherness in the American national imaginary. It is perhaps the paradigmatic example and illustrative case for my earlier contentions about Asian American ethnography. For many Americans, this sequestered and bounded place is seen as the supreme example of how the traditional ethnographic notion of the field is realized within a "Western" setting. In American popular media and in fictional works, Chinatown has been constructed from the bricks of a colonizing gaze—that is, built from a point of view that roots non-American images of yellow faces, calligraphy, pagodas, and other artifacts of alterity within a circumscribed area. In many cases, this area is represented as an hermetically sealed social unit, known only to a few unscrupulous men or a space. Chinatown is a hidden space one stumbles into like a secret staircase or another temporal dimension. Jan Lin (1998, 1) astutely and elegantly noted that Chinatown "traditionally occupied a chimerical position in the American popular imagination . . . [at once being seen as] an extreme archetype of the clannish closed society . . . an Orientalist patina of mystery and danger . . . [a] provincial, overpopulated foreign colony . . . an exotic foreign enclave, [and] a dense rookery of restaurants and street emporiums tucked within the vestigial tenement recesses of the modern metropolis."

Ethnographic studies slowly but surely debunked this myth (e.g., Wong 1982; Zhou 1992). Aiming against the notion of the "closed society," these early ethnographies painted a way of life in these areas that showcased the economic and cultural struggles of a community beset by a history of exclusion from the American mainstream. From the enclave notion of Chinatown, new emerging works have started to consider the ways in which the new post-1965 Chinese immigrants (including Taiwanese and diasporic Chinese from the Caribbean, Asia, and Latin America) have changed the face of Chinatown and the notion of Asian American communities as well. Recent works such as Chen (1992) and Lin (1998) break down the traditional construction of the Chinatown "enclave" as a monolithic self-perpetuating social entity and, in its place, posit and create incisive portraits of new global and local links between capital and cultural institutions.

Organization of the Book: Critical Themes

Asian American ethnography is not only influenced by raging methodological and theoretical debates in the social sciences but, more importantly, to the shifts and changes in Asian American immigration history. After 1965, with the changes and reforms promulgated in U.S. immigration laws, Asian American populations became more variegated in terms of gender (increasing number of female immigrants), occupation (the influx of professionals including doctors, nurses, computer programmers, and scholars), ethnicity (influx of non-East Asians including South Asians, Filipinos, and Southeast Asians), and class (immigrants with significant and powerful material and cultural capital). Recent ethnographic works on Asian American communities reflect these pivotal shifts in the post-1965 Asian American landscape (e.g., Park 1997; Kibria 1994; Lessinger 1997). The essays in this collection are reflective of these historical, demographic, and sociocultural transformations of various Asian American communities.

The book is characterized by a kind of listless itinerancy due in part to the textual form of the essay. The ethnographic essay, as Kamala Visweswaran (1994, 11) notes, provides "an opportunity for sustained analysis that does not attempt the totalizing narrative gestures of the monograph." Therefore, the book's beginning and ending do not constitute a simple linear progression. The essays, while grouped together in three parts, also engage each other on common issues that defy simple categorization. The common issues or spaces that are explored include the constructions and displacements of self, community, and home. Each part maintains some kind of thematic coherence while also evoking—if not provoking—debates and dialogue among the various other essays in the two other parts.

Part One introduces dynamics of the ethnographic project in Asian American communities and its concomitant problematics. Although all the essays in this collection include some kind of reflection on methodology, the essays in this part devote a considerable and consistent engagement with the issues of "observing" and "writing" Asian American cultures. Although the essays are not explicit rhetorical recipes on how to "write cultures," they are, in the first instance, a kind of critical rewriting or reconstitution of the ways Asian American Studies scholars perceive, conceptualize, and engage issues, problems, and practices. While most recent theoretically-inclined scholarship is often not grounded in specific social milieu, the essays' theoretical exercises are embedded in and constitutive of ethnographic limning—the dialectics between ethnographer (the observer) and subject (the observed).

The essays by Andrea Louie, Linda Trinh Võ, and Miliann Kang explore the methodological and theoretical implications of shifting identities—or, more appropriately, conjunctural identities of ethnographers and informants. All three essays, while explicitly reflexive in terms of methodological, practical, and ethical concerns, are also meditations on the exigencies of home and self. Central to this meditation is the description and analysis of the ethnographer as subject. In various ways Louie, Võ, and Kang pose these queries: What are the advantages and the parallel downside of being a co-ethnic or a native ethnographer doing work "among one's own?" What are the ethical dilemmas of this kind of ethnographic work? Who speaks for whom? How does one negotiate personal and political agendas—activism and academic concerns? As Linda Trinh Võ poignantly states in the first essay, for minority/native ethnographers the field is a space one never leaves behind. Evoking Visweswaran's notion of "homework," the three essays in Part One render the field as a site of identification and disidentification, of belonging and rejection. Here the shifting and changing boundaries of self and community become paramount, glaring realities.

As a second generation Korean American woman conducting fieldwork among female workers in Korean nail salons in New York City, Miliann Kang faces not only the advantage of being a co-ethnic where her heritage opens some doors, she also encounters ethical challenges for being "one of them." Her field is rendered as a fruitful yet volatile space where situations of identification and disidentification exist side by side. She examines the kinds of moral situations that arise when the women approach her for help in addressing their needs in scenarios ranging from a daughter's school problems to accessing immigration legal services. These situations uncover the possibilities and limits of this kind of research project.

Linda Trinh Võ's field experiences portray the shifts and transformations her identity undergoes when she studies several community organizations of varying Asian American ethnicities including panethnic ones. Võ analyzes situations of panethnic or intra-ethnic identification that lead to particular coalitional possibilities and, conversely, forms of exclusion. She complicates and goes beyond the simplistic outsider/insider dichotomy by demonstrating the complexities of negotiating racial versus ethnic categories.

Andrea Louie attempts to make sense of the temporal and spatial boundaries that mark her off as being both Chinese and yet a particular sort of Chinese in her exploration of her "home" province in mainland China. As a second generation "overseas" Chinese American, Louie's multisited exploration of "Chineseness" allows her to critique the idea of the boundedness of Chinese identity in time and space as well as to nuance questions of "authenticity" and "authority."

As these three essays suggest, for native ethnographers there are no clear lines or ready formulas to follow, but as Kang (this volume) cogently observes, co-ethnic or native ethnographic research "provides a flexibility and openness as well as [gestures] to new ways of enriching both empirical and theoretical undertaking." In many of the succeeding essays, this assertion becomes quite evident.

Part Two, the largest section, involves essays that locate diverse kinds of ethnic, class, racial, gender and/or sexual identity articulation, and community building. In this section, social institutions from nonprofit agencies to newspaper offices to the home as well as racialized subjects such as women workers, homosexuals, and clinic patients are intensely scrutinized from rigorous yet sensitive vantage points. Here, the notion of site inevitably connotes traversing several geographic, cultural, and economic and/or political spaces.

Ethnography is well positioned in this important juncture of Asia and America more so because of the fact that recent debates concerning ethnography mirror the same issues around scholarship in regard to Asian Americans. These same issues provide the fulcrum for propelling a critical discussion of "community." In many college courses and texts on Asian American issues, "community" occupies a central and yet largely uninterrogated space.[6] Critical discussions about ethnographic representation and textualization have questioned the classic construction of community as a solid, homogeneous, and consensual group within one specific locale or place. All the essays in this collection reclaim an idea of a contested community, intensely engaged with power dynamics both local and global. Power is confronted through the prisms of gender, class, gender, sexuality, ethnicity, and most importantly race. Following Burawoy's (1991, 271–90) extended case method, these prisms are held against and critically linked to larger structures of power on the national and transnational levels.

"Politics" as the struggle for power in its broadest term is the theme for Rick Bonus's and Gina Masequesmay's essays. Rick Bonus's essay focuses on the vibrant and hybrid negotiated practices of Filipino American intra-ethnic political traditions. Seemingly inchoate and full of contradictions, Bonus uncovers the cultural logic behind Filipino American political practices such as beauty pageants and the impact of that logic on the group's sense of national belonging and community cohesion. Political agency as demonstrated through organized activism in AIDS services provides the grist for Gina Masequesmay's study of a community organization dedicated to providing AIDS services to Asian American communities. Masequesmay utilizes observations about mundane, everyday situations as a means to understanding disputed ideas about sexuality, illness, gender, and race in the politics of AIDS work. Moreover, Masequesmay links "everyday identity work" in the organization as a "racial project" and suggests that these situations in the organization reify race as inextricable from larger national struggles with an unequal racial hierarchy.

Gender, as it articulates with race and ethnicity, is the central vantage for the essays of Aihwa Ong and Kyeyoung Park. However, their essays do not merely deploy gender as the sole means for analysis but rather show the intricate and complex interconnections with other identities, practices, and institutions.

Aihwa Ong's fieldwork with Cambodian women analyzes various material and ideological struggles in the medico-cultural field when these women attempt to access Western medical services in the San Francisco Bay Area. Cambodian women resist the disciplining gaze of Western medical systems and personnel through varied practices. Ong suggests that these women's engagements and negotiations with the medical establishment are part of a larger struggle for cultural citizenship in America, an attempt to forge a sense of belonging in the national context.

Kyeyoung Park's essay, on the other hand, examines the transformation of marriage ideology and practices among Korean American immigrants. As gender roles change particularly around women's work, the strictures of marriage as an institution begin to unravel especially for Korean Americans. However, the essay refuses a traditional as-similationist narrative by centering the ideological and material contestation involved in this process.

Benito Vergara's essay echoes the previous essays' concern about the issue of cultural/national citizenship by examining how a sense of belonging is mediated through practices of consumption and the semantics of money for the immigrant Filipino middle class in Daly City, California. Vergara suggests that Daly City invokes particular imagined and material connections based on these Filipinos class dreams and desires around immigrating to America and living memories of the homeland. Anticipating the final three essays of the collection, Vergara troubles the easy connection between material and symbolic capital by juxtaposing complicated intersections of Filipino transnational imaginings.

While the essays in Part Two weave necessary counternarratives to the debates around nationhood, family, gender, sexuality, ethnicity, and race in Asian America, Part Three extends these tales into a questioning of location and positionality in expansive terms. The three essays in this final section critically position Asian America within a transnational and diasporic context. Most importantly, these essays destabilize the notion of "Asian America" that goes beyond the "national order of things" while, at the same time, paradoxically reinvigorating it.

Part Three amplifies what has been suggested by the previous essays—working against the idea of the United States as the ultimate or final site of modernity as well as the end/starting point of transnational circuits. This anthology's title juxtaposes Asia(n) with America, which suggests not only the strength of transnational cultural, economic, and political ties, but also the reformation and revision of traditional "areas" of research and study.

Karen Leonard and Louisa Schein, following the emergent theoretical innovations of multilocale ethnography and travel/transnational theories, explore variegated experiences of identity formation as they examine competing perceptions of "tradition" and "modernity" in analyzing diasporic survival in Chinese, South Asian, and Hmong communities. Karen Leonard explores the ways in which generation and gender operate as points of identity articulation for Hyderabadi and Punjabi Americans. Leonard argues for a kind of diasporic perspective where two distinct Indian immigrant groups have contrasting and complex relationships with the homeland and with America. Indeed, this comparative study leads to interesting lessons about the negotiations and intersections of identity across generational lines, historical trajectories, and national spaces.

Louisa Schein's essay is an exploration of method and concept within a transnational cultural context. Schein departs from the notion of multisited and traditional forms of ethnographic method by elaborating what she calls a "siteless" or "itinerant" anthropology that depends on "event" and not "locale" as the basis for fieldwork. She also diverges from the mainstream conception of the transnational by focusing on a nonelite or grass roots form of cosmopolitanism among Miao in China and Hmong in the United States mediated by particular forms of exchanges or flows such as videos and brides. Here, the kinds of identity production and articulation stand apart from dominant images of globalizing and globalized mediated cultural forms that dominate cultural studies today.

The book ends with an essay by Timothy Keeyen Choy that reins in the idea of Asian America and home (or third time-space) in all its fraught and troubled dimensions. Choy questions the "Asian American" identity category through an imaginative reading of the Asian American comic book. At the same time, Choy, together with Schein and Louie, trouble the notion of the "field" by deliberately choosing the space of a comic book used in the pedagogy of Asian American panethnic awareness as the "site" of his fieldwork. Using the comic's narrative, Choy argues for a destabilized notion of an Asian American "home base" (instead of home) that is fluid and more inclusive of divergent practices from various Asian American communities. He cautions against the possible dangers of panethnic bridging and points to the fragility and possibilities of coalitions and the building of multiple "home bases."

Following numerous feminist scholars (Martin and Mohanty 1986; Kondo 1997), the essays in the collection refuse the illusion of a "coherent" home or a "stable" Asian America. Moreover, the essays do not flinch in engaging the violence, exclusion, difference, and power relations that nostalgic musings might elide. It is to this space of Asian America that the essays keep returning.

While by no means an exhaustive or comprehensive survey of all Asian American communities, this collection provides the beginnings of a critical dialogue about ethnography and Asian American communities.[7] These essays aim to trace, chart, and possibly point to other travels within and beyond Asian America. Future projects on Asian American ethnography should continue to build on these essays while exploring other areas and sites. Among the possible sites for such "alternative futures" include the lived experiences and cultures of Pacific Islander communities, Asian American gays and lesbians, inter- and intragenerational experiences (particularly second- and third-generation Asian Americans), cross-ethnic and cross-racial groups and institutions, repatriates, elites, and homeless people.

Unlike the popular notion of a cartographic project, the ethnographic project is never a close-ended endeavor or one that aims to "pin down" or to definitively define contours. A critical ethnography of Asian America enables multiple strategies and readings that are productive and expressive of political struggles, cultural critiques, and social change—that is, it includes processes of home-making and the creation of new worlds for peoples. Within the context of the multicultural debate, the ethnography of Asian America, therefore, is the quintessential example of "homework" that has the potential of unraveling the complications and complexities of demystifying America to itself.

Notes

1. Asian America and Asian Americans are vexed terms especially as they are set against official designations that include Pacific Islanders. This collection focuses on Asian American communities.

2. See Hoyt Zhia's (1999) essay for a cogent analysis of the questioning of national loyalty and the bestowal of the "spy" label to Asian Americans in recent political situations. To locate Asian Americans within the anti-immigrant rhetoric see Reimers (1998).

3. I agree with Marcus's contention (1998) that while postmodern theory has precipitated debates within the social sciences particularly around the issues of ethnography, there are still very few ethnographic works that may clearly be categorized as "postmodern." Much of postmodernism's influence on ethnography has focused on the textual basis of the ethnographic enterprise.

4. While I do not suggest that Marcus (1998) only refers to the physical or geographic dimensions of sites and locales, I want to de-emphasize his overvalorization of the geographic to the detriment of other dimensions in his theorization of multisited ethnographic research imaginary. However, I still recognize the creative and provocative potential of his formulation.

5. Here, I take my cue from Homi Bhabha's short but effective response to James Clifford's (1992) presentation/essay, "Traveling Cultures." This trenchant insight is located after Clifford's essay published in the massive tome entitled *Cultural Studies* where the transcript of the discussion after Clifford's presentation is provided. Bhabha is concerned with limits of deploying travel as the paradigmatic notion for marginalized peoples who need to effect what he calls a dynamic of "non-movement" in order to survive.

6. See Hirabayashi's (1995) essay for an important critique of community research in Asian American Studies.

7. As in any anthology project, several potential contributors on Japanese Americans, Southeast Asian, Pacific Islanders, and other groups opted out for various reasons.

References

Abu Lughod, Lila. 1991. Writing against Culture. In *Recapturing Anthropology*. Edited by Richard Fox. Santa Fe: SAR Press.

Almirol, Edwin. 1985. *Ethnic Identity and Social Negotiation: A Study of a Filipino Community in California*. New York: AMS Press.

Anzaldúa, Gloria. 1987. *Borderlands/La Frontera*. San Francisco: Aunt Lute Books.

Appadurai, Arjun. 1992. Putting Hierarchy in its Place. In *Rereading Cultural Anthropology*. Edited by George Marcus. Durham, N.C.: Duke University Press.

Burawoy, Michael. 1991. The Extended Case Method. In *Ethnography Unbound*. Edited by M. Burawoy et al. Berkeley: University of California Press.

Chen, Hsiang-Shui. 1992. *Chinatown No More: Taiwan Immigrants in Contemporary New York*. Ithaca: Cornell University Press.

Clifford, James. 1992. Traveling Cultures. In *Cultural Studies*. Edited by L. Grossberg, C. Nelson, and P. Treichler. New York: Routledge. 96–115.

Clifford, James, and George Marcus, eds. 1986. *Writing Culture: The Poetics and Politics of Ethnography*. Berkeley: University of California Press.

Geertz, Clifford. 1973. *The Interpretation of Cultures*. New York: Basic Books.

Gupta, Akhil, and James Ferguson. 1997. *Anthropological Locations: Boundaries and Grounds of Field Science*. Berkeley: University of California Press.

Hirabayashi, Lane. 1995. Back to the future: Re-framing community-based research. *Amerasia Journal* 21(1&2).

Kibria, Nazli. 1994. *Tightrope: Vietnamese American Lives*. Ithaca: Cornell University Press.

Kondo, Dorinne. 1997. *About Face*. New York: Routledge.

Lavie, Smadar, and Ted Swedenburg, eds. 1996. *Displacement, Diaspora, and Geographies of Identity*. Durham, N.C.: Duke University Press.

Lessinger, Johanna. 1997. *From the Ganges to the Hudson: Indian Immigrants in New York City*. New York: Allyn and Bacon.

Lin, Jan. 1998. *Reconstructing Chinatown: Ethnic Enclave, Global Change*. Minneapolis: University of Minnesota Press.

Lowe, Lisa. 1996. *Immigrant Acts.* Durham, N.C.: Duke University Press.

Manganaro, Marc. 1990. *Modernist Anthropology: From Fieldwork to Text.* Princeton: Princeton University Press.

Marcus, George. 1992. Past, Present and Emergent Identities: Requirements for Ethnographies of Late Twentieth Century Modernity Worldwide. In *Modernity and Identity.* Edited by Scott Lash and Jonathan Friedman. London: Blackwell.

———. 1998. *Ethnography through Thick and Thin.* Princeton: Princeton University Press.

———, and Michael Fischer. 1986. *Anthropology and Cultural Critique.* Chicago: University of Chicago Press.

Martin, Biddy, and Chandra Talpade Mohanty. 1986. Feminist Politics: What's Home Got to Do with It. In *Feminist Studies: Critical Studies.* Edited by Teresa de Lauretis. Bloomington: Indiana University Press.

Narayan, Kirin. 1992. *Storyteller, Saints and Scoundrels.* Delhi: Motilall Banarsidass.

Palumbo-Liu, David. 1999. *Asian/American: Historical Crossings of a Racial Frontier.* Stanford: Stanford University Press.

Park, Kyeyoung. 1997. *The Korean American Dream: Immigrants and Small Business in New York City.* Ithaca: Cornell University Press.

Reimers, David. 1998. *Unwelcome Strangers: American Identity and the Turn against Immigration.* New York: Columbia University Press.

Visweswaran, Kamala. 1994. *Fictions of Feminist Ethnography.* Minneapolis: University of Minnesota.

Wong, Bernard. 1982. *Chinatown: Economic Adaptation and Ethnic Identity of the Chinese.* New York: Holt, Rinehard, and Winston.

Yanagisako, Sylvia. 1985. *Transforming the Past: Tradition and Kinship among Japanese Americans.* Palo Alto: Stanford University Press.

Zhia, Hoyt. 1999. "Well, is he a spy or not?" *New York Times.* May 26, p. A33.

Zhou, Min. 1992. *Chinatown: The Socioeconomic Potential of an Urban Enclave.* Philadelphia: Temple University Press.

Part I

Writing Asian America: Locating the Field and the Home

Linda Trinh Võ

1   Performing Ethnography in Asian American Communities: Beyond the Insider-versus-Outsider Perspective

What are the methodological and analytical implications of third-world scholars from first-world academic institutions studying third-world communities in the first-world? At one time, fieldwork for sociologists and anthropologists meant studying exotic others and their cultures, in many cases colonial subjects in faraway lands. In more recent periods in the United States, sociologists have discovered that the urban neighborhoods of American cities provide an ideal setting to conduct social science research, and anthropologists have moved home as well to study their own society (Messerschmidt 1981). Among researchers doing what has become defined as insider sociology or native anthropology have been scholars of color studying their own racial or ethnic groups, which has raised new dilemmas and debates.

The general debate over the distinction between insiders and outsiders or between natives and non-natives is discussed in terms of constructed boundaries—whether cultural, political, social, or economic—and is most often framed in terms of how one can cross these boundaries (Aguilar 1981). For example, native ethnographers claim that they can be trusted with personal information because of their insider status, while outsiders claim it is precisely because they are removed from the inner circle of gossip that they can be trusted; therefore, trust (or distrust) is a claim that both have used to validate their position. Epistemological concerns have been raised that insiders are "too close to home" and will miss the obvious, whereas outsiders curious about their new environment will make valuable discoveries (Aguilar 1981, 16). One's lived experience can make what would seem like an extraordinary occurrence seem ordinary; in other words, native researchers essentially fail to notice incidents that are familiar as worthy of evaluation. Yet outsiders, after a period of initiation, can become immersed in the setting to the extent that the unfamiliar becomes familiar and the noticeable becomes unnoticed as well (Whyte 1943, 321).

For the most part, theoretical debates over racial and ethnic scholars studying their own groups followed this lead and tended to emphasize and reinforce this oppositional framework. Merton (1972) contributed to the insider/outsider debate in his essay on the sociology of knowledge by challenging Black scholars' rights to monopolize research on Black communities, based on their claims that they have privileged forms of knowledge unattainable by outsiders. Wilson (1974) questions the privileged insider principle that claims "individuals of a particular race or ethnic group have a greater intellectual understanding of the experiences of that group," since collection and interpretation of data do not necessarily require firsthand knowledge of a group's experience.

Even those who defend the role of scholars of color to study their own group maintained this oppositional framework (Moore 1973; Ladner 1977). For example, Blauner and Wellman state:

> There are certain aspects of racial phenomena, however, that are particularly difficult—if not impossible—for a member of the oppressing group to grasp empirically and formulate conceptually. These barriers are existential and methodological as well as political and ethical. We refer here to the nuances of culture and group ethos; to the meaning of oppression and especially psychic reactions; to what is called the Black, the Mexican-American, the Asian and the Indian *experience*. (Blauner and Wellman 1977, 329)

Although she does not discount the role of the White researcher, Stack (1974, xiv) cautions that outsiders bring biases to the cultures they study, and White researchers often do not analyze their data according to the perspective of minority communities and fail to comprehend the impact of institutional racism. Zinn (1979, 212) argues that there are empirical and methodology advantages to studying a group that one identifies with and is familiar with, but adds: "This is not to suggest that such researchers' understanding or experience will substitute for more systematic knowledge, rather that it may generate hypotheses and discovery of data precluded from traditional frameworks and the experiences of outsiders." Discussions by scholars of Asian ancestry studying Asians in the United States have been cursory (Maykovich 1977; Loo 1980), and rather than exploring the multilayered complexities of this project they have instead supported the binary model.[1]

Most of the self-reflexive fieldwork accounts focus on what techniques White researchers use to conduct research abroad in non-Western nations (Rabinow 1977; Wolf 1992) or concentrate on Whites studying minority communities in the United States (Liebow 1967; Wax 1971; Stack 1974; MacLeod 1987). They, too, have also inadvertently relied on this binary distinction. Previously it was suggested that non-native ethnographers "go native" by immersing themselves into the native scene to become members; however, this methodological strategy has been criticized, since the non-native will always be considered an outsider (Gans 1968; Wax 1971). Although the concern is with non-natives studying natives, the underlying assumption is that researchers who share a similar racial or ethnic background to those being studied are automatically insiders or natives.

In this essay, I analyze the outsider-versus-insider debate, focusing on the methodological and interpretative dilemmas of doing research in what is defined as one's own ethnic community. Drawing on my experiences carrying out research as a participantobserver in San Diego's Asian American community and my lived experiences as an American citizen of Vietnamese ancestry, I want to dislocate the centrality of the bipolar insider-versus-outsider model by problematizing this opposition. By critiquing the insider or native distinction, I show how this framework reinforces essentialized conceptions of racial and cultural groups. As a researcher of Asian ancestry studying the Asian American community, I could be considered an insider, which is beneficial in attaining rapport with individuals. Yet there were noticeable differences— including ethnic, cultural, political, generational, class, educational, and gender— that were acute reminders of the differences between Asian individuals who were my informants and myself. So I do concur with the idea that the actual process of data collection and the quality of the materials gathered are influenced in crucial ways by a researcher's personal and social characteristics, which can also affect the interpretation of data, but what is needed is the recognition of the multilayered, shifting, and competing similarities and differences between native or insider researchers and their communities—a process that is shaped by simultaneous, ongoing negotiations.

An Introduction to the Debate

There is a long history of Black scholars (Wilson 1974), and to a lesser extent Chicano scholars (Zinn 1979), completing field studies of their own communities, but works by Asian American scholars have only begun to flourish in more recent decades. Miyamoto's (1984 [1939]) research of the Japanese American community in Seattle was one of the few case studies published on Asian Americans. In more recent years, Asian American scholars have pursued and published field research projects on a variety of ethnic communities (Kim 1981; Kwong 1987; Chen 1992; Zhou 1992; Kibria 1993; Fong 1994; Takezawa 1995; Saito 1998). Actually studying one's own ethnic group is not a new phenomena. European American scholars have completed studies of European immigrants in the United States; many were completed by those from the Chicago School (Wax 1971, 38–41). Yet it became controversial for empirical and theoretical reasons when minority scholars entered the field and began studying their own ethnic groups (Reyes and Halcón 1988, 76–77). Reacting to outsiders' misrepresentations, minority communities and scholars questioned the right of White scholars to study minority communities. This occurred simultaneously with the development of the internal colonization models and as people of color challenged the exclusionary policies of universities towards minorities (Blauner and Wellman 1977; Hirabayashi 1995).

The line between personal and academic agendas often becomes blurred, and combining political commitment with research is not a new phenomena invented by scholars of color, although it is one of the most common criticisms directed at ethnic researchers. In an effort to replace myths or stereotypes about their communities, those from minority communities are often working against previous studies that distort or misrepresent their lives (Ladner 1971; Gwaltney 1981). Insider research has been criticized for being inherently biased, since its objective is to foster ethnic pride—a goal that can lead an ethnic insider to select and interpret information accordingly by "functioning as advocates rather than scientists" (Aguilar 1981, 16). Yet other scholars have agendas such as improving conditions for women, the homeless, or workers, or other political causes. Their research can be influenced by funding sources or public policy objectives; however, these scholars do not garner similar criticism even though they can hardly be defined as dispassionate observers. For example, Thorne (1978) was able to justify her role as a participant in the draft resistance movement and the instrumental purposes of doing sociological research, and Gitlin's (1980) participation in the Students for a Democratic Society is seen as beneficial, if not crucial, to his study. Strangers are often perceived as disinterested and can be more objective (Beattie 1964; Merton 1972); however, as I discuss later, at some levels ethnic insiders can be strangers in their community as well.

Like other scholars, I had personal as well as scholarly reasons for choosing my research project. Realizing that ethnic histories of Asian Americans are ignored, devalued, or exoticized, I wanted to capture the voices and actions of activists in one community and to dispel the common misconception that Asians are passive and apolitical.[2] My intention was to understand the dynamics of Asian American political mobilization by focusing on a variety of social, economic, and political organizations in one community. I was interested in what larger structural transformations and internal changes within the Asian American population affect their ability to mobilize as a pan-Asian population. With the increasing diversity of the population and its divergent interests, why have Asian Americans chosen to sustain and expand pan-Asian networks and organizations?[3] I conducted a case study to provide a contextualized analysis of the socioeconomic and political forces that generate change in pan-Asian mobilization and to understand how Americans of Asian ancestry respond to, and are shaped by, these changes (Võ 1995).[4]

Entering Our "Native" Backyards

Fieldwork is considered a collaborative enterprise, not as a neutral one-way encounter, but as a process of dialogue between researcher and those being researched (Burawoy 1991; Emerson 1988, vii). According to Wax, it is "a social phenomenon (involving reciprocity, complex role playing, the invention and obeying of rules, mutual assistance, and play)" (1971, 363). In Goffman's (1959) terms, the dramaturgic elements of doing fieldwork can be viewed like a performance on a stage, especially since ethnographers are like actors concerned with impression management and role playing. My encounters in the field indicated that I was not an automatic insider, since some Asians clearly imagined me as an ally, while others perceived me as a stranger and were suspicious of my intentions. Like all ethnographers, I realized that observation and participation is circumstantial and that each researcher must constantly negotiate her or his interactions while in the field—it is not something that can be mapped and followed according to a step-by-step process in which one starts merely as an outsider and gradually moves to becoming an insider.

For the most part, researching an Asian population felt familiar and comfortable, but the research context was actually a new environment for me. I was regarded as an ethnic and cultural member, but also as a social stranger (see Aguilar 1981). In San Diego, I frequented Asian restaurants, markets, and other businesses and had taken language classes at a Vietnamese language school, yet I was unfamiliar with the organizational infrastructure of the community. I had moved to the area to attend college, so the majority of my interactions were with Asian Americans involved in the academic community; therefore, I had minimal contact with the larger Asian community before I began my project in 1992.[5] Initially, I considered myself an outsider since I was a more recent resident, but because many other Asians were also new migrants or immigrants to San Diego, I realized that being a newcomer was common for a community experiencing a demographic transition.[6] Yet as a researcher who wanted to "hang around" the Asian American organizations, I did not fit into an easily identifiable role, since I did not own a business, was not a professional, did not work for a nonprofit organization, was not interested in being an Asian political representative or politician, and was not looking for a job in the community.

My ethnic credentials helped me gain entrée into the community, although I quickly learned that this was only one criterion. Ethnic communities can be suspicious and distrustful of researchers not from their ethnic group (Blauner and Wellman 1977; Couchman 1973). Yet ethnic researchers do not automatically gain the trust of co-ethnic communities or organizations (Loo 1980). Initially, I contacted the only pan-Asian organization I knew of at the time, a pan-Asian social service agency. The new director, a Japanese American, was wary of researchers prying into the agency's programs, even after I assured her that this was not the objective of my study. In exchange for allowing me access, she wanted me to help them do research or write grants, and because the organization had negative experiences with researchers (some of whom were minorities) in the past, she wanted final approval of my writings before publication. She was receptive to including me in the organization because I was Asian but was suspicious of my status as a researcher.[7]

Fortunately, my second contact was more beneficial, and in this case both my ethnic and academic credentials were seen as an asset. A non-Asian graduate student in my program recommended that I contact a Filipina activist she had met at her nephew's birthday party who was trying to find an Asian American researcher to study the local Filipino American or Asian American communities. After a three-hour meeting with this woman at her home, I felt totally overwhelmed; she had bombarded me with information on individuals, organizations, events, and controversies. Most importantly, she invited me to several events and allowed me to use her name as a form of introduction. The first event I went to was a tour given by the Chinese Historical Society of the San Diego downtown area once occupied by Chinese, Japanese, and Filipino communities, and I was able to establish more contacts. I began attending pan-Asian events consistently, informing people that I was a sociology graduate student gathering data for a dissertation on Asian American organizations. The majority were receptive to the idea that I was studying them, and many accepted me because my presence showed that I valued their ideas and actions.

The Interplay of Participation and Reciprocity

At this stage I was only interested in being an observer. However, as someone identified racially as Asian, I could not be a detached bystander; they expected me to become more than merely an outside observer. After attending a few Asian Business Association (ABA) meetings, I was asked if I could contribute to their newsletter an article about the preservation and restoration project of what was once the Asian section of downtown San Diego, since I had also attended some meetings on this project. After the article was published, I was asked to become the editor of the newsletter and because of this position I automatically became a board member of the business association and served on several committees. They compensated me for my voluntary efforts by allowing me to be a part of the organization and by covering dinner events, membership dues, and other related expenses. I believe organization members saw their role as beneficial, since they were mentoring someone who could assist the community as well as helping me in my research project. A quid pro quo relationship can be valuable for a research project (Pollner and Emerson 1988, 238), and this was the situation in my case. In this way, we formed a mutually beneficial relationship, and while it allowed me to reciprocate in some way, I felt I gained much more than I gave.

As both an observer and a participant, I was allowed situational flexibility in identifying myself in the field. Depending on the circumstances, I could identify myself as a researcher affiliated with the university, as a member of ABA, as the editor of the ABA newsletter, or merely as an Asian American interested in organizational issues. Like other fieldworkers, my involvement gave me a sense of the backstage—of what goes on behind the curtains of the organization—allowing me access to a wealth of information. I was included on mailing and fax lists, which helped me keep in touch with a community that was essentially nonterritorial and in which individuals were dispersed throughout the county. Being a participant, I had justification for being at particular gatherings, especially small ones when the role of an observer would have been intrusive. With new participants joining community activities and new organizations emerging, it was easy for Asian Americans to incorporate another stranger into the community structure. The business organization gave me networks to other Asian American associations and connections with individuals involved in a wide array of single-ethnic and pan-Asian organizations that were essential to my dissertation project.

Relative Involvement or Detachment

Some scholars (Miller 1952; Gold 1958; Gans 1968) argue that objectivity is derived from neutrality, distance, and emotional detachment from those one studies, since personal involvement can lead to distortion of the data and bias in interpretation. Other scholars, however, particularly feminist researchers (Andersen 1993; Olesen 1994), argue for more self-consciously engaged methodological practices of constructing knowledge, since the criteria that makes a researcher subjective or objective is relative. Gans states that "I would go so far as to say that the participant-observer cannot study his own people" (1968, 304), yet in his study of Levittowners he shared commonalities such as values, age, occupation, income, education, and even race with those he studied. He argues that he was only a research resident in that community and thus was an objective outsider, a point that can be contested. Maintaining neutrality or emotional marginality is often not possible for researchers in general, and this is also the case when studying groups in which one is racially affiliated; rather, involvement and detachment are situational and in constant interplay.

Being from the same racial group one studies requires maneuvering between one's personal beliefs and those of the larger group. Pollner and Emerson note that "the fieldworker is inevitably present *in* the interactions that are the focus of observation" (1988, 236), so distance and detachment can be a constant struggle, one that I contend differs for someone racially identified with a group. For the most part, I abstained from getting involved in conflicts, which could involve personality differences or strategic disagreements, and was careful not to take sides on issues that could distance me from individuals or groups. A longtime activist in the community with strong political allegiances, who later decided to conduct a research project in the same community, would use a different approach (see Kwong 1987). I did not always agree with the political opinions, ideologies, or strategies of the Asian Americans I studied. It was particularly bothersome for me when they claimed to be representing the Asian American community, which included me at some level, especially when I was opposed to their position or approach to particular issues (for instance, the anti-union views of some leaders).

As researchers, our role is not to lecture the people we research about how to conduct their lives; rather, our intention is to find out what people think and do, and why (MacLeod 1987, 172). Some might find this issue debatable, but our role is not the same as the one we play at our academic institutions—it is not one of "professor" in the field lecturing to "students." At the more personal level, there were instances in which my silence bothered me, particularly when Asian Americans made disparaging comments about other racial groups. Rather than challenge them, I tried to probe them further about why they held these stereotypes in order to analyze how these perceptions reflected their understanding of racial issues and their views on building coalitions with other minority groups. Although this strategy helped my research goals, it was troubling but not surprising that prominent Asian American leaders—even those who worked to forge alliances with Black, Latino, and Native American community leaders—espoused these views given their exposure to the dominant racial ideologies in the United States (see Abelmann and Lie 1995). If I am to understand that my objective is to record and understand their perspectives, not to impose my values on them, then I feel justified in my inaction.[8]

I had to balance my role as a researcher, which meant that I did not interfere with the direction of the organization, yet I had concerns as an Asian American woman as well. There were times when I wanted to more openly express my opinion on issues related to gender—for example, to point out that more women were needed on certain committees or that women were doing the work behind the scene while men were receiving the recognition—but as a researcher, I also wanted to maintain a more detached or quiet role in the community. My personal inclination to be more vocal and not to live up to the stereotypes about demure Asian women clashed with the responsibility of being a researcher. Fortunately, other women voiced these concerns and, at times, men did as well.

There were numerous instances when I felt the Asian American activists or their organizations were being treated unfairly, but it disturbed me most when they failed to respond to these incidents. My reaction was personal, hardly as an unbiased, disinterested, or dispassionate researcher. I vividly remember that when a politician running for mayor was asked—during a political forum sponsored by the Filipino American community and then in another forum sponsored by the Asian American community—how he would deal with the Asian American community if elected, he responded that he had learned to communicate with his deaf son and would use the same approach with the Asian American community. In both cases, the audience politely applauded, but no one contested this analogy. I recorded in my field notes my personal anger at this individual, who had shown little sensitivity toward or understanding of the Asian American community's needs in the past, and my frustration at those in the audience for not questioning his insulting comparison. While some privately grumbled about it afterwards, I felt they should have confronted him publicly. Their political actions or inactions can potentially affect the lives of all Asian Americans, myself included. Scholars are warned against overrapport (Miller 1952), but this is oftentimes unavoidable for ethnic researchers; however, it does not necessarily invalidate their study. Like other researchers who may identify, or even empathize, with those they research, we need to evaluate these situations and incorporate these predicaments into the study.[9] From this experience, on the analytical level, I learned about the dilemmas that confront Asian activists on a daily level and the conflicts over political representation; on the personal level, I learned that I could not separate my individual and academic identities, nor was it necessary or even possible.

While other researchers (Gans 1968) are concerned about overidentification with people they are studying, as an ethnic researcher I was more concerned about people overidentifying me with the group, which was beyond my control. I conducted thirty in-depth semistructured interviews with Asian American activists concerning their life history, their ethnic identity, their political opinions, and their organizational participation. During interviews, when interviewees discussed Asians in general, they would use inclusive terms such as "we" or "us." In other instances, they assumed that I knew what they meant because I was from the same racial group, which helped interviewees reveal valuable information but sometimes also led to moments of awkwardness because I had to ask them to explain what they thought should be obvious to an ethnic insider (see Zavella 1987, 28). Feminist and ethnic scholars (Oakley 1981; Matsumoto 1993, 14) have encouraged interviewers to incorporate their own backgrounds into the interview process. I often found I did not have to initiate a discussion of my personal history; interviewees would redirect my questions—such as "When did *you* immigrate to the U.S.?" or "What do *you* think Asian Americans have in common?"—back at me throughout the interview process.

My similar racial categorization with those I studied enhanced the rapport, but this was based on their assumptions of my racial identity, not necessarily something that was formally articulated, and as I discuss later, this shared commonalty can be a matter of perception. They assumed we shared common frames of reference, perhaps in terms of being an Asian in the United States, so they felt comfortable and could "let down their guard." Yet this is only based on my personal experience; it is difficult to generalize that this would occur with all Asian interviewers or that they would not have divulged similar or other personal information to non-Asian interviewees. I must concede that in many settings, especially in all-Asian ones, my presence was accepted because I was Asian, whereas had I been a non-Asian, my role as an observer or participant would have been difficult. Being Asian helped because when they saw me among the group, they were seeing all Asian faces.[10] It was more than visual dynamics, though; in my informal and formal discussions, some Asians revealed to me that they felt uncomfortable interacting with or being in the presence of Whites or other non-Asians. It was not a matter of likes or dislikes, but because most of the family members, friends, and coworkers they interacted with were Asian and they felt more at ease in this social environment. My observations supported this to some extent, since many of the Asian American leaders were more vocal in settings in which Asian Americans were the predominant group.

Liebow states that "the degree to which one becomes a participant is as much a matter of perceiving oneself as a participant as it is of being accepted as a participant by others" (1967, 256). At times I was treated as a member of the community—to some extent, as "one of them." In one instance, I was contacted by a Filipina from a nonprofit loan company who berated me for not including her on the panel that discussed making low-interest loans available to Asian Americans and stated that the other representatives had no track record of serving the Asian American community. Although I was a member of the planning committee that was responsible for selecting the panelists, I had little control over the selection of panelists, a fact she refused to believe. Several activists who tried to recruit me to be an officer in a newly-formed Democratic Asian American organization could not understand how my affiliation with the organization could jeopardize my research.[11] A fair number of Asian activists were Republican, and although I knew they would grant me an interview, I wanted to be sure they would express their political opinions openly. Even though I wanted to maintain some semblance of marginality and neutrality,[12] I realized this did not fit with how others perceived my role, and the fact that I was from the same racial background as those I studied contributed to their confusion.

Belonging and Race

As ethnic researchers, we must contend with questions concerning what researching our own community means; however, I believe it is not so much the external criticism that is significant, but rather that it is the internal skepticism that has become central. As the discipline grows and the diversity of the population increases, new groups of academics are entering the field, which complicates how Asian Americans will define an authentic ethnic insider or outsider. Some scholars have avoided these dilemmas directly and instead strategically pointed out that their research projects were strengthened because they shared common experiences of immigration, adaptation, and discrimination with their informants. For Nazli Kibria (1993, 31) a Bangladeshi American, being a minority made the Vietnamese families she studied more receptive to her. Shiori Ui (1991) discusses how being a Japanese national helped her gain rapport with the Cambodian refugees she was studying in Stockton, since she shared their experiences of living in "a foreign land." Usha Welaratna (1993) found that her experiences as an immigrant from Sri Lanka, along with being a Theravada Buddhist, enabled her to establish a trusting relationship with the Cambodian refugees she studied in northern California. In these cases, the researchers could be considered racial insiders, but they also could be regarded as ethnic outsiders. I suspect that these contestations over whether or not Asian American scholars can adequately study a subgroup other than their own will continue to engage those of us in the discipline.

What I think is even more telling is to notice how Asian Americans relate to one another and what they reveal in terms of their feelings about other Asian ethnics, which can also be an indication of how they perceive the researcher who is supposedly one of them. My project required that I interact with and analyze other ethnic groups, such as Chinese, Japanese, Filipinos, Laotians, Koreans, Thais, Asian Indians, Laotians, and Cambodians. The Asian American or Asian Pacific American label is a contentious one with ongoing debates over which groups actually "belong" in this racialized category. I interviewed acculturated Asians who had negative perceptions of the Vietnamese "boat people" and had been misidentified as refugees themselves, so they had tried to distance themselves from this group although they agreed that the Vietnamese belong in the Asian American category. Others influenced by the Asian American movement and the anti-Vietnam War movement of the late 1960s and early 1970s identified with the Vietnamese for ideological reasons, even though they had few personal interactions with the Vietnamese. I found that Asian Americans disagreed as to whether or not South Asians, Filipinos, or Pacific Islanders should be included in or with the Asian American rubric, which could ostensibly affect a researcher's reception. Furthermore, the participants I studied included multiracial people with Asian ancestry and participants of mixed Asian heritage who had varying opinions about how they were treated by other Asians. Although the process of racialization has forcibly lumped together these individuals and ethnic groups, these examples indicate how malleable and situational the multiple boundaries are for this diverse group; therefore, categorizing the Asian American researcher as a native, half-native, or non-native is too simplistic.

Asian Americans can differ substantially in their immigration and generational experiences, and this points to the complexities of exclusion and inclusion for researchers. We may be studying individuals from a similar ethnic background, but their immigrant histories may vary substantially from our own. Recent examples include a study completed by a Japanese national of the Japanese American Redress movement (Takezawa 1995) and a study by a U.S.-born Chinese of Chinese immigrants (Fong 1994). In my research project, I found that some participants were born abroad and immigrated here recently, while others, like myself, came to the United States with their parents, and then there were others who were born in the United States. At one of the monthly business association meetings, I discovered that as a result of the diaspora of the Asian population, all eight individuals dining at my table, myself included, did not take a direct route from Asia to the United States. As first generation or as one-and-a-half generation Asian immigrants, a term used to describe those born abroad who arrive with their parents, we do not fit the general immigration patterns for our particular ethnic group. These experiential differences challenge boundary constructions and problematize the dichotomous model.

We may be placed within a singular racialized group; however, Asian ethnic groups vary in terms of their socialization processes, and within this group there exists a multiplicity of cultural practices. As someone who does not conform to the phenotypic, visual image of an "all-American," I learned by experience that there are various ethnic labels applied to me: Vietnamese from South Vietnam, Vietnamese, Vietnamese American, Southeast Asian, Indochinese, Asian, Asian American, American, Oriental, minority, person of color, woman of color, non-White, foreigner, immigrant, migrant, or refugee. Like those I researched, I am cognizant of racial and cultural differences. However, it cannot be assumed that, unlike a non-native researcher, it is unnecessary for me "to learn" about Asians or "become socialized" with Asian customs, since I am already immersed in the community. Although I am familiar with certain traditions, I am not well versed in the customs and cultural practices of each ethnic group. For example, even though various Asian ethnic groups acknowledge the changing seasons or the coming of the new year, they celebrate it on different days and in various ways. Moreover, it is not always clear what cultural aspects an Asian individual accepts or chooses to reject.

Ethnic scholars may encounter suspicion and resentment by co-ethnics in terms of their level of acculturation or assimilation; therefore, researchers are not absolutely inside or outside of an homogeneous sociocultural system (Aguilar 1981). During my fieldwork, I heard Asians make disparaging remarks about other participants being too culturally Americanized or too foreign. These judgments did not always correlate with the perceptions that individuals had of themselves. For example, a Chinese immigrant who thought he was quite acculturated was ridiculed for being too Chinese, whereas a fourth-generation Chinese who identified strongly with his ethnic heritage was not ethnic enough according to others. There are elderly Asians who have lived in the United States for twenty years in an ethnic enclave and are less acculturated than a young immigrant living in an exclusive suburb who arrived from Asia a year ago. So, how do we measure who is more "Asian" or, for that matter, who is more "American"?[13] This raises problematic issues of having to define who can be classified as authentically or inauthentically Asian.

Deciding what criteria to use to measure ethnic validity is complicated further by global cultural influences. For example, during interviews, an immigrant woman from Hong Kong discussed how she grew up idolizing American rock-and-roll icons, while a third-generation Korean American born in Hawaii stated that as a kid his role models were Bruce Lee and Mao Zedong. The boundaries of who is authentically Western (American) or Eastern (Asian) is blurred, and the legacy of colonialism or neocolonialism and transnational interconnections make it difficult to separate that which is purely West from non-West or East from non-East. Native cultures do not develop in isolation in the homeland, and they are not simply transplanted to the land of the colonizer without being affected by the immigration experience. They are shifting and multilayered—not static—cultural entities. Additionally, it was confusing for participants when they interacted with immigrants of Asian ancestry raised in Cuba, Peru, and Mexico who were fluent in Spanish and shaped by Latin American cultures. As Rosaldo (1993, 44–45) points out, in the postcolonial situation, ethnographers are conducting research in societies with "open borders" rather than "closed communities" with hermetically sealed cultures or national boundaries.

To assume that being racialized as Asian makes one an ethnic insider essentializes the Asian American experience and the Asian American community—denying the fact that there are multiple experiences and cultures. And although I have been using the term "Asian American community," I am not speaking of a discrete, bounded one, but of a socially constructed community, or rather communities. Defining distinctions between Asians and non-Asians, particularly in the articulation of an Asian American identity, can lead to a tendency toward essentialism and overgeneralization, and reinforces the dominant discourse that homogenizes this racialized group (Lowe 1991) as well as supports the false insider/outsider binary.

Being "Vietnamese"

Being Vietnamese can provide one with entrée, yet it does not give one instant rapport with other Vietnamese. The Vietnamese in the United States, like all Asian ethnic groups, are not an homogeneous group but are marked by religious, linguistic, cultural, political, economic, sexual, regional, gender, and emigration differences, especially as these populations in the Asian rubric become more diverse in the post-1965 period. Thus, researching one's own community can bring myriad unexpected complications. The Vietnamese I encountered who were involved with pan-Asian affairs were primarily older traditional male leaders who were first-generation refugees, a profile that differed from my own as a young, one-and-a-half generation female immigrant. While most of the older generation were representing Vietnamese organizations within the larger pan-Asian coalitions, the younger participants joined on their own accord as individuals. Like other refugee populations or other displaced groups, one's status in the home country is still important, and introductions with compatriots often involve questions to ascertain one's former class and political status, such as "When did you come to America (1975 or in later waves)?"; "What region (north, central or south) or village are you from?"; and "What was your previous occupation or your family's occupation in Vietnam?" The answers provide co-ethnics with a frame of reference that can result in positive or negative reactions, and I received both depending on their perspective. For example, my own educational background was incongruent with my family's class position in Vietnam, and my loss of the native language was often perplexing to expatriates since it disrupted homeland hierarchies and traditional expectations. Yet being born in South Vietnam was seen favorably by anti-Communist expatriates. This shows the limitations of a dichotomous boundary; they saw me both as an insider who was on the outside and as an outsider who was on the inside.

As ethnic researchers, there are often expectations that we will contribute or give back something to our single-ethnic group, an expectation not automatically assumed of other researchers. While researchers have often been asked to complete research that could be of use to minority communities, the demands on ethnic researchers often extend themselves beyond the parameters of the research project. Scholars (Blauner and Wellman 1977; Zinn 1979) have discussed the exploitative nature of research on minority communities and suggest that researchers reciprocate in some way, yet reciprocation differs according to how one is identified with those they study. Even though I was not studying the Vietnamese population per se, I was expected to do advocacy work for them on issues that were not my area of expertise. Loo (1980, 20) argues that a researcher's motive, political perspective, ethnic identification, and ethnic consciousness contribute to a community's sense of comfort or discomfort with the researcher, but I believe that it is not an unidirectional social relationship but, rather, one of exchange.

I was surprised when I attended a Vietnamese Tet Festival and a Vietnamese leader admonished me for spending time working on Asian American organizations, rather than helping the Vietnamese with organizing the festival and working on other local agendas.[14] I considered his suggestions until I realized during an informal discussion with him that many of the views he expressed personally and as a community leader were in opposition to my own. Although I was admittedly concerned about the community's reception towards me and my viewpoints, I was more overwhelmed contemplating how I would contend with the longstanding frictions among leaders within the Vietnamese and Southeast Asian community and how I would find the necessary time to devote to such commitments. It is interesting to note that non-Vietnamese Asians did not have the same expectations of me, and even when they requested my assistance, I did not feel the same responsibility to contribute my energy and time. As ethnic researchers, we must continually balance the expectations of others, in addition to our own desire, to do advocacy work versus the demands of completing a research project and fulfilling the requirements of the academic institution, which oftentimes does not reward us for community activism.

Beyond Just Race

Differences between the researcher and those being researched are often conceived of as a gradual scale in which "the extent of relative 'insidedness' and 'identity' between researcher and subject is best conceived of as a continuum from virtual oneness to a marginal nearness" (Messerschmidt 1981, 8). Perhaps on the abstract level this model of positionality works, but in reality identification or disidentification does not follow such a linear or incremental process. Wax comments that a "fieldworker's gender, age, prestige, expertise or ethnic identity may limit or determine what he or she can accomplish" (1979, 513), but much of this depends on the subject of study and the circumstances of the investigation (Cicourel 1964). Or, as Amadiume (1993, 182) puts it, researchers have "multiple selves" that determine their methodology, and it is necessary to interrogate these in the practice of ethnography.

In addition to race, my status as a young married woman affected the dynamics of rapport. I was not competing with those being researched for resources such as jobs, marriage partners, or power—elements that can cause conflicts. Although the majority of those I interacted with were men, women held a fair number of leadership positions and many of them served in multiple organizations. Had I been studying traditional single-ethnic organizations—many of which consist primarily, if not exclusively, of older male leaders and members—rather than pan-Asian organizations, it would have been difficult for me, as a young female, to gain access. Some of the older men and women treated me like a daughter and went out of their way to help me with my research project (see Facio 1993, 84). For the most part, I had little difficulty interacting with the younger men since we were similar in age, but my experiences depended on factors such as their profession, education, marital status, and values. My rapport with the younger women was evident from the beginning; we shared more experiences in common because of our age and gender.

My status as a graduate student placed me in contradictory positions because my academic credentials elevated my social status, but my economic level lowered my status within the community. Many of those I encountered, even briefly, were proud that an Asian was pursuing graduate studies in the social sciences, which is still considered a nontraditional major for Asians (see Zavella 1987, 27). As a researcher living in subsidized graduate student housing and dependent on a teaching assistant and research assistant salary, my income was limited in comparison to many of those I researched. I should clarify that even though I was studying elites in leadership positions in the Asian community, they were not necessarily wealthy, especially if compared to others in the community-at-large. Most activists, at least at the level I was studying, came from a variety of class backgrounds, but none were from the poorest groups. So, although I had more academic credentials than the majority of those I studied, I was on the economic margins of the group. It was not just ethnicity, then, that determined whether or not I was part of the in-group or out-group, but clearly class, age, gender, sexual preference, and other aspects are all contributing factors. Fieldwork is based on the culmination of individualized interactions; it is a continuous, ongoing series of interactions and negotiations (Johnson 1975).

Involved Interpretation and Accountability

The dilemmas of fieldwork for a native or inside researcher are interconnected to the process of interpreting and writing as well. This "involved interpretation" means that native researchers, or "halfies" as Abu-Lughod defines them, are "speaking for and speaking from" their respective communities because of the process of racialization (1991, 142). In terms of "speaking from," there are assumptions that I am speaking not about "them" but about "us"—in other words, not about "their community" but about "my community." To some extent, as Aguilar points out, "whatever the researcher writes about them is also true of the researcher. . . . The ethnic-insider researcher is seen as being in the same sociopolitical boat as the subjects" (1981, 18). Given the racial dynamics of this country, I have come to accept that I do have an investment in what is presented, but at the same time I am still learning to question and resist this imposition of "speaking from"; however, I find the issue of "speaking for" a more difficult one to confront.

Not only are we as academics, in this case as a sociologist, expected to record life histories and community events, but we are also expected to present critical theoretical analyses of these communities. Our task is to study social situations and turn observations into explanations and data into theories. Yet, how would I represent the participants' lives and interpret their actions to Asian American academics and to the general Asian American population as well as to the community I studied? Asian participants saw me as preserving their history, and I do feel a compelling obligation to "get it right," yet I struggle with this knowing that I am presenting just a personal perspective through a selective and partial collection of facts and interpretations.

The act of writing is an interpretative enterprise since "any and all description is inevitably *partial* and *selective*" based on "a theory-informed re-*presentation* of that thing" (Emerson 1988, 20–21). Clifford also argues that ethnographies are true fictions since "ethnographic truths are thus inherently partial—committed and incomplete" (Clifford 1986, 7). Studying one's own racial group may represent a more equitable relation of power since it displaces the usual racial hierarchy, but ultimately the researcher is still in a position of authority to control the interpretation, analysis, and presentation of the data.

We labor under pressure to conform our work to the theoretical demands of our disciplines, but as ethnic scholars we must also be accountable to the expectations of the community or communities that we research. Matsumoto states it quite succinctly: "Perhaps scholars should be reminded that we, no less than those we study, are actors in history, making choices that affect the lives of others" (1993, 224). As a scholar of color, I do feel an obligation to give something back to the community and ponder how useful my academic writings will be for the community itself. As scholars doing fieldwork, we know that it is these works—in the form of articles and books—that contribute, in large part, to us attaining employment, promotions, and tenure (Blauner and Wellman 1977; Thorne 1978). Whereas some research provides direct benefits, such as completing a study that justifies the need for more social service funding for Asians, oftentimes ethnographic studies lend themselves more to indirect benefits, perhaps giving voice to a silenced population or breaking the Black-White racial dichotomy that still seems to permeate racial discourse in this country. I suppose I must reveal my partiality when I defend ethnographic studies that do not lend themselves to immediate remuneration for a particular community but may provide intangible long-term benefits for Asian Americans.

Conclusion

I went into the field unprepared to deal with all the contradictions and complexities I encountered as a researcher, and as is often the case, fieldwork transforms the fieldworker (Clarke 1975, 118). My research experiences profoundly affected my understanding of the Asian population in the United States, beyond just a textual understanding and clearly beyond my own lived experience. It was a learning process for all—I was trying to negotiate my role as a researcher of Asian ancestry while Asians in San Diego were learning how to negotiate differences among themselves. As I saw them grappling with their cultural, social, and political identities, I was also confronting the ambiguities of my own identities. I realized that the insider-versus-outsider perspective provides a starting point, but that it is a false dichotomy that we need to reframe and move beyond.

As scholars of color, we can contribute to the scholarship on the communities with which we are identified or with which we identity. This does not mean that I advocate only ethnics studying ethnics. Studies of Asians by those classified as non-Asians, who are aware of the racial intricacies and implications of their project, have added and can add to the discipline. For similar reasons, I think it is imperative for Asian Americans to study other racial groups and to study interactions between Asians and other racial groups. Doing fieldwork allows scholars of color to capture snapshots of daily interactions between individuals as well as between individuals and institutions, yet we as ethnic scholars must acknowledge that the process of data collection and interpretation can create differing images and meanings according to our multiple and simultaneous connections and disconnections to our communities.

As researchers, we can retreat back beyond the academic walls and leave behind our research sites and the people who generously shared their lives with us. Yet, for minority researchers, these issues are not something we can merely leave behind or toss aside. Racial inequities and injustices, issues that are most often intertwined with our understanding of racial and ethnic communities, are mirrored in the academic institutions where we work and in the sites where we conduct our daily lives. Even though I have left the field, so to speak, I will never leave the field behind.

Notes

I wish to express my deep appreciation to the members of the Asian American community in San Diego for sharing their life experiences with me. They made my research project enjoyable and possible. I am grateful for support I received from the University of California, Berkeley Chancellor's Postdoctoral Fellowship, and the University of California Humanities Research Institute Fellowship. My thanks to William Ross, Karen Mary Davalos, Antoinette Charfauros McDaniel, William Norris, Rick Bonus, and Michael Omi for advice in the various stages of preparing this chapter.

   1. The focus of this paper is on Asians in the United States. For insightful discussions on the dilemmas Asian Americans doing ethnography in Asia encounter, see Dorine K. Kondo, *Crafting Selves: Power, Gender, and Discourses of Identity in a Japanese Workplace* (Chicago: University of Chicago Press, 1990); and Matthew Masayuki Hamabata, *Crested Kimono: Power and Love in the Japanese Business Family* (Ithaca: Cornell University Press, 1990).

   2. I was also interested in doing a study of political mobilization outside of what has been considered the usual "sites" for the Asian American movement, such as San Francisco, New York, and Los Angeles.

   3. I did not intend to capture the experiences of all Asian Americans; instead, my goal was to focus on individuals who felt compelled to take action on these issues, particularly those involved in pan-Asian organizations.

   4. I consider my work an historically situated ethnography that merges several methodologies. Since it was impossible for me to employ participation-observation methods when studying organizations that were no longer in existence or when studying the formative years of an established organization, I relied on documents and oral interviews to inform my discussions about these earlier events.

   5. Previously, I had gone to high school in San Bernardino, California, where I worked in my parents' mom-and-pop run oriental food market that catered to all Asians, but especially to Southeast Asian refugees.

6. According to the 1990 Census Race and Hispanic Origin: Population Change 1980–1990 (San Diego Association of Government [SANDAG] Info, March—April 1991), in 1990 Asian and Pacific Islanders numbered 198,311, representing 7.9 percent of the total San Diego County population, up from 4.8 percent a decade ago.

7. I decided against her offer and sought other organizations to study. Although I was discouraged at the time, I realized that she was concerned about protecting her agency, which relied on private and public funding. Eventually, after I had established myself in the community, she realized my intent was not to scrutinize social service programs, and she gave me one of the best interviews as well as uncontrolled access to the organization's valuable collection of historical records.

8. Of course, in other contexts outside of the research setting, I do not hesitate to express my viewpoints.

9. I found that I am better able to evaluate my fieldwork project after leaving the fieldwork site, and I am still in the process of analyzing these situations in my manuscript.

10. Elliot Liebow in *Tally's Corner* makes a crucial point in his discussion of the importance of visual imagery: "My field notes contain a record of what I saw when I looked at Tally, Richard, Sea Cat and the others. I have only a small notion—and one that I myself consider suspect—of what they saw when they looked at me. Some things, however, are very clear. They saw, first of all, a white man. . . . I am not certain, but I have a hunch that they were more continuously aware of the color difference than I was. When four of us sat around a kitchen table, for example, I saw three Negroes; each of them saw two Negroes and a white man" (1967, 248).

11. There are greater possibilities for participation had this been a collaborative effort by multiple researchers. See John Horton with the assistance of Jose Calderon, Mary Pardo, Leland Saito, Linda Shaw, and Yen-Fen Tseng, *The Politics of Diversity: Immigration, Resistance, and Change in Monterey Park, California* (Philadelphia: Temple University Press, 1995).

12. As a graduate student I was able to maintain a more noninterventionist role, but the situation would have been different had I been a faculty member. This was evident to me when an Asian American professor did some preliminary fieldwork in the Asian community in San Diego. The residents expected him to use his status and clout in leadership positions.

13. Recognizing that they are inexact criteria, I am using measurements of acculturation, such as English language ability, interaction with non-Asians, and area of residence.

14. He also disapproved of my affiliation with a Vietnamese-based organization. For personal reasons, I did volunteer work for an organization that raised money to send medical supplies and build clinics and schools in Vietnam, mainly central Vietnam. This was at a time when many anti-Communist Vietnamese abroad disapproved of any relations with Vietnam.

References

Abelmann, Nancy and John Lie. 1995. *Blue Dreams: Korean Americans and the Los Angeles Riots.* Cambridge, Mass.: Harvard University Press.

Abu-Lughod, Lila. 1991. Writing against Culture. In *Recapturing Anthropology: Working in the Present.* Edited by Richard G. Fox. Pp. 137–62. Santa Fe: School of American Research Press.

Aguilar, John L. 1981. Insider Research: An Ethnography of a Debate. In *Anthropologists at Home in North America: Methods and Issues in the Study of One's Own Society.* Edited by Donald A. Messerschmidt. Pp. 15–28. Cambridge, U.K.: Cambridge University Press.

Amadiume, Ifi. 1993. The Mouth That Spoke a Falsehood Will Later Speak the Truth: Going Home to the Field in Eastern Africa. In *Gendered Fields: Women, Men, and Ethnography.* Edited by Diane Bell, Pat Caplan, and Wazir Jahan Karim. Pp. 182–98. New York: Routledge.

Andersen, Margaret. 1993. Studying across Difference: Race, Class, and Gender in Qualitative Research. In *Race and Ethnicity in Research Methods.* Edited by John H. Stanfield, II, and Rutledge M. Dennis. Pp. 39–52. Newbury Park, Calif.: Sage.

Beattie, J. 1964. *Other Cultures: Aims, Methods, and Achievements in Social Anthropology.* New York: Free Press.

Blauner, Robert, and David Wellman. 1977. Toward the Decolonization of Social Research. In *The Death of White Sociology.* Edited by Joyce A. Ladner. Pp. 310–32. New York: Random House.

Burawoy, Michael. 1991. Reconstructing Social Theories. In *Ethnography Unbound: Power and Resistance in the Modern Metropolis.* Edited by Michael Burawoy et al. Pp. 8–28. Berkeley: University of California Press.

Chen, Hsiang-Shui. 1992. *Chinatown No More: Taiwan Immigrants in Contemporary New York.* Ithaca: Cornell University Press.

Cicourel, Arron V. 1964. *Method and Measurement in Sociology.* Glencoe, Ill.: Free Press.

Clarke, Michael. 1975. Survival in the field: Implications of personal experience in field work. *Theory and Society* 2: 95–123.

Clifford, James. 1986. Introduction: Partial Truths. In *Writing Culture: The Poetics and Politics of Ethnography.* Edited by James Clifford and George Marcus. Pp. 1–26. Berkeley: University of California Press.

Couchman, Iain S. B. 1973. Notes from a white researcher in black society. *Journal of Social Issues* 29 (1): 45–52.

Emerson, Robert M. 1988. Introduction. In *Contemporary Field Research: A Collection of Readings.* Pp. 1–16. Prospect Heights, Ill.: Waveland Press.

Facio, Elisa. 1993. Ethnography as Personal Experience. In *Race and Ethnicity in Research Methods.* Edited by John H. Stanfield, II, and Rutledge M. Dennis. Pp. 75–91. Newbury Park, Calif.: Sage.

Fong, Timothy. 1994. *The First Suburban Chinatown: The Remaking of Monterey Park, California.* Philadelphia: Temple University Press.

Gans, Herbert. 1968. The Participant-Observer as a Human Being: Observations on the Personal Aspects of Field Work. In *Institutions and the Person.* Edited by Howard Becker, Blanche Geer, David Riesman, and Robert Weiss. Pp. 300–17. Chicago: Aldine.

Gitlin, Todd. 1980. *The Whole World Is Watching: Mass Media in the Making and Unmaking of the New Left.* Berkeley: University of California Press.

Goffman, Irving. 1959. *The Presentation of Self in Everyday Life.* Garden City, N.J.: Anchor Books.

Gold, Raymond L. 1958. Roles in sociological field observations. *Social Forces* 36: 217–23.

Gwaltney, John L. 1981. Common Sense and Science: Urban Core Black Observations. In *Anthropologists at Home in North America: Methods and Issues in the Study of One's Own Society.* Edited by Donald A. Messerschmidt. Pp. 46–61. Cambridge, U.K.: Cambridge University Press.

Hirabayashi, Lane Ryo. 1995. Back to the future: Re-framing community-based research. *Amerasia Journal* 21(1&2): 2103–18.

Johnson, John M. 1975. *Doing Field Research.* New York: Free Press.

Kibria, Nazli. 1993. *Family Tightrope: The Changing Lives of Vietnamese Americans*. Princeton: Princeton University Press.

Kim, Illsoo. 1981. *New Urban Immigrants: The Korean Community of New York*. Princeton: Princeton University Press.

Kwong, Peter. 1987. *The New Chinatown*. New York: Noonday Press.

Ladner, Joyce A. 1971. *Tomorrow's Tomorrow: The Black Woman*. New York: Doubleday.

Liebow, Elliot. 1967. *Tally's Corner: A Study of Negro Streetcorner Men*. Boston: Little, Brown.

Loo, Chalsa. 1980. Community Research among Asian Americans: Problematic Issues and Resolutions. In *Issues in Community Research: Asian American Perspectives [Occasional Paper Number 5]*. Edited by Alice K. Murata and Juanita Salvador- Burris. Pp. 15–22. Chicago, Ill.: Pacific/Asian American Mental Health Research Center.

Lowe, Lisa. 1991. Heterogeneity, hybridity, multiplicity: Marking Asian American differences. *Diaspora* (Spring): 25–44.

MacLeod, Jay. 1987. *Ain't No Makin' It: Leveled Aspirations in a Low-Income Neighborhood*. Boulder, Colo.: Westview Press.

Matsumoto, Valerie J. 1993. *Farming the Homeplace: A Japanese American Community in California, 1919–1982*. Ithaca: Cornell University Press.

Maykovich, Minado Kurokawa. 1977. The difficulties of a minority researcher in minority communities. *Journal of Social Issues* 33 (4): 108–19.

Merton, Robert K. 1972. Insiders and outsiders: A chapter in the sociology of knowledge. *American Journal of Sociology* 78 (July): 9–27.

Messerschmidt, Donald A. 1981. On Anthropology "at Home." In *Anthropologists at Home in North America: Methods and Issues in the Study of One's Own Society*. Edited by Donald A. Messerschmidt. Pp. 3–14. Cambridge, U.K.: Cambridge University Press.

Miller, S. M. 1952. The participant observer and "over-rapport." *American Sociological Review* 17: 97–99.

Miyamoto, S. Frank. 1984 [1939]. *Social Solidarity Among the Japanese in Seattle*. Seattle: University of Washington Press.

Moore, Joan W. 1973. Social constraints on sociological knowledge: Academics and research concerning minorities. *Social Problems* 21 (Summer): 64–77.

Oakley, Ann. 1981. Interviewing Women: A Contradiction in Terms. In *Doing Feminist Research*. Edited by Helen Roberts. Pp. 30–61. London: Routledge and Kegan Paul.

Olesen, Virginia. 1994. Feminisms and Models of Qualitative Research. In *Handbook of Qualitative Research*. Edited by Norman K. Denzin and Yvonna S. Lincoln. Pp. 158–74. Thousands Oaks, Calif.: Sage.

Pollner, Melvin, and Robert M. Emerson. 1988. The Dynamics of Inclusion and Distance in Fieldwork Relations. In *Contemporary Field Research: A Collection of Readings*. Edited by Robert M. Emerson. Pp. 235–52. Heights, Ill.: Waveland Press.

Rabinow, Paul. 1977. *Reflections on Fieldwork in Morocco*. Berkeley: University of California Press.

Reyes, María de la Luz, and John J. Halcón. 1988. Racism in academia: The old wolf revisited. *Harvard Educational Review* Vol. 58, no. 3 (August): 299–314.

Rosaldo, Renato. 1993. *Culture and Truth: The Remaking of Social Analysis*. Boston, Mass.: Beacon Press.

Saito, Leland T. 1998. *Race and Politics: Asian Americans, Latinos, and Whites in a Los Angeles Suburb*. Urbana: University of Illinois Press.

Stack, Carol B. 1974. *All Our Kin: Strategies for Survival in a Black Community*. New York: Harper and Row.

Takezawa, Yasuko. 1995. *Breaking the Silence: Redress and Japanese American Ethnicity*. Ithaca, N.Y.: Cornell University Press.

Thorne, Barrie. 1978. Political activist as participant observer: Conflicts of commitment in a study of the draft resistance movement of the 1960s. *Symbolic Interaction* Vol. 2, no. 1 (Spring): 73–88.

Ui, Shiori. 1991. "Unlikely Heroes": The Evolution of Female Leadership in a Cambodian Ethnic Enclave. In *Ethnography Unbound: Power and Resistance in the Modern Metropolis*. Edited by Michael Burawoy et al. Pp. 161–78. Berkeley: University of California Press.

Võ, Linda Trinh. 1995. Paths to Empowerment: Panethnic Mobilization in San Diego's Asian American Community. Ph.D. dissertation. University of California, San Diego.

Wax, Rosalie. 1971. *Doing Fieldwork: Warnings and Advice*. Chicago: University of Chicago Press.

———. 1979. Gender and age in fieldwork and fieldwork education: No good thing is done by man alone. *Social Problems* 26 (5): 509–22.

Welaratna, Usha. 1993. *Beyond the Killing Fields: Voices of Nine Cambodian Survivors in America*. Stanford: Stanford University Press.

Whyte, William F. 1943. *Street Corner Society*. Chicago: University of Chicago Press.

Wilson, William J. 1974. The New Black Sociology: Reflections on the "Insiders and Outsiders" Controversy. In *Black Sociologists: Historical and Contemporary Perspectives*. Edited by James E. Blackwell and Morris Janowitz. Pp. 327–38. Chicago: University of Chicago Press.

Wolf, Margery. 1992. *A Thrice-Told Tale*. Stanford: Stanford University Press.

Zavella, Patricia. 1987. *Women's Work and Chicano Families: Cannery Workers of the Santa Clara Valley*. Ithaca: Cornell University Press.

Zhou, Min. 1992. *Chinatown: The Socioeconomic Potential of an Urban Enclave*. Philadelphia: Temple University Press.

Zinn, Maxine Baca. 1979. Field research in minority communities: Ethical, methodological and political observations by an insider. *Social Problems* 27 (2): 209–19.

Miliann Kang

---

2   Researching One's Own:
Negotiating Co-Ethnicity in the Field

If we do not interrogate our motives, the direction of our work, continually, we risk
furthering a discourse on difference and otherness that not only marginalizes people
of color but actively eliminates the need for our presence.
   —bell hooks, *Yearning: Race, Gender, and Cultural Politics*

The first time you came here, I thought you were Korean but I usually don't ask.
Actually, I don't like having Korean customers—especially *i-sei* (second generation).
Some of you have forgotten where you come from. . . . I let you do your research
here because you are Korean, but sometimes it makes the customers uncomfortable. I
agreed to let you do it but it would be good if you finish up soon.
   —Mary, Korean nail salon owner, December 5, 1998

Introduction

Ethnographic studies of post-1965 "new" Asian immigrant groups comprise some
of the most exciting emergent scholarship on race and ethnicity. A significant and
increasing portion of this research is conducted by "co-ethnic" scholars who are themselves first- or second-generation immigrants of the groups they are studying. This is
especially true for studies of the Korean immigrant community (Yoon, 1997; Min 1996;
Park 1997; Abelmann and Lie 1995[1]; Kim 1981). The following discussion draws from
my research as a second-generation Korean American woman examining personal
service interactions in Korean-owned nail salons in New York. Although my research
was grounded in theoretical and empirical understandings, I focus on the practical
aspects of researching co-ethnics and its implications for the development of minority
scholars and improving relations between the university and the community.[2] Rather
than attempting any prescriptive statements, this article is meant to foster more open
discussion among emergent scholars who are involved in the complex process of
"researching one's own."[3]

The identification of co-ethnic scholars with their research subjects, their ties to these communities, and their investment in the issues they are investigating challenge traditional views of social science research as objective, distant, and dispassionate. While the negotiation of co-ethnic relations in the field can, on the one hand, foster a more informed, nuanced "insider's" perspective and provide greater access to informants, such negotiation can also prove to be an ambivalent experience for both the researcher and the research subjects. Furthermore, the political implications of these studies for policy and intergroup relations often reach far beyond the boundaries of academic discourse. Qualitative studies involving in-depth interviews and participant observation are particularly fraught with complex personal and professional dilemmas for the investigator. For the co-ethnic researcher, debates on the construction and politics of identity are more than academic and often necessitate placing his or her own identity under the research lens.

Reconceptualizing Insider versus Outsider Positions

In her article in this volume, Linda Trinh Võ provides a thorough review of the debates regarding the ethnic "insider-versus-outsider" perspective in ethnographic studies. Problematizing this simplistic binary framework, she criticizes this debate for reproducing essentialized notions of racial and cultural groups while glossing over other important issues (such as class, generational, and political differences) that influence the collection and interpretation of data. Rather than reiterating concerns regarding insider overidentification and outsider misrepresentation, she argues that "what is needed is the recognition of the multilayered, shifting, and competing similarities and differences between native or insider researchers and their communities—a process that is shaped by simultaneous, ongoing negotiations."

Building on Võ's incisive critique, I also seek to reconceptualize the category of "insider-versus-outsider," utilizing the contributions of critical social theory, symbolic interactionism, and feminist and cultural studies to inform specific concerns regarding co-ethnic studies by and about Asian Americans. In agreement with the theoretical approach of Michael Burawoy, I regard ethnography as a distinctive form of social science inquiry that bridges two competing models of science—positive and reflexive. Positive science "works on the principle of the separation between scientists and the subjects they examine" whereas reflexive science "takes as its premise the intersubjectivity of scientist and subject of study" (Burawoy 1998, 4). Based on these two models, Burawoy illustrates the shifting and overlapping nature of the researcher's subject position in a discussion of his extended case method. He suggests from his own experience—as both an employee of the Zambian copper industry's bureau of research on policy and industrial relations and a white British expatriate engaged in covert research—that all ethnographers are potentially both insiders and outsiders based not on their physical or cultural attributes but on their position and orientation toward their research subjects and field sites. Thus, an ethnographic "insider" is one who enters reflexively into the world of the research subjects and excavates situational knowledge from close involvement in interactive social processes. The ethnographic "outsider" would then be one who asserts the separation of participant and observer; refrains from influencing the field site and the lives of the respondents; targets a standardized, representative sample of the population; and strives for the elimination of any context effects.

There is much to be gained in adopting Burawoy's stance of basing insider/outsider locations not on shared characteristics with research subjects but instead on principles of scientific inquiry. This framing provides more objective criteria for evaluating research findings, shifting discussion away from a researcher's group membership (ethnic or otherwise) to how rigorously and responsibly he or she endeavors to fulfill the principles of reflexive research. It simultaneously frees up the individual researcher from having to prove an "insider's" personal history to gain legitimacy with certain audiences while having to deny the very same to pass the scrutiny of others, thus refocusing the debates on the actual merits of data collection and interpretation.

I am in no way discounting the importance of the co-ethnic relationship in ethnographic studies or counseling its complete subordination to principles of science. While I am in favor of reconceptualizing the basis of insider/outsider status based on the researcher's method of scientific inquiry rather than on individual characteristics, I am not arguing that the co-ethnic relationship is insignificant for ethnographic work. The salience of co-ethnicity in the field is evidenced in the persistence of affective ties, the advantage these ties can confer on the data gathering process, and the ongoing political sensitivity of the social locations of those who represent people of color and their concerns. Failure to recognize the unique relationship of co-ethnic researchers to their own ethnic communities risks revivifying exclusionary academic discourses and practices while sabotaging nascent forays by scholars into previously inaccessible substantive and theoretical domains.

bell hooks, by rigorously interrogating her own cross-cutting gender and racial locations in relation to those she studies, underscores the political dimensions of insider/outsider research as resistance against domination. In a debate with the contributors to the edited volume *Writing Culture: The Poetics and Politics of Ethnography*, hooks argues that the contemporary critique of essentialism by white, male academics can backlash against "indigenous ethnographers" if it is invoked as "a means to dismiss differences or an excuse for ignoring the authority of experience" (hooks 1990, 130). Citing the exclusion of black ethnographers in the volume, she argues that for cultural studies to serve as a critical intervention in the dominant discourse rather than degenerating into "the latest hip racism," they must actively seek institutionalization of marginalized voices while simultaneously remaining vigilant toward the influence of existing power structures.

These issues are particularly significant for Asian American Studies given the recent emergence of research and institutional support, not to mention support from the communities themselves. Asian American scholars are actively engaging in debates regarding reflexivity and are contributing both theoretical frameworks as well as empirical studies informed by these debates (Omi and Takagi 1995; Lowe 1996; Palumbo-Liu 1999). Reflecting on the tradition of community-based research, Hirabayashi comments on the difficulties ethnic scholars have encountered in attempting to satisfy both traditional social science standards and ethnic political agendas:

> In short, in order to control the impact of tacit or explicit biases, reflexivity provides a set of techniques that help researchers bring their assumptions and positionings, whether intellectual or political, to the forefront of their research. The object, then, is not to eliminate biases but rather, to make them explicit, that they may be more fully understood in terms of their role in the overall research process. (Hirabayashi 1995, 113)

I support a somewhat contradictory approach to co-ethnic research that valorizes both the general and the particular. While calling for an alternative framing of the insider/outsider debate that grounds itself not on co-ethnic ties but on reflexive, interpretivist practices, I also believe that the domain of co-ethnic studies possesses certain unique characteristics that demand particular methodological and theoretical approaches, as well as consideration of the social and political contexts in which the research is situated.

Impact of Co-Ethnicity on Data Collection and Interpretation

My fieldwork in New York City nail salons investigating service interactions between Korean female service providers and black and white customers illuminates some of the complex processes involved in negotiating personal, professional, and political concerns in co-ethnic research. Seeking to discern contrasting patterns of interactions according to racial, ethnic, gender, class, and spatial locations, for fourteen months I used the site of nail salons to interrogate dominant discourses and categorizations of intergroup relations, particularly regarding the "Korean-black conflict" and the Asian "model minority." The research questions examined how racially-distinct actors construct categories of self and other, how these constructions influence intergroup relations, and what factors lead to conflict or accommodation. Employing the methodologies of in-depth interviews and participant observation to produce "thick description" (Geertz 1973) of these sites, I addressed the language dynamics, embodied interactions, and influence of the public sphere in the everyday construction of race and contextualized them within broad processes of international migration and the development of the service economy.

Throughout the research, I engaged in reflexive interrogation of the impact on the subjects and findings of my own background as a middle-class, second-generation Korean woman. This has involved attentiveness to my biases and blind spots and accounting for these in the research design. I discovered several examples of how the co-ethnic relationship both facilitates access to subjects and complicates the research findings. The richest insights regarding the identity constructions of the Korean respondents emerged through participant observation of mealtimes with them in the salons. At most of the sites, the women each bring one dish from home and they share a communal Korean-style lunch; after the noontime rush dies down, the women rotate lunch shifts for food and conversation in a small backroom equipped with rice cooker, microwave, and refrigerator. It was during these shared meals that I formulated theoretical questions and gathered empirical findings regarding the Goffmanian contrast between the "frontstage" and "backstage" of the salons (Goffman 1959). The women often revealed attitudes regarding the customers, owners and coworkers as well as of the work itself that were not observable in the performance of service provision. Oftentimes, their backstage comments and behavior contradicted what they revealed in formal interviews as well as in their public presentations of self.

While common taste in ethnic food hardly serves as an indicator of similar subject positions, the knowledge that I was Korean brought forth an invitation to enter into these backstage mealtimes. I would not go so far as to say that only a Korean could have gained such access, but I do believe the co-ethnic relationship facilitated a certain rapport that enabled more intimate access and deeper understandings of the research site. Furthermore, although most owners tend to possess at least basic English conversation skills, the lack of full fluency in the English language on the part of most of the manicurists necessitates at least a working knowledge of the Korean language for in-depth communication. Even in the case of a non-Korean person fluent in the Korean language engaged in participant observation of this kind, I assert that certain cultural affinities and understandings beyond language would still confer advantages to the co-ethnic researcher, allowing him or her a more naturalistic view of the setting.

Several illustrations of the mask conferred by my Korean ethnicity that enabled me to fit somewhat unobtrusively into the research site emerged during my fieldwork. In one salon, the customers inferred from my constant presence and engagement in activities such as answering the phone or going out and buying coffee that I was the daughter of the owner. This prompted them to direct complaints and requests to me, which both facilitated and constrained interaction. Among customers, I encountered respondents who were either noticeably reticent or extremely impassioned when responding to questions regarding stereotypes of Koreans and their success in small business. In either case, it became clear that I was being communicated to not as an objective researcher but as a perceived representative of my ethnic group.

These factors influenced the kind of data collected. The most charged customer responses revolved around perceptions of the 1990 boycott of the Korean-owned Red Apple Market in Brooklyn. The following quotes reveal two very different positions on this issue. The first quote is from an Afro-Caribbean resident of East Flatbush, age mid-thirties, and active in community politics; the other quote is from a Jewish social worker, age mid-fifties, whose Russian parents fled the former Soviet Union:

I'm an NAACP member, so I was involved with it [the boycott]. Has it changed? I don't think I've seen the kind of progress I would have hoped to see. I think we were able to contain it, in terms of damage control of an explosive situation. On the part of the Koreans, initially there was quite a rush to deal with the situation, then the urgency died down and there was no follow-up. I really don't think *your people* have gotten what this is about. (October 8, 1997, emphasis added)

You know, I'm a Russian Jew—so I have a special feeling toward people coming and trying to make a new life in a new country. To attack people based on their ethnicity because they're trying to earn a living—they [blacks] could have done that too [started small businesses]. . . . I admire the ability of *you Koreans* to pull together group resources, to help each other. I'm always open to people who work hard and take care of themselves. (October 1, 1997, emphasis added)

Both sets of comments were aimed, I feel, at the desire to communicate a particular message to me as a Korean, or at least conditioned by that desire. I do not believe that this fact then invalidates the findings, but I do believe this dynamic must be recognized and its impact on the data evaluated and discussed.

In contrast to relations with customers, shared ethnicity creates a different kind of dynamic with the manicurists, allowing them to address me in Korean using the casual grammatical form (*ban-mal*) as well as to make work-related requests of me. Nonetheless, I do not overstate these examples to argue that the co-ethnic researcher does not also alter these settings or that merely possessing common ethnic status as a Korean thereby eliminates class, educational, generational, and cultural differences or the anomalous effects of the researcher's very presence.

One particular field experience crystallized the importance of controlling for co-ethnic biases and subjecting the research design to reformulation. Although the nail salon industry is dominated by Koreans (estimated at 70–80 percent),[4] Chinese, Vietnamese, and Russians also occupy a significant part of the niche. I had not visited any but Korean salons, however, until I was approached by a Korean journalist who needed English language assistance in interviewing non-Korean owners for an article he was writing about increasing ethnic competition among the nail salons. The occasion served not only as an opportunity to reciprocate for his help with initial contacts and information but also opened up new avenues of inquiry. It underscored the importance of working controls into my research design, not so much because I am particularly interested in comparing and contrasting the Korean salons with those operated by other ethnic groups (although this may prove a fruitful future line of research) but because comparing my observations in Korean versus other ethnically-owned salons engages important reflexive processes.

While I am not sure to what degree the precise issues can be predicted in advance, the tendency toward either glossing over tensions in collecting and interpreting data on co-ethnics or seeing the issues as insurmountable only serves to sabotage the research agenda. Specific measures that can be taken to control for co-ethnic bias while upholding the unique contributions of this perspective include incorporating questions that allow for comparisons between co-ethnic and other similar sites, utilizing both co-ethnic and non-co-ethnic research assistants for multiple perspectives, and incorporating and evaluating secondary sources that represent a variety of methodological approaches and theoretical frameworks conducted by diverse researchers.

Relations with Co-Ethnic Research Subjects

Establishing and maintaining relations between the co-ethnic researcher and research subjects presents another area that places particular demands on the co-ethnic researcher. As with any human interaction, in the course of fieldwork a degree of rapport can develop between researcher and respondents and strict boundaries between participant observation and personal interactions become hard to maintain and decipher. In many cases, the greater degree of familiarity and sense of relatedness with subjects imposes higher standards of reciprocity on co-ethnic researchers. In my research, invitations to respondents' homes, churches, or outings constituted rich occasions to gather data but also obscured traditional research boundaries and ethical standards. On one occasion, I spent an afternoon with a distressed manicurist whose teenage daughter was having difficulties in school, but I politely declined her request to meet the daughter in person and tutor her with her homework. In another incident, a manicurist asked for help in securing a work visa. I made a few phone calls on her behalf to government agencies and referred her to a Korean-speaking immigration lawyer who answered a few questions pro bono but asked for payment in order to process the actual application. In both these cases, I felt acutely that my co-ethnic respondents were not satisfied with the degree and kind of response I offered. These women had allowed me into their personal and professional lives, shared their insights and experiences, and provided me with access to their social networks and resources, without which my research would not have been possible. While recognizing their contributions and my indebtedness to them, in the end I believe it was a prudent, albeit painful, decision not to become overinvolved in situations for which I lacked professional expertise as well as personal resources to follow through.

In short, because both researchers and subjects are only human, a certain kind of personal exchange is bound to occur in the field. This human exchange is, in fact, what makes the fieldwork experience meaningful but also messy. The degree to which the researcher successfully maneuvers through these murky waters most often depends on an awareness of general principles of conduct in social science research combined with a willingness to forego strict rules in favor of flexible responses to the immediate issues that arise in the field site. Achieving this co-presence often involves actively restraining the desire to steer conversations toward those topics that are beneficial to the research agenda and, instead, exercising an openness to engage in conversations that seemingly make no direct contribution to the data. For me, these have included sharing information about the college application process for the women's children, serving as a sounding board for their complaints about their families and work, assisting them with personal business requiring usage of the English language, and making referrals or phone calls to social service agencies or immigration offices.

While often time consuming, these conversations ease my own anxiety, establish trust with the research subjects, and often unearth surprising findings that end up informing the data or even redirecting the research design. More importantly, they can make a real difference in the lives of the respondents. In the end, the guidelines for ethical co-ethnic fieldwork involve basic principles of respect and reciprocity that are not so different from the etiquette governing other forms of research and general social life.

The Politics of Co-Ethnic Research

While the relational aspects of co-ethnic research may conform more or less to general principles involving ethical treatment of human subjects, the politics of co-ethnic research often involve attention to special concerns and complex dynamics of racial and ethnic relations in the United States. The various struggles throughout the country for ethnic studies expose the ongoing institutional resistance toward the goals and principles of these programs and the kinds of knowledge they produce. Thus, recognizing that our work is situated within a highly politicized context, co-ethnic researchers must anticipate the possible readings and misreadings of our research and the implications of findings for our communities.

No matter how much a researcher conditions her statements as not speaking for the whole community, both her academic findings and public statements are often automatically imbued with some kind of authority behind their limited pretensions. The tendency of the broader public to cast co-ethnic researchers as spokespeople for their communities thus raises the standard of accountability. While I am painfully aware of my limitations in understanding the New York City Korean American community with which I identify, those who are complete outsiders most often will not question my credentials and instead will tend to take what I say at face value. On the other hand, respect from recent immigrants and community workers for the expertise and authenticity of academics is not something that can be taken for granted; instead, the researcher must earn such respect.

The various stages of development of my own research have underscored these lessons. The nail salon project emerged not from purely intellectual interests but from activism in various Asian American community organizations, particularly the Committee Against Anti-Asian Violence (CAAAV)—a New York City-based pan-Asian organization dedicated to advocating for the rights of victims of bias-related crimes—with which I served as a board member. The April 1992 events in Los Angeles following the verdict in the Rodney King case were still freshly imprinted, and individuals and organizations engaged in work with the Korean American community were undergoing a painful reassessment of crisis-oriented advocacy that mobilized a mostly college-educated, English-speaking, politically progressive constituency. In searching for more organic, proactive, indigenously-led structures to respond to community tensions, CAAAV initiated a workplace literacy project for recent Asian immigrants. The vehicle of holding regular English language classes in locales such as garment factories and nail salons was to serve as the basis for understanding and expanding relations with members of the immigrant community, especially women employed in low-wage, unstable, hazardous jobs.

As the organizing project developed, CAAAV made the decision to focus efforts more on the garment factories and not to pursue the nail salon sites. At the same time, my own research interests in examining microinteractions within the beauty service industry were beginning to crystallize around the nail salons. This precipitated what seemed at the time an agonizing choice between continuing on with the organizing work versus prioritizing my own research agenda, which in hindsight need not have been an either/or decision—or at least not a tormented one. Nonetheless, the tensions of negotiating the demands of community needs versus professional advancement are certainly real and potentially at odds.

The act of researching one's own ethnic group thus imposes various hurdles even beyond the already strenuous demands of completing an advanced degree program or gaining tenure. The lack of institutional support and individual mentoring translates into far too many up-and-coming scholars abandoning worthy projects at their most critical stages, or failing to get them off the ground. Concerns about lending potential ammunition to distasteful political positions and fears of doing violence to self and community cause many researchers to flounder on the shoals of personal contradictions regarding the projects that are nearest and dearest their hearts. This process often exacts an unnecessarily high personal toll on individual researchers, which then translates into high attrition rates, avoidance of the most challenging and important research questions, and the resulting impoverishment of academic disciplines.

Clearer guidelines and more open discussion would contribute greatly to encouraging more scholars to persevere and complete what can often seem daunting and undoable projects and programs. This requires recognizing and prioritizing the need to establish genuinely supportive networks of like-minded colleagues, co-ethnic and otherwise. Rather than assuming the strength of co-ethnic ties, it is essential to acknowledge the difficulties of establishing trust and cooperation both within a competitive academic environment and between the academy and community, and to work actively toward transcending distrust and divisions. In addition, while often enervating and frustrating, seeking out new audiences is crucial to the success of co-ethnic scholars. Preaching to the converted risks further marginalizing research that is already too often ignored or discounted.

In my research, I have tried to salvage some of the earlier political concerns of the project by continuing to ask questions about workplace conditions and occupational-related illnesses resulting from exposure to toxic chemicals in the salons, even though these questions are somewhat out of synch with the current research design. Given the kind of impact the research can have on the community, I have tried to be especially attentive to issues of anonymity, disclosure, and consent and to subject the work to informed scrutiny by other politically engaged researchers. I have also shared my findings with members of the community in the form of written materials and informational meetings with various individuals and organizations.

Satisfactorily negotiating these relations with the community remains one of the most difficult and unresolved issues I have faced in co-ethnic research. I am fortunate to have had the positive experience of collaboration between co-ethnic researchers and community-based organizations. Through the work of Korean Immigrant Worker's Advocates, a labor rights organization in Koreatown, we produced a modest bilingual booklet, *A Bridge Toward Unity*, that is aimed at fostering street-level dialogue between the embattled Korean community and the citizenry of Los Angeles. Whatever the ultimate effectiveness of these efforts, this invaluable experience remains my model of the potential for fruitful cooperation among co-ethnic researchers, organizers, and community members.

Much of the passion underlying co-ethnic research is a desire to contribute to the development of the next generation of Asian American students through the sharing of hard-won insights and common struggles. In addition to researching and publishing, I have found that interacting with students in the classroom has pushed me to own and reconcile the competing roles and responsibilities of co-ethnic research. These students affirm the founding beliefs of Asian American Studies that research responsive to the lives and concerns of students and community achieves the highest standards of academic excellence and relevance.

Although the process of conducting co-ethnic research is challenging, it can also be transformative for the researcher, students, ethnic community, and university, engendering a deeper, more meaningful exploration of self and social world. While I still grapple with feelings of being an imposter or interloper, the rich interactions with respondents and engagement with the enterprise of producing new knowledge about issues of personal concern provide a counterbalance. Despite my assertion that insider/outside status should not be conferred according to the characteristics of the individual researcher, I am clearly distanced from my research subjects by undeniably "American" aspects of my identity, such as limited fluency in the Korean language, lack of knowledge of aspects of Korean culture, and physical isolation from the Korean community. These very limitations, however, have also helped to bridge class and educational barriers—many of the nail salon women assumed a kind of maternal or big sister role in vigorously correcting my Korean and offering tips about how to approach my research—while enabling the perspective necessary for fueling the sociological imagination.

The demands of co-ethnic research thus need not translate into paralysis and instead can inspire new ways of envisioning both empirical and theoretical undertakings. A constant balancing act is called for that gives attention to professional exigencies, political commitments, and personal care. One friend and colleague, who is researching the politics of ethnicity and sexuality in the provision of services to persons with HIV and AIDS while he is also involved in the struggles of this community as a gay Asian male, summed it up eloquently: "I don't care if it takes longer; I want to make sure the soul stays in my work."

Notes

1. While Abelmann is a Korean-speaking white American, Lie identifies himself as a Korean born in Seoul who grew up in Tokyo and Honolulu (Abelmann and Lie 1995, xii).

2. For a more in-depth presentation of my research, see Kang 1997, "Manicuring Race, Gender and Class: Service Interactions in New York City Korean-owned Nail Salons."

3. This statement in no way suggests that theory is not important for co-ethnic studies of Asian Americans, but rather merely indicates the limited focus of this article. For a fuller discussion of these issues, see Omi and Takagi 1995, "Thinking Theory in Asian American Studies."

4. Interview, nail industry spokesperson, September 10, 1997.

References

Abelmann, Nancy, and John Lie. 1995. *Blue Dreams: Korean Americans and the Los Angeles Riots.* Cambridge, Mass.: Harvard University Press.

Burawoy, Michael. 1998. The extended case method. *Sociological Theory* 16(1): 4-33.

Geertz, Clifford. 1973. *The Interpretation of Cultures: Selected Essays.* New York: Basic Books.

Goffman, Erving. 1959. *The Presentation of Self in Everyday Life.* New York: Penguin.

Hirabayashi, Lane Ryo. 1995. Back to the Future: Re-framing Community-based Research. *Amerasia Journal* 21(1&2): 103–18.

hooks, bell. 1990. *Yearning: Race, Gender and Cultural Politics.* Boston: South End Press.

Kang, Miliann. 1997. Manicuring Race, Gender and Class: Service Interactions in New York City Korean-owned Nail Salons. *Race, Gender and Class: Asian American Voices* 4(3): 143–64.

Kim, Illsoo. 1981. *New Urban Immigrants: The Korean Community in New York.* Princeton, N.J.: Princeton University Press.

Lowe, Lisa. 1996. *Immigrant Acts: On Asian American Cultural Politics.* Durham, N.C.: Duke University Press.

Min, Pyong Gap. 1996. *Caught in the Middle: Korean Communities in New York and Los Angeles.* Berkeley: University of California Press.

Omi, Michael, and Dana Takagi, eds. 1995. "Thinking Theory in Asian American Studies." *Amerasia Journal* 21(1&2).

Palumbo-Liu, David. 1999. *Asian/American: Historical Crossings of a Racial Frontier.* Stanford, Calif.: Stanford University Press.

Park, Kyeyoung. 1997. *The Korean American Dream: Immigrants and Small Business in New York City.* Ithaca, N.Y.: Cornell University Press.

Yoon, In-Jin. 1997. *On My Own: Korean Businesses and Race Relations in America.* Chicago: University of Chicago Press.

Andrea Louie

3   Chineseness across Borders:
     A Multisited Investigation of
     Chinese Diaspora Identities

Ethnographic fieldwork has traditionally served as a rite of passage for new anthropologists. It is an endeavor in which the countless hours spent familiarizing oneself
with the history and theories of the discipline, and even the careful attention paid
to ethnographic work produced by the respected elders of the field, prove to be of
disappointingly and discouragingly little use.

In the days in which the bounded community was still thought to exist, it was
believed that an anthropologist could just settle down in a small island or village with
a tent and typewriter, become fluent in the local language, immerse him or herself in
the culture, and return home to write a definitive monograph on his or her "people."
This Malinowskian style of ethnographic research, although still upheld as a model
for participant observation, was exposed as involving more complex dynamics by the
recent publication of his diary, which added a revealing subtext to the authoritative
account of Trobriand life he presented in his monograph (Marcus and Fischer 1986).
Increasing attention has been paid to recognizing the subjectivity of the ethnographer.
The current trend toward reevaluating the project of ethnography in the field of
anthropology is largely a response to this questioning of the ethnographic authority
of the fieldworker, the recognition of the power relations enacted by his or her very
presence as a more privileged (often colonial) outsider, and the subjective nature of
knowledge and its production.

Some things about fieldwork have remained the same. One still deposits oneself
into a "community," and despite how clear the project seemed in the countless *proposed*
methodologies written for grant proposals, one basically has to "wing it."[1] But what
constitutes a field site has changed, and so has the methodology used, the questions
asked, and the way they are asked. Increasing attention to transnational processes—

flows of capital, people, and ideas across national borders (Basch, Schiller, and Stanton-Blanc 1994)—have made it evident that the local is no longer local, and as many would argue, has never been. Bounded communities no longer exist, as nonlocal, broad-scale social, economic and political forces impinge on even the smallest places: the global on the local. Fieldwork informants move; they migrate or travel and become aware of things outside their locality through their TV sets or stories from others who have traveled. The speed at which information, goods, and people travel makes it difficult to make judgments about where one's fieldsite begins and ends and what constitutes the "culture" that one is studying. Anthropologists not only study across (as in transnational) but "study up" (Nader 1972), looking at relations of power and the influence of corporations and institutions on people's lives.

The model of the bounded, isolated community is no longer appropriate as a focus for ethnographic fieldwork. Emphasis has turned toward imagined and invented aspects of communities and traditions (Anderson 1983; Hobsbawm 1983), as well as the impact of traveling discourses on peoples whose lives don't connect on an immediate, face-to-face basis. Anthropologists have paid increased attention to issues of place, space, and identity within the context of globalization—the way that cultures are seen as "occupy[ing] naturally discontinuous spaces" (Gupta and Ferguson 1992, 6)—and to the ideas about culture change and contact that follow from these assumptions. Gupta and Ferguson write that

> the special challenge here is to use a focus on the way space is imagined (but not imaginary!) as a way to explore the processes through which such conceptual processes of place making meet the changing global economic and political conditions of lived spaces—the relation, we could say, between place and space. (1992, 11)

Below I address some of these theoretical and methodological issues through a discussion of my dissertation fieldwork experience in the San Francisco Bay Area and in the Pearl River Delta Region of Guangdong Province, P.R.C.[2]

The Two Parts: Evolution of a Project

My field research began as a two-part examination of the relationship between mainland Chinese and the Chinese abroad. The first part, based on field research in the United States, intended to explore the formation of American-born Chinese American identities in relation to mainland China through focusing on the San Francisco-based "In Search of Roots" program. The second was to investigate mainland Chinese attitudes toward the Chinese abroad, in terms of conceptions of the relationship between overseas Chinese and their ancestral villages (jia xiang, ji guan)[3] in China. This part was based in the Pearl River Delta region of Guangdong Province, the area from which a large number of emigrants originated and whose economy is now booming due to economic reform, its proximity to Hong Kong, and overseas investments.[4] This project has since evolved into a study of the renegotiation of the relationship between Guangdong (Pearl River Delta) Chinese and the Chinese abroad, within the context of the massive changes that have occurred in the relationship of this particular part of China with the "outside" world since Deng Xiao Ping initiated the Open Policy and economic reform in 1978. Below, I trace the evolution of this project—of how the "two parts" developed as parts of a single question: the "changing meaning of being Chinese today" (Tu 1994).

The "In Search of Roots" Program

I first became interested in the Roots (Md. *xun gen*/C. *chahm gan*) program as a participant in the 1992 cohort. This program, for American-born youths of Cantonese descent aged sixteen to twenty-five, provided a structure for the exploration of Chinese American ancestral roots and identities. It was conceived jointly by the Chinese Culture Foundation and Chinese Historical Society of San Francisco and sponsored in addition by the Office of Overseas Chinese Affairs (*Qiao Ban*) of Guangdong province in China. Its format consisted of a series of bimonthly seminars on Chinese American history and genealogical research techniques conducted over a period of four months. The internship culminated in a two-week summer trip to China during which each participant's village was visited in turn under the sponsorship of the Guangdong Province Office of Overseas Chinese Affairs.[5] Family trees and narratives were publicly displayed in a Chinese Culture Center exhibit the following Chinese New Year.

The Roots program was unique for a number of reasons: its localized focus on the Pearl River Delta area in Guangdong province, the region from which most of the early Chinese immigrants to America emigrated; its rooting of Chinese American history in China; and its focus on researching and writing family narratives that combine the tracing of Chinese American family history and roots to an ancestral village in China and personal reflections on one's Chinese American identity.

As a participant, I visited my ancestral village in Heshan (C. *Hoksan*) county, Guangdong Province and met my second grand- uncle (C. *yi suk gung*) and his family in Guangzhou for the first time. Our group also took part in a summer camp program (*hai wai hua yi qing nian xia ling ning*), sponsored by the Chinese government's Office of Overseas Chinese Affairs (*Qiao Ban*), a two-day event consisting of a banquets, site-seeing, and performances that brought together youth of Chinese descent from all over the world. Participation in these activities placed our group at the receiving end of the Chinese government's more structured attempts at influencing the identities of the visiting Chinese Americans (*hua yi*, or descendants of overseas Chinese), based on their assumptions about the loyalty and dedication of the Chinese overseas in building China.

Shenzhen, Guangdong, China

The September following my summer Roots trip in 1992, I arranged to teach spoken English at a high school in the Special Economic Zone of Shenzhen, China, near the Hong Kong—China border. Thus began a process of learning about mainland

Chinese perceptions of overseas Chinese, as I was in various ways contextualized
as an American-born person of Chinese descent by my colleagues and students at
the school. These conceptions usually involved ambiguous, loose, and sometimes
conflicting usages of the English word "Chinese" and the Chinese words *hua ren,
zhong guo ren, hua qiao,* and *hua yi*.[6] The following anecdotes from my field notes
describe typical encounters surrounding my arrival at the school.

> The teachers and students didn't know quite how to place me. They had heard that the
> new English teacher from America was coming, but before I had been introduced officially,
> they wondered who this new arrival to the school was. Some thought I was a new teacher
> from somewhere else in China and asked others what province I was from. One student
> of Senior 2, Class 4, thought I was a new classmate when I took a seat in the back of the
> classroom to observe. Others thought I was the girlfriend or little sister of one of the young
> male teachers who was showing me around.

> A few weeks later, an eighth-grade teacher in her fifties from northern China told me
> that when I had first come, she had thought I was from inland China (*nei di*), Anhui
> province, to be specific. When I asked her about it again later, she said that she'd had no
> idea that I was from overseas. My hair, long and straight and tied in a ponytail with a
> simple band, and low-key demeanor had led her to believe I was "An hui, nong cun de"
> (from the countryside of Anhui province). Another time she told me that I looked "more
> beautiful" than when I first arrived, attributing it to bathing in and drinking the water of
> my home country.

The first few weeks in Shenzhen were part of a process of being contextualized into
the unit (*dan wei*) of Shenzhen City School, not only as the new foreign teacher, but also
as someone of Chinese ancestry and American citizenship. For the students, teachers,
and staff of the school, various preconceptions about the Chinese abroad were put to
a "reality test," as ideologies about Chineseness as racial, cultural, or political were
somewhat confounded when used to understand me in relation to themselves and
the other Chinese they knew. My special status as the invited foreign teacher and a
nonfluent Chinese speaker increased perceptions of me as an outsider. However, I also
didn't fit neatly into preexisting conceptions of a *wai ji lao shi* (foreign teacher)—that
is, blond and blue-eyed. While as a *mei ji hua ren*, an American of Chinese descent,
there existed a political and cultural category into which I could be placed, the fit was
by no means exact. Few of the teachers or students had actually met a foreign-born
person of Chinese ancestry, especially someone who "looked Chinese" but spoke
broken Mandarin and was not fully competent in negotiating daily life in China.
From the same individual's mouth I would hear, "I am glad to help you because
you are Chinese" and at other times, "You don't have to do that because you are
a foreigner."

Being "rewritten as Chinese" was a process that involved marking various traits I
was perceived as having as "Chinese"—my quiet demeanor, the way I dressed, my
values, and my physical features.[7] However, the most common way of contextualizing
me, after having established that I was an American citizen of Chinese descent, was to

ask how many generations ago my ancestors had emigrated to the United States, and where they were from in China. Soon, people I had not told directly somehow knew that my ancestral village was in Guangdong province, Heshan county. I realized later that in this immigrant city of Shenzhen, everyone was identified in terms of his or her native place and that these *lao xiang* (native place fellow) ties were of both practical and symbolic significance, and were extended to the Chinese abroad. I also learned that the concept of *xun gen* (C. *chahm gan*), or searching for roots, had its own culturally and historically based meaning in China, and I began to want to explore more deeply both the politically and the culturally defined conceptions of Chineseness that underlay the Chinese government's more obvious motives for setting up the summer camps that I had attended earlier that summer.

Fitting the Pieces Together

I returned to graduate school from teaching English in China intending to continue researching these culturally and politically rooted conceptions of "Chineseness" from both sides of the Pacific, through focusing on these two groups (American-born Cantonese Americans and Guangdong Chinese) who were brought together around the idea of roots-searching by the Chinese government. I planned to explore Chinese American identities within the politics of multiculturalism in the United States and as structured through programs like Roots, and then investigate mainland Chinese conceptions, both official and folk, of the Chinese abroad. Throughout various attempts to conceptualize this research problem, I struggled to find a framework that would connect the various geographically and culturally scattered parts of the project. I was not studying a physically, politically, socially, or culturally bounded community. In fact, few American-born Chinese had spent an extensive amount of time in mainland China, and fewer Guangdong Chinese had come into close contact with Chinese born abroad (with the exception of Hong Kong Chinese), especially those of the third and fourth generations. The extent to which this could even be referred to as an "imagined community" (Anderson 1983) was sketchy. Asian American identity politics advocated empowerment through U.S.-based identities with an aversion to petty subgroup loyalties that were viewed as divisive to common goals as minorities in the United States.[8] A large number of American-born Chinese saw themselves as "Americans" who had, like generations before them, "melted" into U.S. society. At the same time, many Guangdong Chinese would claim they knew little about the Chinese abroad, only that they were probably richer than they were and that some had "returned" to invest in China. The racial constructions of Chineseness that fueled modern Chinese nationalism, and cultural conceptions that perhaps predated it, were extended to conceptions of overseas Chinese in often subtle, ambivalent, unconscious ways.

Both Chinese Americans and mainland Chinese formed conceptions of the Chinese or Chinese American "other" at a distance, not through direct contact and interaction, but with second-hand information filtered through Chinese government constructions of the Chinese abroad and Western discourses on the "Orient." Linkages had to be sought more often through shared histories and genealogies than through current shared political or cultural ideals, thus rendering this attempt at structuring a community vulnerable to deconstruction should its parts actually be brought together for a kind of "first contact" (Schieffelin and Crittenden 1991).[9]

In 1995 I returned to the Pearl River Delta area of Guangdong to continue with my research, somewhat unclear about how to proceed with an investigation of people's attitudes toward the Chinese abroad, and about the more abstract topics of roots-searching and native place ties. I planned to find out to what extent socialist reforms had brought about new forms of social identities through the suppression of tradition, and bureaucratic practices and controls that had supplanted more "traditional" closed-community, lineage-based forms of identification. Had shared urban identities controlled through the *hukou* (household registration system) and *dan wei* (work unit) systems made ties to native place less significant? I wanted to see through what mechanisms and practices links to overseas Chinese relatives and friends were viewed, if not through more historically-rooted ties of shared place, property, and ancestors. On what foundation were these relationships perceived as being based—other than obligation as kin? In other words, how were status and power relations enacted within these kinship relations? Conducting fieldwork in an urban setting where relations and trust depended largely on personal networks, it was difficult to know where and how to start asking questions about such abstract issues. I needed to ground my fieldwork in issues more relevant to people's daily lives.

Most informants in Guangzhou, upon initial inquiry, would say they knew little about overseas Chinese, and that I should really talk to Mr. "Li" who had a brother in Indonesia. However, further more casual inquiries led to more complex and nuanced conceptions of the Chinese abroad discussed in relation to their own status in China. I was told that overseas Chinese were no longer as special. Since the Open Policy, more people have had opportunities to emigrate. The phrase "nan feng chuang" (southern breeze window), formerly used to represent the window of opportunity provided by having a relative abroad, was no longer in fashionable use because these opportunities were no longer as pronounced. Previously, having relatives outside mainland China gave one access to the privilege of buying duty-free goods such as televisions and washing machines that brought great status to the families who owned them. Now these items were available openly on the Chinese market to anyone who could pay for them.

Many Guangdong residents from more prosperous areas of the Pearl River Delta reflect on changes that have occurred in their understanding of the lives of their friends and relatives abroad. "Outside" (overseas) used to be seen as a "heaven" (*tian tang*). But now many said, "We know that things aren't necessarily better there. I can be a 'first class citizen' [*di yi deng gong min*] here in China. In the United States, Chinese have to work long hours washing dishes and are discriminated against. Ten years ago, we were very poor, but now I can make money here in China. Some people are choosing to stay here." These shifts in attitude coexisted and sometimes conflicted with pre-Open Policy attitudes toward the Chinese abroad.[10]

Reframing the Question

How can the impact of these changes in living standards that have accompanied the Open Policy and economic reforms be measured on a social and cultural level? It is evident that Guangdong Chinese are in the process of reworking old conceptual-izations of overseas Chinese as privileged sons whose flexibility of movement and opportunities for earning foreign capital and attaining higher living standards has in the past made them the objects of blind envy (*xian mu*) for those who feel they have been left behind. Increased access to information about the "outside" world combined with improvements in living standards at home have resulted in more multidimensional assessments of the status of overseas Chinese, fostering a sense of relativism about the development of China in relation to the West and a critical assessment of which lifestyle may be appropriate for themselves. This involves an understanding of the conditions of living as a minority in a non-Chinese country.

Given these shifts in orientation, attempting to discuss second-, third-, and fourth-generation Chinese Americans in relation to Guangdong residents seemed an even more farfetched attempt to connect two populations linked only a few generations back in the villages of rural Guangdong. But American-born Chinese Americans—even those who (at an extreme) are not sure whether they are "Cantonese" or "Man-darin," think *ju yuk beng* (Md. *ji rou bing*) is a type of meat loaf, and learn about Chinese culture from *gung fu* films—are increasingly connected to mainland China in new ways through processes accompanying globalization. The rise of the Pacific Rim as a global economic power, the appearance of China in the news around issues of trade and human rights, the increase in the number of immigrants from the Pacific and accompanying controversies over immigration policies in the United States, and accelerated flow of information and people across national borders have brought the image of mainland China more to the forefront of the American public. More historically-rooted Orientalist images of the "Far East" continue to shape images of China on another level—as an exotic, mysterious, and underdeveloped region. For these new generations of Chinese Americans who in many ways learn more about "Chinese culture" outside the home than from their parents, these discourses have a heightened impact. Ien Ang, an Indonesian-born Dutch citizen of Chinese descent, comments, "I have always had to see it [China] as *my* country, even if only imaginarily" because "throughout my life, I have been implicitly or explicitly categorized, willy-nilly, as a 'Chinese.'" Regardless of the degree to which the Chinese abroad choose to identify as "Chinese" or "Chinese American" or with China as a place of origin, motherland, or the seat of Chinese culture, there is, according to Ang, a "pressure toward diasporic identification with the mythic homeland" that problematizes the label of "Chineseness" for the Chinese abroad (Ang 1994, 5). Ang proposes a reconcep-tualization of this label to free people of Chinese descent from this forced identification.

At this point it became necessary to ask not how the two parts of my research project fit together, but rather how and why they didn't. In what ways did conceptualizations of diaspora no longer suffice to explain the "many ways of being Chinese" in the world and the relationships among those called or who call themselves Chinese? It was perhaps more appropriate to focus on problematizing the various hegemonic definitions of Chineseness defined through discourses of homeland and diaspora produced by the Chinese state, the international media, and intellectuals, and to examine the shifting connections and relations of power within and affected by these constructions. It is necessary to problematize conceptions of "Chineseness" through reworking unidimensional definitions of Chineseness within a Chinese diaspora "community" to which members, to differing degrees and in different ways, think of themselves as belonging. It is also necessary to examine the processes through which different parts of the world interact based on preconceptions formed at a distance, and the ways mainland Chinese and the Chinese abroad become "other" to each other through processes of comparison.

As people become more mobile, the boundaries between the categories "Chinese" and "overseas Chinese" (or the Chinese abroad) become increasingly blurred for many, as people shift from one category to the other and back. Cultural practices and identity are no longer necessarily coincident with descent, geographical location, or citizenship. A Chinese of foreign citizenship can return to China from abroad, and Chinese citizens can go abroad for business, travel, or study. Some Chinese try to establish foreign citizenship for the flexibility it will allow them when they move back to China to conduct business with foreign companies. The relations between people of Chinese descent in different parts of the world are changing, perhaps most prominently in southern China where post-Open Policy development and flows of information and capital from the "outside" are resulting in a renegotiation of the relationship between Guangdong Chinese and overseas Chinese.

The process of developing my field site and research problem brought out some of the methodological and theoretical difficulties of taking on the transnational question of the Chinese diaspora. The cohesiveness of this concept as an academic or intellectual construct is betrayed by the actual diversity within it, making it impossible to study the Chinese diaspora as an undifferentiated whole. Below I place these issues within a more analytical framework by discussing in further detail the necessity of a multisited perspective, the problem of ethnographic authority and cultural authenticity, and finally, issues relating to doing fieldwork within one's "own group."

Multisited Fieldwork: Perspectives and Questions for Transnational Studies

My research focused on a transnational, diasporic "community" in that it involved field research conducted in both the United States and mainland China. However, unlike many studies of transnational communities that follow migrants in their back-and-forth movements, the connections between the various geographical sites of my study were less clear-cut. I looked at extreme ends of what has been called a diasporic, transnational community that is being reconnected as various parts of the world interact in new ways. This "community" of multigenerational Cantonese

American youth and residents of the Pearl River Delta area in Guangdong, China (the ancestral region of both populations), has been separated through both geographic and historical circumstances but can be connected within the imagined space of "Chineseness" in relation to the imagined "place" of China.

The study of transnational, diasporic communities has necessitated the need for multisited ethnographic work to take into account these nonlocal spaces. Nontraditional methodologies and perspectives are required to understand the connections and influences between the various sites of production and traveling discourses that influence the scattered parts of communities, which are often defined in different ways by people both within and outside of them. In my research it became evident that China as a symbolic center of Chineseness had an effect on American-born Chinese, just as imaginations (Appadurai 1990) of life overseas influenced Guangdong Chinese perceptions of their own life conditions. Special attention had to be paid to conceptions of historical memory and connections that subjects drew between themselves and others in their imagined community.

I conducted research in San Francisco, Shenzhen, Hong Kong, and Guangzhou and purposely did not define a geographically-bound field site. Because the Cantonese "community," especially through its imaginings, cannot be centered or situated in one place, my research was theme-focused and multisited. I interpreted daily experiences at scattered research sites as research materials presented methodological issues concerning the boundaries of my field site and resultant questions arose concerning verification, validity, and limits of interpretation of my data. But, given the nature of transnational flows, and because identity is always situated, under negotiation, and never complete, the exploration of identity exploration at specific sites and at specific moments of contact became more important than delineating a fixed geographical site. It was necessary to trace connections, following the contours of ideas and social actors by moving among these people and ideas that were also in motion.[11]

On Ethnographic Authority and Cultural Authenticity

Since the publication of *Anthropology as Cultural Critique* (Marcus and Fischer 1986), *Writing Culture* (Clifford and Marcus 1986), and other theoretical works that called into question the ethnographic authority of the fieldworker, increasing attention has been paid to questions of power and positionality in the conducting of field research. Attempts have been made to demonstrate an awareness of these issues thorough the use of forms of reflexive and dialogic ethnographic writing.

A particular challenge in recognizing the power of ethnographic authority is the need to engage in an interpretive analysis beyond mere reflexivity while still recognizing the potential effects of one's academic authority. Too much attention to power and positionality can render one paralyzed to speak for or about others because of the exercise of power this act represents. Conversely, in speaking with any degree of authority about the people one is studying, one runs the risk of representing them in an essentializing and judgmental manner. These issues become magnified when dealing with phenomena of cultural production, invention, and authenticity. In such cases, emphasis on the imagined or invented aspects of culture places much of the interpretation of these processes, again, under the interpretive authority of the ethnographer. Ethnographic monographs can become powerful bases for the canonization and commodification of cultures (Handler 1988; Jackson 1995), especially for minority or formerly colonized peoples who are struggling to revive their "traditional" cultures. Authoritative descriptions of cultures and authentic traditions chronicled by anthropologists and historians in their academic work often become models against which the authenticity of these revived cultures is measured (Borofsky 1987; Handler 1988; Handler and Linnekin 1984; Jackson 1995). In such cases, these descriptions of cultures and traditions as "imagined" and "invented" can sometimes become synonymous with judgments of "inauthenticity," which both downplays cultural continuities and portrays these processes of cultural change as involving the invention of fictitious identities.

How, then, is it possible to recognize the dynamic, fluid nature of culture without invoking comparisons between more and less authentic forms of cultural practice? This question comes to the fore when studying diasporic, multisited communities in which one first has to define what holds the community together before attempting to study and analyze it. My research is linked by the common thread of "Chineseness"—the ways it is used as both an inclusive and exclusive concept, empowered as racial discourse, used to reinforce a sense of rootedness, or turned into a commodity; the way it is sometimes stretched to include the many people of the diaspora, and at other times to distinguish one group from many others normally included in this category. Chineseness, like all forms of identity, is not a fixed or bounded category, and its meaning only becomes relevant as people use it as a tool to define themselves in relation others. For this reason, this research needed to be not only comparative and contextualized, but also attentive to the dynamics of constructions of "Chineseness." In its analysis of "Chineseness" this research had to work around commonly-found conceptualizations—both folk and academic—of "Chinese culture" as a static, objectified set of cultural beliefs and practices, and the notions of cultural change that accompany such perspectives. As Ien Ang observes, perceptions of China as the center of Chineseness imply that there are ways of being more and less pure and authentically Chinese:

> The symbolic construction of "China" as the cultural/geographical core of "Chinese identity" forces "westernized" overseas Chinese to take up a humble position, even a position of shame and inadequacy over her own "impurity." (Ang 1994, 13)

In working with the diversity of expressions and conceptions of Chineseness in this project, I found it essential to address the often imagined, invented traditions of "Chineseness" among American-born Chinese along with more China-centered views of Chineseness that hold more authenticity and cultural capital, being careful not to judge one as more "Chinese" than the other.

Field Stories: Anthropologist as Subject

In the fieldwork process, all knowledge is filtered through the lens of one's own experiences, interactions, and perceptions. The extensive use of oneself as a "subject" and filter for observations is a concern inherent to the process of anthropological research. These issues were intensified for me—a Chinese American researching Chinese American identity (and a Chinese from abroad investigating mainland Chinese contextualizations of overseas Chinese). As an American-born Chinese of Cantonese descent, I hesitantly but unavoidably placed myself within the analysis of my fieldwork. However, despite temptations to indulge in postmodern reflexivity, the study was not about me.

Concerns over representation and positionality and the close relationship between my family and personal history to the topic necessitated that I situate myself within the research. Through positioning myself both as a researcher and a subject, obtaining a diversity of points of view from both Chinese Americans and mainland Chinese, and through employing a variety of field methods, I collected information while recognizing it not to be fully objective or representative. The most valuable insights were obtained through informal participant observation, as others reacted to and interacted with me as an American-born Cantonese American. As such, my "problem" traveled with me; whether sitting in the school's barbershop, talking with students and teachers, riding on a train to Congqing, or visiting relatives in Guangzhou or Hong Kong.

I spent a great deal of time in the barbershop, attached to the high school where I taught English and run by an entrepreneurial young woman from Guangzhou named A Xiang. Customers would often ask A Xiang who I was and proceed to ask me questions directly. One customer asked whether I liked China because everyone has "yellow skin and black hair." Another time, a customer asked if I was a white foreigner because I was speaking English with one of the teachers. Another friend replied in Cantonese, "She's one of us Guangdong people." Students commented to me that "you should stay here longer because this is your motherland" and theorized that I should learn Chinese more quickly than did the previous foreign teacher, a white American, because of my Chinese heritage. One teacher at the school asked me if it weren't for my family and friends in America, where would I choose to live (China or America)? She also asked if China and America were at war, who would I want to win?

The last day of my class, the students in one section held special activities to mark the occasion. One student sang John Denver's "Country Roads" because "Andrea is Chinese and China is her homeland." Another who had to draw a picture of me for a game drew a simple sketch of a woman and colored the face yellow. She said, "I'll explain. Andrea is Chinese so she has yellow skin and black hair."

I had conversations with my Hong Kong relatives about their changing relationship with their mainland relatives, who in their eyes were much better off in recent years than they had been in the past, and conversations with my grand uncle's family in

Guangzhou regarding how they felt about meeting my cousins from the United States, many of whom they could not communicate with because of the language barrier.

The train ride for a research trip to Congqing proved to be an experiment in itself, as I and an Anglo American colleague from Berkeley accompanied a young woman from a village near Congqing, Sichuan Province, back to her hometown. There we were, a "foreigner," an "overseas Chinese," and a "local" person occupying three hard sleepers across from three strangers. One of the most interesting moments was when one of our bunkmates commented to me about how impressed she was with my American friend's good Chinese (not realizing that mine was no better).

Being of Chinese, specifically Cantonese, descent affected my research in numerous ways. It allowed me to participate as an intern in the "In Search of Roots" program and to observe not too conspicuously and with genuine personal interest and relevance as a researcher at later meetings and events. In China, my Chinese and, more often, my Cantonese descent was used as a basis for establishing familiarity or closeness, based more often on perceptions of shared heritage and "blood" than culture or experience.[12] As a *hua yi* (descendant of overseas Chinese), I was not fully expected to know about my Chinese heritage and could therefore get away with asking "stupid" or "obvious" questions, and then be taught the answer as part of my training for becoming a proper Chinese. My questions were viewed as less intrusive because they were about issues of "Chineseness" that were seen in some ways as applying to me, my relatives, or ancestors. Associates at the university I was affiliated with in Guangzhou commented that I was in a good position to do this research, since many people would not talk to a regular "foreigner" about these issues, nor would a "foreigner" have as much access to interviews with the Office of Overseas Chinese Affairs (*Qiao Ban*). Nevertheless, my position as an overseas Chinese most likely also imposed limitations for my research, as I represented in many ways the privileged overseas Chinese from which many informants differentiated themselves. The subtle relations of power that were enacted by my holding an American passport undoubtedly altered how I was perceived and treated, and the attitudes shared with me.

On a final note, it is important to remember that the necessity of positioning oneself within one's research should be balanced by a caution to do so in a strategic manner. In ethnic studies, unlike most other disciplines, ethnographic authority is often drawn from membership in a particular minority group, based on the belief that these experiences are an integral part of understanding, studying, and engaging in activism for that group. While lived experiences undeniably do provide a basis of knowledge and authority, it is also because of these dynamics that the line between scholarship and personal agenda becomes hard to draw. The difficulty of separating the two becomes more problematic for Asian Americans engaged in ethnographic research in which the researcher by nature becomes entangled in questions of the effects of one's own subjectivity on the outcome of his or her research. Being perceived as too close to the issues, and therefore not objective, is a common dilemma of "native" anthropologists, with the added potential of being accused of engaging in the study for reasons of personal exploration. It may be necessary to think about in what other ways it is possible to gain legitimate academic authority without invoking one's ethnicity.

Notes

1. An archaeologist friend pointed out the irony that cultural anthropologists aren't better prepared for their field research. It seemed strange to her that archaeologists appeared to receive more training in methodology than sociocultural anthropologists, especially because "we're working with inanimate objects, but you guys are working with living people."

2. Throughout this analysis, I will attempt to strike a balance between engaging in the self-indulgent, autobiographical tone that characterizes many reflexive meditations on positionality and the acknowledgment of the implications of my own subjectivity on my research.

3. Chinese words are in Mandarin Chinese and are transcribed according to the *pinyin* system, unless otherwise noted. If Cantonese and/or both Cantonese and Mandarin pronunciations are given, the Cantonese is denoted by a "C." and the Mandarin by an "Md."

4. Guangdong, the southernmost province of China (with the exception of Hainan), is located on the South China Sea near Hong Kong. The Pearl River Delta area (*Zhujiang san jiao zhou*) is an alluvial plain system formed by the west (*xi*), north (*bei*) and east (*dong*) tributaries of the Pearl River.

5. This organization is represented at all administrative levels of government in most parts of the Guangdong province, from district (*zhen*) to province. It also is an official branch of the national government's central committee.

6. *Hua ren* refers to anyone descended from a Han Chinese, whether residing in China or abroad. *Zhong guo ren* brings connotations of citizenship, incorporating all nationalities—Han and minority—living on Chinese land. *Hua qiao* is a political term that refers to a Chinese national who has lived abroad for more than two years. *Hua yi* are descendants of overseas Chinese.

7. My barber friend even told me that I had a "Cantonese head" (*Guangdong tou*), characterized by the degree to which it protruded in the back. Even my "quick" progress in learning Cantonese was attributed to my heritage.

8. This Asian American cultural nationalist viewpoint has received less emphasis recently in favor of a perspective that emphasizes diasporic connections between Asian Americans and their ancestral countries. See Sau Ling C. Wong (1995).

9. In their book *Like People You See in a Dream*, Schieffelin and Crittenden (1991) describe "first contact" between European explorers and the natives of Papua New Guinea, who had never before seen a white man. While the European world view had a place for these tribal New Guineans in the categories of the "primitive" and "savage" peoples living in undeveloped areas of the world, the New Guineans struggled to understand the coming of the Europeans in a manner consistent with their own cosmology.

10. Guangdong province has spearheaded economic reforms that have made China the fastest growing economy in the world. Since Deng Xiao Ping's decision in 1978 to implement economic reforms and the open door policy, the province has undergone dramatic changes in all sectors. Its proximity and ties to nearby Hong Kong led to the decision to open three special economic zones (SEZ)—Shenzhen and Zhuhai in 1978, Shantou in 1980—that have focused

on market reforms and infrastructure building (Yeung and Chu 1994) and stimulated foreign investment through an incentive system. Changes were not limited to these zones. Reforms have also been made in rural and urban sectors outside of the SEZs, and many industries have moved to smaller urban centers in the Pearl River Delta area, such as Dongguan, Zhongshan, and Jiangmen where labor is cheaper and immigration controls for workers from inner provinces less strict.

Statistics dramatically demonstrate this economic growth. While the real economic growth for China between 1981 and 1991 averaged 8.8 percent per year, Guangdong's was 12.8 percent. Guangdong's GDP (gross domestic product) grew by 7.12 times. (Yeung and Chu 1994, 6). In 1978 the difference in wages between Guangdong and neighboring provinces was 10 percent, but by 1990 it ranged from 35 to 70 percent (1994, 9). The result has been massive labor migration from poorer areas within Guangdong and other provinces. Estimates put the growth of this mobile population at 12.95 percent per year from 1979 to 1989.

11. Email became a primary way of communicating with Chinese American "informants" in the United States, just as the telephone was for informants in China.

The following anecdote is an example of subjects in motion. One of my last days in Hong Kong at the end of my fieldwork, I decided to venture into Mong Kok's Fa Yuen Gai outlet district to do some last minute shopping for bargain brand name clothing made for export. Feeling quite anonymous among the throngs of pedestrians on this crowded street, I reeled with surprise when I heard my name called in Chinese. I turned around to see Mr. Ruan, the Qiao Lian (Overseas Chinese Union) official who had, days earlier, accompanied me to my maternal grandmother's ancestral village in rural Duan fen, Taishan, approximately a three-hour ferry and one-hour bus ride from Hong Kong. He said he was here for business and travel; this was his second visit to Hong Kong. He seemed not nearly as disconcerted as I was with the differences in setting between the small, poor, agricultural district in Taishan and this bustling city street in Kowloon.

12. I was "incorporated" into a group of teachers and staff from the Pearl River Delta region and referred to by many of them as *"ji gei yahn"* (Md. *zi ji ren*), a term that I was told often literally referred to one's own kin, or people from one's own region. The application of this reference to me probably stemmed from a combination of my Cantonese ancestry and my efforts to speak Cantonese with both teachers and staff, and their efforts to establish friendship and familiarity with me.

References

Anderson, Benedict. 1983. *Imagined Communities: Reflections on the Origin and Spread of Nationalism.* London: Verso and New Left Books.

Ang, Ien. 1994. On not speaking Chinese. *New Formations* 24 (Winter).

Appadurai, Arjun. 1990. Disjuncture and difference in the global cultural economy. *Public Culture* 2 (2):1–24.

Basch, L., N. Glick Schiller, and C. Stanton-Blanc. 1994. *Nations Unbound: Transnational Projects, Postcolonial Predicaments and Deterritorialized Nation States.* Langhorne, Penn.: Gordon and Breach.

Borofsky, Robert. 1987. *Making History: Pukapukan and Anthropological Constructions of Knowledge.* New York: Cambridge University Press.

Clifford, J., and George Marcus, eds. 1986. *Writing Culture: The Poetics and Politics of Ethnography.* Berkeley: University of California Press.

Gupta, Akhil, and Ferguson, James. 1992. Beyond culture: Space, identity, and the politics of difference. *Cultural Anthropology* 7(1): 1–23.

Handler, Richard. 1988. *Nationalism and the Politics of Identity in Quebec.* Madison: University of Wisconsin Press.

Handler, Richard, and Linnekin, Jocelyn. 1984. Tradition, genuine or spurious. *Journal of American Folklore* 97:273–90.

Hobsbawm, Eric. 1983. Introduction: Inventing Traditions. In *The Invention of Tradition.* Edited by Eric Hobsbawm and Terence Ranger. New York: Cambridge University Press.

Jackson, Jean. 1995. Culture, genuine and spurious: The politics of Indianness in the Vaupes, Colombia. *American Ethnologist* 22(1): 3–27.

Marcus, George, and Michael Fischer. 1986. *Anthropology as Cultural Critique: An Experimental Moment in the Human Sciences.* Chicago: University of Chicago Press.

Nader, Laura. 1972. Up the Anthropologist: Perspectives Gained from Studying Up. In *Reinventing Anthropology.* Edited by D. Hymes. New York: Pantheon.

Schieffelin, Edward L., and Robert Crittenden. 1991. *Like People You See in a Dream: First Contact in Six Papuan Societies.* Stanford, Calif.: Stanford University Press.

Tu Wei Ming, ed. 1994. *The Living Tree: The Changing Meaning of Being Chinese Today.* Stanford, Calif.: Stanford University Press.

Wong, Sau Ling C. 1995. Denationalization Reconsidered: Asian American Cultural Criticism at a Theoretical Crossroads. In the series "Thinking Theory in Asian American Studies," *Amerasia Journal* 21(1&2).

Yeung, C. M., and David Chu, eds. 1994. *Guangdong: Survey of a Province Undergoing Rapid Change.* Shatin, N.T., Hong Kong: Chinese University Press.

Part II

The Sites of Identity
and Community

Rick Bonus

4   Of *Palengkes* And Beauty Pageants: Filipino American-Style Politics in Southern California

> *Nakita mo na . . .'di ba parang palengke?*
> *Anong say mo? Bukas, lalo na!*
> *Coronation ng Miss USA-Philippines!*
>
> [So you see . . . isn't it like a marketplace?
> What can you say? Tomorrow, even more!
> It's the coronation of Miss USA—Philippines!]
>   —Interview excerpts, 1992–1995

To ask about "politics" and where it could be found, or what shape it takes, is to ask some rather complicated questions. Whenever conversations with my informants turned into what they thought about politics, I usually got a wide spectrum of responses about topics ranging from presidential performance to what was on TV last night. Occasionally, there would also be blank stares or queries made in return: "What do you mean by politics, *hijo* [son]? What are you thinking about? Are you referring to what people do out there in Congress and the White House? Or, do you mean the weekly meetings we have here in National City?"[1] During my fieldwork, as I'm sure has been the experience for other fieldworkers, I have encountered numerous incidents like this when expectations of clear-cut answers turned into diverse and complex narratives that invariably propelled the ethnography into unforseen directions. Needless to say, these episodes have also compelled me to reflect upon and rethink taken-for-granted assumptions about ideas and concepts learned in academia and the ways in which the tales of the field invalidate, complicate, or temper them.

In this essay, I use these occasions to work through partial and selected accounts of what constitutes "politics" and "politicking" among Filipino American immigrants in Southern California, subjects of a three-year ethnography I carried out as part of a larger project on the area's cultural politics of ethnicity. Specifically, I offer here a set of striking connections between the manners in which respondents expressed their ideas about "politics" and how these related to their social sense of themselves as Filipinos in America. Hence, it is in the fundamental sense of evoking a "Filipino American style of politics" that I employ as a wedge for understanding articulations of identities as Filipino Americans. In writing about these frequent interlocutions between "politicking" and "Filipino Americanness," I also situate the significant negotiations across these poles within the dialogues I had with respondents. My primary aim in doing this is to make more apparent than usual the dynamics of sense-making that occur on the level of conversation: for example, how meanings were negotiated especially when their notion of "politics" competed with mine. Note that in emphasizing the multivalances of such a notion, I have thus referred to it always with quotation marks.

While acknowledging the multiplicity of perceptions my respondents had in thinking and speaking about "politics," I limit my discussion to two levels or sites of articulating "politics," not so much to minimize other narratives that do not neatly fall into the category of relevance or significance but to highlight the frequency and force of certain patterns of responses that point to specific and shared understandings among the people with whom I interacted. As the quotation above suggests, references to "politics" are usually made in terms of its character—*palengke* [marketplace]—as well as one of its venues—the beauty pageant. I explore these two intersecting arenas of meaning-making to argue that "doing politics" for these Filipino Americans points to particular practices and sites of significant negotiations of Filipino Americanness among themselves and in dialogue with the larger society. These practices reveal local registers of resistance to mainstream forms of "politicking" that, on one hand, defy mainstream protocols and impede full inclusion into the American "body politic," but on the other, encourage alternative forms of community building that are predicated upon gestures that circumscribe and navigate through the dynamics of participation and access.

Palengke-Style Politics

In many encounters I have had with first-generation Filipino American residents in San Diego, there have been occasions when our conversations about "politics" would center on opinions about what happened in the latest get-together of the Council of Pilipino American Organizations of San Diego County, Inc. (COPAO), which held meetings of its House of Delegates every second Thursday of the month in National City. Even though I usually made it a point to refer to "politics" by quickly adding "whatever that means to you," many respondents who live around San Diego would mention, at least, some connection to activities pertaining to COPAO, the local site of Filipino American "politics." "What you need to see," said Roger Alano,[2] "if you really want to see the politics we have, is to go to COPAO meetings, the *palengke* of FilAm politics, *'ika nga* [as they say]."[3]

"What do you mean by *palengke*?" I asked. "*Palengke . . . e 'di parang palengke! Nakapunta ka na ba sa palengke sa atin? Ganoon! Labu-labo! Kaniya-kaniya.*" [Palengke . . . well it's like a marketplace. Have you been to a marketplace in our country? It's like that! It's a melee! To each his or her own.] I began resurrecting images of how I remember *palengkes* in the Philippines: wet markets in the city where tons of fresh produce would be hawked by sellers screaming for attention, yelling out prices of goods, names of vegetables, fish just delivered, meat that just came in; vendors and buyers haggling at all hours of the morning; filth and stench; and edibles and garbage alike inches away from each other. I was appalled for a moment. Then, Mr. Alano continued:

> You should go and attend the meetings we have. People from as far as North County[4] all the way to the [Mexican] border make it a point to be there. You'll get to see how we do our own kind of politics here. You'll get to see these personalities and celebrities. . . . Oh, they could be real dirty there, you know. Plus, you'll catch the latest gossip, and God knows what's the next thing they're up to. Most of the time, there's so much yelling, screaming, and . . . what do you call that? Feuding . . . public feuding. It's really a *palengke.*

My initial shock quickly turned into a mixture of excitement and apprehension. I have heard about COPAO through articles about its activities reported in community newspapers and also by word of mouth through several key informants. Many other interviewees have indeed referred to COPAO as some sort of *palengke*—an idiosyncratic Philippine wet marketplace where, according to them, "anything and everything goes." But Mr. Alano added more spice to the description, which made me further inquire about the loaded terms he employed in talking about COPAO. Minutes later, he revealed to me that he happens to be an officer of that organization, so I quickly asked him how he felt about the ways he "negatively" portrayed a group of which he is a part. He replied:

> Oh, was I painting the organization in a negative light? *Hindi oy.* [Not really.] I was merely describing how we do our own stuff here. *Siempre, maraming sigawan.* [Of course, there's a lot of yelling going on.] But I think we get things done, too. Why do you think I remain [committed] to the group for over five years now? *Siguro* [perhaps], you're thinking about the congressional and senate meetings you see on C-SPAN which, by the way, has a lot of screaming, too. Well, we do it the same way . . . and in different ways, too. You should go and see us. Even if we're not in Congress yet, you'll see what we're doing.

Quickly, I alerted myself to preconceived notions of "politics" that somehow conflicted with what Mr. Alano was trying to explain to me. Indeed, I was looking for a version of "politics" a la C-SPAN where leaders held institutionally-sanctioned positions and deliberated with each other in some orderly fashion. Obviously, Mr. Alano recognized my textbook application of political activity owing to the fact that he knew I was a university student—a recognition he immediately seized to express a kind of "politics" that he thought was different from and yet similar to what I was thinking of. To him, this difference is constituted in the double sense of a "politics" that is "of our own," or as something that is markedly Filipino (through the invocation of a place that originates from the homeland—a *palengke*) and, on the other, a "politics" where "things get done" not in spite of but through the idiosyncrasies and apparent disarray of the *palengke*. The assurance Mr. Alano gives about how "things get done" is important since both of us do have some understanding that in a *palengke*, market transactions are usually undertaken with a lot of hawking and screaming. On the surface, one could easily ask how things could possibly get accomplished in the midst of the chaos and confusion associated with the *palengke* atmosphere. But to these Filipinos, it is precisely the place where things do get done. To "get things done" in a *palengke*, one can almost refer only to a few quick steps: the arrival in the market, the screening of goods, the haggling and some gossiping, and then the eventual purchase. To someone who is not familiar with the *palengke*'s "hidden transcripts," it is difficult to imagine how one arrives at a productive end with such bewildering means, a kind of order in the midst of confusion, and a practice that makes good sense to those who engage in it so much so that it's brought over and transformed in the new place.[5]

"There's just too much preoccupation with order here [in the United States]," Rose Sison said. As a former officer but current active delegate of COPAO, Sison, in her words, "has gone through thick and thin" despite the seeming "*kaguluhan* [disarray] of FilAm politics here." And through it all, she claimed:

> I have seen the best and the worst *sa mga meeting* [in the meetings]. Sometimes, *magulo* [it's in disarray]. *Pero kahit magulo, alam naman ng lahat kung nasaan ang mga limits.* [But even if it's in disarray, everyone knows where the limits are.] We always try to be *desente* [decent] with each other. *Pangit naman 'yung sobrang maayos.* [It's not nice if it's too orderly.] *Siempre, tayo-tayo, nagkakaintindihan kung ano ang babagay sa atin.* [Of course, we know what will suit us.]

Here, Sison's characterization of the meetings' apparent disarray is emblematic of the *palengke*'s surface attribute of frenzy. But the transcript of "knowing where the limits are" invariably transforms this kind of marketplace of excess into a productive endeavor where the understanding of "decency" towards each other qualifies as a baseline criterion of social conduct. Complete order in this case becomes a suspicious and repulsive exercise ("it's not nice"), something that is marked as alien and misplaced in the meetings, and therefore appropriately replaced or often supplemented by moments of disorder tempered by the assurance that "we know what we're doing."

"We try to keep things in perspective *naman* [even then]," added COPAO secretary Daisy Perez. "We make sure we record meetings. . . . We also make sure we have an agenda that's distributed to members before the meetings." A casual perusal of the minutes of previous meetings reveals a concise but comprehensive listing of previous activities and discussions delineated according to issue. And in such meetings that I attended, organizers always made sure copies of the agenda were distributed, listing the order of activities for the 7:30 p.m. deliberations. Always, the top of the agenda began with "Call Meeting to Order," because prior to 7:30, members would slowly walk in and engage in discussions with each other. The formal start of the meeting then proceeded with an "Opening Prayer," "Introduction of Guests," and "Approval of Last Meeting's Minutes." By the time the meeting progressed to the central aspects of the agenda, delegates commenced with their more active roles by voicing their opinions, questions, and suggestions about the items listed. "That's the time when you see this [kind of] *palengke* rolling along," Perez added. "So there's order and disorder at the same time."

Of course, understanding and working within and through these polarities de-mands a particular facility in social relationships of this nature on the part of players and attendees, something that the minutes of any COPAO meeting reveal is difficult to capture. While "knowing what we're doing," keeping things in perspective, and "decency" serve as veritable indices of social behavior in the meetings, they are most often unsaid. If they are ever mentioned in those rare instances of outright public misconduct, it is in the context of delegates reminding one another that "decency," for example, is something that is expected and assumed as a requisite for participation. Two meetings come to mind as illustrations of how these expectations cohere into accepted rules of conduct.[6]

In one instance, a delegate from one of the associations suddenly raised his hand and, upon acknowledgment, said that he wanted to start a discussion of a particular issue different from what was currently being talked about. Realizing the impropriety of such a gesture, the chair responded to him by making a reference to the agenda that was made public beforehand, and imploring him (as well as everybody) that matters outside of the list would be accommodated after the agreed-upon activities were deliberated and settled. "You are out of order," he said to the man. "And you should know how we do business here." The rest of the audience, including myself, hissed for a moment, until one of us said out loud, for a moment appearing also out of order, "*Pasyensya na kayo, baguhan lang siya!* [Be patient, he's just new!]"[7] "Well then, he should brush up on our rules. Give him a copy of our by-laws!" retorted the chair. "*Maging maayos naman po tayo.* [Let's be orderly.] *Konting* decency *naman ho.* [A little bit of decency here, please.]"[8]

A resort to "order" was also implored in another incident during a delegates' meet-ing when members of the audience, including myself again, persisted in talking to each other as the deliberations on the floor were ensuing. Here, the apt word is "*chismisan*," or gossiping, which caught the ire of the officers— especially since the topic being discussed related to suspicions of COPAO funds being pilfered and embezzled by certain members. The handling of the organization's money has traditionally been contentious among these people, and COPAO's history, as revealed in its previous minutes dating back to the 1970s, has been fraught with incidents of funds lost, stolen, or embezzled. Members have a good sense of this history and regard it with contempt in light of the ways in which bribery and corruption they see prevalent in the Philippines find their way into the new land. Definitely, the urge to make side comments about this issue, while it was being formally discussed by the officers, was too hard to resist. Wanting to contain an imminent condition of *chismisan* about to reach disastrous proportions, one COPAO officer yelled out: "*O, chismisan na lang ba ang gusto natin? Itigil naman po natin iyang mga chismis na iyan. Maging desente naman tayo sa isa't isa.* [Oh, is it just gossip that we want here? Let's please stop that kind of gossiping. Let's be decent to one another.]" The tone of this man's voice came out so forcefully that everybody immediately stopped speaking. In a way, his interjection defined the limits of disorderly conduct, articulated in the gossiping that ensued for a moment, and was quickly quelled in the name of decency. People afterwards resented the way this man raised his voice but understood that he did it for a reason. A delegate said, "*Siempre, baka mauwi na naman tayo sa palengke. Kaya niya ginawa iyon. . . . Atin 'to. Dapat lang pag-ingatan natin ito. Sayang din naman. Konting gulo, okey lang. Pero konting ayos din, mas maigi.* [Of course, we might end up as a *palengke* again. That's why he did that. . . . This is ours. We ought to take care of it. Let's not put it to waste. A little bit of disorder, it's just okay. But a little bit of order, it's better.]"

Yet, what appears to be a chaotic site of "politics" connoted by the *palengke* has its historical roots in the social and political conditions of Filipino immigration to and settlement in the United States, so much so that this kind of "politics" also finds articulation in another double instance: one that is demarcated as characteristic of Filipino "politics" whose remnants bespeak of "frequent yelling," but at the same time, a kind of "politics" that finds its way into what Mr. Alano casually infers as American—which "has a lot of screaming, too." Evident here is not only the synergy of "politicking" culled from at least two different systems, but a congruence that is forged out of a relationship of exclusion ("we're not in Congress yet") that makes possible an alternative form of politics in the absence of more legitimated positions of political representation. "I don't think they're ready for us," quips a frequent COPAO delegate. "They won't take us right now. We can only work through little steps one at a time."

In many ways, these "little steps" have found manifestation in terms of increased participation. Attendance in COPAO has grown over the years since its formal organization in 1971. "Built from the bottom," as one founding member said, COPAO started only with a few community leaders of several provincial and professional organizations. In the 1960s and 1970s, when the number of Filipinos in San Diego grew as a consequence of U.S. military and industrial development, associations defined by Philippine hometown origin arose primarily to bring together people from the same town or province who happened to share yet another common fate of moving and settling in the same city. Aida Santos, a member of the San Diego Cavite Association since 1968, remembers how isolated and lonely she felt upon coming over to work as a nurse in a local hospital. "I was looking all the time for people who looked Filipino," she said. She continued:

I really wanted to see someone familiar. I was so sad being with people who didn't look like me. Then, I met this man whom I recognized as someone from a town near where I grew up. He's from the Navy, he said. Just seeing and talking to him did a lot to me. He said there are a lot of Caviteños here.[9] So I met them all in a party. *Diyos ko!* [My God!] I was so glad to be with them . . . and I really had a nice time. Just being there with all those people from Cavite. . . . At that time, it was just party-party. Then, we decided to be more formal. . . . They set up this thing called San Diego Cavite Association . . . and I became an official member later on.

Similar to most experiences of early immigrants to a new place, Aida Santos found in her association of province mates a community bonded by a common thread of dislocation and misery mitigated by the comfort and security engendered just by being with people who shared her ethnicity. These kinds of associations would later flourish, especially within Filipino American communities elsewhere.[10] "We are known for having a lot of organizations, I think," Ben Vargas, a Filipino community paper editor told me. "We have a lot . . . and we have too many." According to his estimate, in 1992 there were more than 150 organizations in San Diego County alone, and more than two hundred in the Los Angeles area.[11] Formed mostly as social organizations of Philippine towns, cities, regions, and provinces, many other Filipino American organizations are also organized as alumni associations by gender, age, occupation, profession/trade, and recreational interest. "We even have an association of associations!" Vargas added. Referring to COPAO, he further mused: "We just can't get enough. But also, we want to be organized. You know, [we want to] organize the organizations!"

In the COPAO House of Delegates meetings I attended, constituting a quorum was never an issue. The meeting hall, which also housed the COPAO offices, occupied the second floor of a two-story building in National City where delegates from numerous organizations came together to discuss and deliberate issues pertinent to their needs and interests. As an umbrella organization of more than 125 associations, COPAO's reach has expanded to accommodate members' shifting particular interests and conditions. In its earlier years, there was a focus on alleviating poverty, the effects of the Vietnam War on the Filipino community, and the plight of the Filipino American farm workers. In the 1980s and 1990s, with new leaders coming in and new issues affecting the communities, civic programs targeting the health and well-being of senior citizens and pursuing the welfare of the youth took center stage. But the general primary goals have always been clear and consistent: "to build and support networks of alliance among ourselves," as said by one of its officers. And further, as the slogan accompanying the COPAO letterhead goes: "Community Development through Self-Reliance."

This impetus for self-reliance draws its intensity from the specifics of Filipino immigration history. Here, I make an historical digression momentarily to provide the context in which this discourse of self-reliance operates. Sociologist Elena S. H. Yu, in an article that traces the nature of Filipino migration and patterns of community organization in the United States, claims that the varying characteristics of each migratory wave of Filipinos and their differing adaptation experiences have resulted in fragmentary, unsustained, and unorganized Filipino communities.[12] The mobile character of first-wave agricultural contract laborers (1900s to 1930s) who mostly depended on the demands of migratory work in the West Coast, for example, deterred them from settling permanently in any one place to establish long-lasting affiliations. The second wave of military migrants enlisted mostly in the U.S. Navy and Army (1940s to 1960s) also had difficulty in sustaining ethnic organizational ties owing to their regimented and mobile tours of duty. And with the professional immigrants of the 1960s and onwards, Yu points to their career orientations (usually, earlier, in the medical field) that necessitated dispersal into and confinement in urban and suburban locales for social and financial gain. There are clear generational, class, and gender divisions (first and second waves were comprised predominantly of males) across these temporal swells, which Yu alludes to as factors that have made Filipino community formations in the United States quite peculiarly disaggregated.[13]

I would argue against her, however, by suggesting that what complicates this history of migration further are the social-political conditions in the United States that Filipinos faced upon arrival—conditions that fundamentally rendered them as racialized subjects (Orientals, little brown people, etc.) regardless of generation, class, and gender and that, on an important level, bridge their migratory differences.[14] I am not implying that only one form of racism existed in all three waves, nor am I suggesting that all Filipinos who came to America experienced racism the same way, if at all. But to many of my respondents, there is an acute consciousness of racism as either personally experienced (and oftentimes, painfully told) or known to have happened to some other Filipino. The Filipino immigrants in Southern California I talked to possess a good familiarity with the oppression of Filipino farmworkers, the strikes and boycotts these laborers led and participated in, restaurant and grocery store signs that used to announce "No Filipinos and Dogs Allowed," and the Hollywood depictions of the "wily" Filipino in old movies. "*Alam ko lahat ang mga iyon* [I know all of that]," says Daisy Perez. "*Hanggang ngayon, malakas pa rin ang dating nila. Ang tingin ng mga puti sa atin, kadalasan e itim, o kaya e Mexicano o Intsik. Pati accent, kundi ka slang e masama ang tingin sa iyo.* [Until now, their force is still great. Whites see us as black people, or Mexicans, or Chinese. Even our accent, if you don't speak like them, they look at you in a bad way.]"[15] Contemporary Filipinos' historical knowledge of these "incidents" of racism may not be as detailed as scholarly texts, but a significant awareness of past and present injustices do enable them to find common ground with those who are generations apart from them. COPAO, like many other Filipino organizations established both before and during COPAO's organization, seizes these shared narratives of racism that have rendered them marginal or invisible by deploying a virtue of "self-reliance"; that is, according to Mr. Alano, "If we're always left out, if we are always cast aside, who else can we turn to except ourselves? Who else can we rely upon to make a decent living here except our very own people?"

I have heard such sentiments articulated along similar lines in smaller organizations both in San Diego and Los Angeles. COPAO's northern counterpart, the Filipino American Community of Los Angeles (FACLA) prides itself on being the catalyst for unifying and servicing Filipino immigrants based in California primarily through "*sariling pagsisikap*" [individual diligence]; that is, according to one of its members, through the "efforts of our own little groups." Membership in these organizations is overwhelmingly composed of post-1965 middle-class professionals, with a good number of senior citizens (mostly parents who were petitioned once immigrants have permanently settled), working-class factory workers, and older generation immigrants (who are usually citizens by the time they join). But again, what seems to lend coherence to their generational and class disparities is their awareness of a shared fate voiced by a long-time FACLA officer: "We have come to this nation to seek new or better lives but we have found, instead, a lot of difficulty and a country that mistreats us; since we are on our own here, we can only rely on ourselves." To be sure, there are many ways in which racial exclusion is collectively experienced, but in the realm of what these Filipinos view as "politics," the fundamental evidence lies in the absence of any (or consistent failures in attempting) political representation of their group in most public offices despite their numbers and presence since before the turn of the century.[16]

In response to these overdetermined conditions, the *palengkes* of Filipino American "politics" have served both as avenues for rectifying exclusion and venues for practicing a kind of "politics" figured on Filipino Americans' own terms. I am not implying that these Filipinos merely react to a given set of uncontrollable conditions thrust upon them. Rather, I am suggesting the force of agency that drives *"palengke* politics" in the instances I mentioned, as these Filipino Americans shore up what's familiar to them, adjust it to suit their presumed needs and limitations, and ultimately use it to access a kind of elusive power. This is where I situate a specific style of "politics" that my informants recognize both as Filipino and American. ("This is what makes us Filipinos . . . and Americans, too.") According to a FACLA member:

> *Maganda nga 'yung parang palengke kasi at least, kahit sino, nakakapagsalita. May democrasya baga. Kung meron kang gustong sabihin, sabihin mo kaagad . . . kaya minsan e magulo, kaya ang tawag e palengke. Pero palengke na ang goal ay democracy, American-style baga.* [It's nice to have something like a *palengke* because at least, anyone is able to speak. It's like having a democracy. If you want to say something, you say it right away . . . that's why sometimes, it's a frenzy. But it's a *palengke* whose goal is democracy, American- style, as they say.]

There is a price to be paid for this kind of resistance, as many of my informants are quick to remind me. Mainstream kinds of "politicking" are themselves similarly (or, more so, unequally) staunchly resistant to change and accommodation demanded by marginal groups. "I don't think the big political parties want us," explains Mr. Alano. "We try from time to time, but we never pass the 'little member' stage. And then it takes a lot of money, too, to run for office. How can we make it?" Further, although their exact numbers are difficult to obtain, many constituents are believed to have altogether given up hope in pursuing this strategy by refusing to engage in any of the organizations' activities.

Indeed, the anxieties of the peculiar kind of assimilation (or resistance to it) that I am describing here are certainly managed and localized in the specific workings of *palengke* politics. The borders of this *palengke*, however, are not so strictly demarcated by the organizational headquarters: beyond these spaces lies the arena of the beauty pageant, yet another form of public "politicking" that lends itself to extended practices of political negotiation whose communicative registers rest on ideas about Filipino virtues.

Beauty Pageants

To those Filipino Americans with whom I interacted, beauty pageants are never directly mentioned as synonymous with "politics." That is, beauty pageants are rarely imagined, if ever, as events that pertain to doing strictly "political things." Yet, my conversations with them reveal how closely tied the holding of pageants is to the kinds of *palengke* politics described above. *"Para ding palengke doon* [It's also like a *palengke* there]," remarked Wilma Galvan. *"Bago pa man ding ginaganap e pina-palengke nila 'yung coronation, mula sa pagbili ng ticket hanggang sa katapusan.* [Even before it's held, they turn the coronation into a *palengke,* from the selling of tickets until the end.]" Here, I focus on those beauty pageants that are held primarily to raise funds, similar to those held in towns and cities in the Philippines, and those conducted by other ethnic groups in the United States.[17] During my fieldwork in Southern California, I saw in many instances how pageant organizers and participants always made themselves present in COPAO, FACLA, and other organizational meetings to sell tickets. Small and large social gatherings, whether induction ceremonies for new officers or annual reunions, consistently reserved program spots for, say, the introduction of a beauty titlist, a presentation ("cat walk") of the "hometown pride" (a pageant winner bearing the name of a province, town, or city, as in Miss Batangas—USA or Miss Pride of USA-Ilocandia), or oftentimes, even the emceeing by a beauty queen herself. Organizational meetings also regularly discussed recent or future beauty pageants as part of their agenda. Hence, it may not be the case that they don't see beauty pageants as occupying the same idea of "doing politics," but perhaps they recognize and imagine a *specific* form of "doing politics" in the pageants that are coextensive with their "political" activities in the organizations.

I began to closely pay attention to this notion upon examining previous records of COPAO history. According to several sources, the idea of forming COPAO as an umbrella organization actually originated at a beauty pageant that was held on July 3, 1971, at the El Cortez Hotel in San Diego. Three contestants on the stage surprised the audience by reading "anti-establishment manifestos" they had previously hidden in their bosoms. Right in the middle of the question-and-answer portion of the pageant, they conveyed a message that urged the community to focus on "issues of justice, poverty, the war in Vietnam [a national issue at that time], the plight of the Filipino American farm workers, and equality."[18] This occasion spurred the presidents of seventeen Filipino American organizations to form the President's Circle, which later grew into COPAO upon increased membership and official incorporation.

There is, then, a good indication of such close links between holding pageants and some form of "politics" that have gone since, as evidenced by past issues of Filipino American community newspapers. In the 1990s, the Filipinos I have talked to understand the significance of beauty pageants in this same context. Gloria Miranda, a FACLA officer, stated: *"Iba talaga ang mga Pilipino. 'Yung mga beauty pageant natin . . . iba rin. Kita mo naman, nagmumula sa ganito ang unity natin. Kahit na akala mo e contest-contest lamang . . . aba, seryoso din ang mga ito.* [Filipinos are really different. Our beauty pageants . . . are also different. Just take a look, our unity comes out of things like these. Even though you think it's just a contest . . . oh, these are also serious stuff.]" Beauty pageants to Filipinos like Gloria Miranda carry more weight; they are not really seen as contests in which those who join vie for titles akin to what they see on TV (Miss California, Miss Universe, Miss International, etc.). In most of the pageants I witnessed, people have often been less preoccupied with who was physically the most beautiful, the most elegantly dressed, or the most talented. If they were, these qualities usually were not of primary concern. Rather, in these communities, Filipino Americans regarded such pageants more as venues mainly for bringing people together, generating funds for organizational projects, and, as was in the case above, for expressing particular political agendas. Hence, pageants such as these provide a different dimension of community building.

The coronation of beauty titlists is often an event many people look forward to. But even before that, pageant organizers find their hands full determining its size and scope, depending on the number of people who will potentially support it. Usually, the idea of holding a pageant is driven by the cause an organization wants to generate funds for, so that a contest is held either on a one-time basis because of an immediate and unexpected concern (for example, for the victims of a volcanic eruption or flood in the Philippines) or on an annual basis with different causes every year. At least one cause—and sometimes several causes—is always mentioned along with the announcement of the pageant in flyers and newspaper ads.

The bulk of the work, however, is on selling the tickets for the occasion, something to which organizers and contestants themselves devote a lot of time and energy. A common experience, my respondents tell me, is how frequently they get accosted by these ticket sellers in social gatherings they attend. *"Diyos ko, kahit saan ka magpunta dito, laging may nagbebenta ng ticket para kay Miss ganyan o kay Misis ganito!* [My God, everywhere you go here, there's someone selling tickets for Miss this or Mrs. that!]" said Rose Sison. I have experienced these incidents, too, in many get-togethers of Filipino families, school reunions, organizational meetings, and even FACLA and COPAO House of Delegates sessions. On one COPAO post-meeting social, Violeta Ramos, an officer of one of the town-based organizations, came up to me and inquired: "Are you a member of any organization around here? Why don't you join ours? Are you from Cavite? Well . . . if not, what you can do is buy some tickets from me. There's this beauty contest our group is having . . . or better . . . you should be one of our judges!" And just as others have felt about these solicitations, any kind of refusal is always hard to muster.

Selling tickets, according to many, is just like selling any other merchandise, but one thing that makes this different is the understanding between vendor and buyer that any profit goes to a special cause. This is primarily why the transaction is thought of as charity work, in which a vendor donates time and effort selling tickets (characterized by many as "difficult work") while a buyer is thought of as someone donating cash in turn to someone else other than the seller. But what struck me as more interesting was the way in which this kind of transaction operated, using an idiom of exchange specific to Filipinos. "Come on . . . this is for a good cause. *Makidamay ka naman!* [Be one with us!]" Violeta Ramos told me. This notion of *damay*, a carryover from the Philippines, is usually employed to mean commiseration or sympathy—an expression of "condolence for another's misfortune."[19] "*Nakikiramay po* [My condolences]" is how one would use the word in talking to someone who is grieving because of a death. But in these cases, respondents use *damay* not really to condole with another but to be involved in a *damayan*— an activity or relationship of people helping other people. Historian Reynaldo Ileto refers to this particular register of *damay*, that of "participation in another's work," within the context of nineteenth-century popular movements in the Philippines, but it is not that difficult to find its resonances among Filipinos in twentieth-century America.[20] To *damay* is to enjoin the other to participate in a cause, so that doing so results in having more people helping one another ("*magdamayan tayo* [let's help one another]," I overheard someone say), ultimately reinforcing a bond and creating a sense of oneness with the other (*pakikiramay*). Because one is able to help, one is brought closer into the other's domain. Hence, my translation of "*Makidamay ka naman*" into "be one with us," as stand-in for "participation in the work of another," casts *damay* as a mechanism for co-constructing and sustaining a community.

If the practice of *damay* propels ticket sellers into communities of shared interests and bonds of oneness, the holding of the pageants themselves bring into visible recognition the fruits of such labor. Said one organizer: "*Dito natin makikita 'yung mga nagtrabaho para sa mga contests na ito. Tayo rin naman ang nakikinabang. Tayo-tayo rin ang lumalabas na winners. Tulungan din, 'di ba?* [Here, we see those who have worked for these contests. We're the ones who profit from these. We're the ones who come out as winners. It's helping one another, isn't it?]" Against the spectacle of beauty titlists parading on stage, a strong sense of pride permeates through the audience. Knowing that they have worked towards a goal and have accomplished it so that others may benefit is the source itself of a certain measure of joy that, at the same time, has made possible a community of Filipinos momentarily gathered together as one.

The occasion itself then brings together sellers and buyers, organizers and contestants, and judges and spectators bearing witness to a product of shared labor. "*Siempre*, we have our own *manok*. [Of course, we have our own contenders.] We cheer for them. We want them to win!" according to a ticket seller. Contestants were usually daughters of these first-generation immigrants. Prior to the contest itself, only a few have any idea who will eventually win the titles at stake. Those contestants who have also been engaged in selling tickets might have some clue, but organizers also make it a point to keep the audience riveted. In many pageants that I watched, portions of the program were allotted to swimsuit parades and question-and-answer segments. These were pageants where the number of contestants exceeded the number of titles available. For those pageants in which the number of contestants equaled the number of titles, certain segments were usually dispensed with in favor of a display of talent for each of the contestants. I was a judge for several pageants in both Los Angeles and San Diego, and it took me quite a while to figure out the difference between these pageants. At first, I seriously assigned points for each of the competition portions for all the pageants that I attended. Later on, I realized that for some of them, I only needed to sit and watch. "We tell you in the end who the winners are, the moment we verify who sold the most tickets," Violeta Ramos told me once. "So, just sit back and relax. We're all winners anyway! We're all beautiful!"

The surface impression may be that these pageants are all staged or fixed. True, some of the winners are determined prior to the staging of the pageants themselves. But audiences are not so much concerned about whether the winner or winners are preselected. Rather, audiences that I've seen have always been in the mood to celebrate and socialize, so much so that some of these pageants are also labeled as coronation nights. People come to witness these events to signal their coming together as one, represented by a beauty titlist who, in the end, would symbolize both an elevation of a certain pride personified by a beautiful woman and a job well done. Said one seller: "That's the time we see each other. It's like having fun while raising money!" In the coming weeks, the winners' faces would be strewn over the front pages of the community newspapers, detailing their titles and the causes they have served.

"This is something we are proud of," mentioned one contestant. "We reached out . . . and this title represents that." If you participated, she said, "*tulong mo na rin 'yan sa mga nangangailangan sa atin* [it's also your way of helping those who are in need in our country]." People who have indeed participated realize the gains they are reaping in these events. But more important to them is the kind of work invested in bringing Filipino American communities together—that in the process of helping each other help other Filipinos here and elsewhere, Filipinos are brought closer together. "*Para na ring bayanihan* [It's just like a cooperative endeavor]," noted Mrs. Ramos. "'*Di ba ganyan sa Pilipinas? Ganyan din dito. Tayo-tayo na rin ang magtutulungan. Kita mo, kahit beauty contest e marami rin ang na-eenganyong makisama at tumulong sa isa't isa.* [Isn't it like this in the Philippines? It's also like that here. We're the ones who can help each other. See, even if it's just a beauty contest, a lot of people are motivated to join with others and help one another.]" Here, I wish to make the connection between the notion of *bayanihan* and *damayan* since both ascribe the virtue of helping one another along similar axes. *Bayanihan*'s root word is *bayan*, which in Tagalog means "town, municipality, nation, home, or the public." To imagine *bayanihan*'s full force is to call into action these multiple referents so that "helping one another" in the spirit of *bayanihan* is done within the context of helping someone who comes from the same town or the same nation. In doing so, one is able to build stronger ties with the *bayan*, with the people back home. And, according to many, one ultimately helps in building the *bayan* here with Filipinos in the new country by that very same practice.

I have heard *bayanihan* mentioned along with its other synonyms *tulungan* and *samahan* (COPAO supports a project called Operation Samahan), and the implication has usually been directed towards assurances of mutual aid and cooperative endeavor for the benefit of everyone both here and in the Philippines. COPAO, FACLA, and the funds generated in the beauty pageants support projects targeting health care for seniors, drug abuse programs for the youth, legal services for civil rights cases, and trade and cultural shows. A significant portion of money raised also benefits the poor and the needy as well as victims of calamities in the Philippines. Money is routed to the homeland on a regular basis for scholarship; donations for rebuilding and renovating schools, churches, and sanitation facilities; and seed money for small business enterprises. "A huge bulk of our money goes back to our other home," said another beauty contest organizer. "We owe it to them."

Traversing at least two homes, Filipino Americans find in these pageants social spaces that emplot their tenuous positions as Filipinos who, in their eyes, are not fully American (by virtue of their first-generation immigrant status) and not fully Filipinos either (owing to their departure and distance from the original homeland). The orientation to the *bayan*, both in the context of activities here and in reference to the homeland, is one anchor they hold on to in an effort to mitigate these tensions. Indubitably, however, that kind of orientation is also mired in conflict between, say, those who have chosen to sever ties with the old country and those who insist on strengthening connections wherever possible. Then, there are those who are not able to participate due to lack of time or money. Beauty pageants of this sort require investments of time and money that not everyone can offer.

To those who are able to participate, the motivation, as mentioned above, is predicated on the virtues of helping. Beyond that, beauty pageants are also occasions for power negotiations. The likes of Mrs. Ramos invest money and time to gain a foothold in leadership positions within the community. If their ventures become successful, they realize the potentials in assuming primary roles in community politics, and with their visibility assured, they are liable to command authority and respect from their presumed constituents. Holding these pageants is, thus, fraught with "politicking" as different personalities vie for positions of influence within the communities, hoping that their *manok* or their daughter would win and that enough money would be raised to fund projects. Some respondents find no qualms in describing these contests as *palengkes* in their own right, too. And if a *manok* wins, her sponsors most assuredly win as well with her, as their names as individuals or members of an organization become identified with the beauty queen throughout her reign.

The stakes involved in these kinds of pageants point not only to quests for influential positions, but to representations titleholders potentially draw. Locally, we know how organizers revere beauty titlists to the extent that they embody the processes and effects of *bayanihan* and *damayan* of Filipinos in America. In their terms, "she's something to be proud of in our new home." Her representation in the Philippines, however, is another matter, since more often than not, she would be American-born, or assumed as such when Filipinos back home see her. Usually, if enough money is raised, contest winners are sent to the Philippines to personally deliver donations raised in America. Town officials in the Philippines have been known to eagerly await these bearers of "good will" and treat them with lavishness as soon as they arrive. Some of these winners even take the opportunity to compete in beauty pageants there as representatives of Filipinos in the States. In this vein, the beauty titlist is figured as a prized celebrity, for she not only shares with Filipinos back home some of the fruits of those who have labored in the "land of opportunity," she also personifies access to things American that only a few Filipinos are able to gain. This is a primary reason for the care organizers take in selecting who to send home. For, as one contest judge said, "she [not only] represents us here, how we've been successful here . . . she also represents us there, how we have succeeded here, too."

Both *palengke* politics and beauty pageants of this sort illustrate the nuances of a particular kind of "politicking" familiar to Filipino Americans in southern California. They point to different ways of configuring how Filipino American immigrants meet their own needs within their specific conditions and address these according to their own terms. Navigating through a series of borrowings and appropriations of things considered Filipino and applying them in the context of their conditions and positions in America, these people find creative ways of circumscribing their distance from mainstream forms of "politicking" while actively attending to the potentials of their own kinds of "politics" that would allow them some measure of unity, autonomy, and access. Practicing these versions of "politics," as the *palengke* style shows, demands an alertness in recognizing both the benefits and limits of such syncretic forms. Carried to its pejorative extreme, *palengke* politics has been known to verge on chaotic propensities. Delicately balanced between its poles of order and hysteria, it has also resulted in moments of equitable exchange, of community co-construction closely akin to a democratic public sphere.

I started this essay by musing on the various ways in which Filipino Americans, including myself as an ethnographer, think about "politics." Those with whom I have talked, perhaps realizing how sharply their own kinds of "politics" differed from those of mainstream notions of it, have consistently directed my attention to alternative ways of imagining and handling community affairs. These are the kinds of "politics" that, to them, make possible an orientation to the homeland as a common point of origin and alliance (*"Pilipino tayong lahat."* [We are all Filipinos.]), a source of appropriable virtues (*"Ganyan tayo sa Pilipinas."* [We are like that in the Philippines.]), and a beneficiary of charitable work. Simultaneously, these are also the kinds of "politics" oriented to the new settlements here, with organizations and beauty pageants serving to mobilize Filipinos on terms they could deploy together to address similar conditions and achieve common ends. To these people, such styles of "politicking" open up spaces for negotiating and articulating identities as Filipino Americans.

Notes

1. National City is located south of San Diego.

2. Not his real name. I have concealed the true names of all respondents to protect their privacy.

3. My interviews were conducted between 1992 and 1995 in Los Angeles, San Diego, and nearby vicinities. Almost all of my interviews were conducted in Tagalog, mixed in with some English (the local term is *Taglish*). All Tagalog quotes are supplemented by my own translations.

4. North County refers to the county north of San Diego.

5. I borrow the term "hidden transcript" from James Scott's (1990) *Domination and the Arts of Resistance*, in which he defines "hidden transcript" as "a range of practices . . . [and] discourse that takes place 'offstage,' beyond direct observation by powerholders" (pp. 4, 14). The specific tenor of "hidden transcripts" that I try to employ here is the *palengke*'s linguistic and practiced "disguise" unique to my respondents' conditions that, in some ways, follow Scott's further clarification of "hidden transcripts" as being "the often fugitive political conduct of subordinate groups . . . that [express] dissent to the official transcript of power relations. . . ." (pp. xi, xii, 17).

6. These rules of conduct, while mostly unmentioned, are also codified in COPAO's bylaws. As in most associations of this kind, delegates are expected to abide by them as a condition of membership. Occasionally, conflicts would arise when new members come in and take time to get used to the practice of such laws.

7. The notion of *pasyensya* is difficult to translate here without conveying its idiomatic nuance. Its literal translation is "patience" (from the Spanish *paciencia*) or "to act with patience," but it also calls for "a calm bearing of pain . . . or anything that annoys, troubles, or hurts" (Leo James English 1986, *Tagalog-English Dictionary*). I understand it also to mean "forgiveness" in this particular context, as in "be patient with and forgive him—let it go—since he's just new here and is not used to what we do."

8. The words *po* and *ho* are marks of deference and respect (to elders and the general public, in this context) that I roughly equate with "please."

9. Caviteños are Filipinos who come from Cavite, a province in the Philippines.

10. Part of this history of community organizing among Filipino Americans is narrated and illustrated in Fred Cordova's (1983, esp. pp. 175–227). In his chapter "Community Activities," Cordova begins with: "It has been said that whenever two Pinoys had gotten together, they formed a club" (p. 175). I have heard that line mentioned by several of my informants as well, so much so that community organizing of this sort is traditionally viewed as uniquely Filipino American.

11. Vargas's estimates concur with my research figures and those of Yen Le Espiritu's. See Espiritu (1980, 25).

12. This particular historical narrative of migration by waves is frequently employed in most materials on Filipino immigration to the United States. I attend to this narrative only to specify the salient patterns of that history while acknowledging its protractedness, complexity,

and problematics. Such a narrative, for example, misses out on numerous other immigrants who do not fit into the waves (such as the "Manila men" who came and settled in Louisiana via the galleon trade in the years prior to 1898) and later generations who intermarried with other ethnic groups and/or self-identified differently. The 1970s also saw the coming of political exiles fleeing the Marcos dictatorship. Their histories are equally important and deserve special treatment in projects other than this. For references, see, for example: Yen Le Espiritu (1986, esp. pp. 1–36); Bruno Lasker (1969); Antonio J. A. Pido (1986).

13. In the same breath, Yu (1980) acknowledges the existence of Filipino American organizations in each of the migration waves that she altogether views as dispersed and inadequate; that is, they are not able to sustain coherence and unity across generations.

14. This point also finds its way in historical, cultural, and literary criticism. See, for example, Oscar Campomanes (1995); E. San Juan, Jr. (1992, esp. pp. 117–30).

15. To Filipinos, speaking in "slang" means speaking like an American-born, that is, with a twang.

16. The latest census figures show 1.4 million Filipinos in the United States, out of which 220,000 are in Los Angeles County and 96,000 are in San Diego County. Filipinos comprise the second largest Asian American group in the nation (next to Chinese), and the largest in California. Apparently, the figures could be larger than reported since many of my respondents believe that the number of undocumented Filipino immigrants is significantly large. Bureau of the Census (1992).

17. See Tyler Davidson (1996) and Fennella Cannell (1995).

18. Elena S. H. Yu (1980, 92); see also "Brief History of the Council" (1974, 1).

19. Reynaldo C. Ileto (1979, 51).

20. Ibid.

References

Brief History of the Council. 1974. *Pahayagan* 1:1 (November/December).

Bureau of the Census. 1992. *1990 Census of Population and Housing Summary.* Washington, D.C.: Government Printing Office.

Campomanes, Oscar. 1995. The new empire's forgetful and forgotten citizens: Unrepresentability and unassimilability in Filipino-American postcolonialities. *Critical Mass* 2:2 (Spring): 145–200.

Cannell, Fennella. 1995. The Power of Appearances: Beauty, Mimicry and Transformation in Bicol. In *Discrepant Histories.* Edited by Vicente L. Rafael. Philadelphia: Temple University Press. Pp. 223–58.

Cordova, Fred. 1983. *Filipinos: Forgotten Asian Americans, A Pictorial Essay.* Dubuque, Iowa: Kendall/Hunt Publishing Company.

Davidson, Tyler. 1996. Chinese peaches. *SF Weekly.* March 13–19: pp. 10–16.

English, Leo James. 1986. *Tagalog-English Dictionary.* Quezon City, Philippines: Kalayaan Press.

Espiritu, Yen Le. 1995. *Filipino American Lives.* Philadelphia: Temple University Press.

Ileto, Reynaldo C. 1979. *Pasyon and Revolution: Popular Movements in the Philippines, 1840–1910.* Quezon City, Philippines: Ateneo de Manila University Press.

Lasker, Bruno. 1969. *Filipino Immigration to Continental United States and Hawaii.* New York: Arno Press.

Pido, Antonio J. A. 1986. *Pilipinos in America: Macro-Micro Dimensions of Immigration and Integration.* New York: Center for Migration Studies.

San Juan, E., Jr. 1992. *Racial Formations/Critical Transformations.* Atlantic Highlands, N.J.: Humanities Press.

Scott, James. 1990. *Domination and the Arts of Resistance.* New Haven: Yale University Press.

Yu, Elena S. H. 1980. Filipino migration and community organizations in the United States. *California Sociologist* 3:2 (Summer): 76–102.

Aihwa Ong

5 Making the Biopolitical Subject: Cambodian Immigrants, Refugee Medicine, and Cultural Citizenship in California

From Absolute Power to Biopolitics

On a sunny afternoon in San Francisco, a young Khmer man wearing a U.S. army jacket told me the nightmare that recurred in his dreams. Some time in the early 1970s, he and his brother had been captured by Pol Pot's troops. One day, he managed to escape. Hiding behind bushes, he saw soldiers kill his brother and another prisoner. Their hearts and lungs were torn out, and hung on a fence as a warning to others. In the silence following the story, the survivor held out his hands, as if cradling the remains of his brother. Then, shuddering imperceptibly, he pulled his army jacket closer.

Under the Khmer Rouge regime (1975–79), millions of Cambodians (primarily Khmers) were forced to be state laborers, while thousands were tortured and killed. By 1979, over a million had died, mainly from illness and starvation in the camps.[1] In their flight from Kampuchea to the United States, Khmer refugees escaped from a regime of absolute power over death to a democratic society defending life. They fled a preindustrial country where the Khmer Rouge regime attempted to institute a modern bureaucracy of terror. The central organ *Angka Leou* depended largely on illiterate, teenage soldiers to enforce rule on an uprooted and traumatized population, and continual surveillance to seek out 'enemies' and document their crimes. These strategies are reminiscent of modern state terrorism like Mao's regime during the

Reprinted from *Social Science and Medicine*, vol. 40, no. 9, Aihwa Ong, "Making the Biopolitical Subject: Cambodian Immigrants, Refugee Medicine and Cultural Citizenship in California," 1995, with permission from Elsevier Science.

Cultural Revolution.[2] Thus for Khmer refugees, most of whom came from rural areas outside Phnom Penh, the United States represented a different experience of state power that presents other kinds of modern predicaments.

Michel Foucault argues that in Western democracies, modern state power is dedicated to ensuring "the 'right' to life, to one's body, to health, to happiness . . . the 'right' to rediscover what one is and all that one can be."[3] These sentiments are expressed in the United States' Declaration of Independence, the most famous guarantees of modern citizenship.[4] From the nineteenth century onwards, Foucault maintains, modern state power has been deployed mainly through social regulation that acts on the heart, mind, and the will, dedicated to making individuals, families and collectivities "governable."[5] Social policy, informed by the human sciences, came to constitute "the social." "Biopolitics" refers to the strategic uses of knowledge that invests bodies and populations with properties making them amenable to various technologies of control.[6] Besides industrial policies,[7] welfare services, public health, educational and housing agencies administering the needs of citizens can be said to participate in the creation of biopolitical subjects of a particular kind. The modern democratic state dominates through the mundane administration and surveillance of individual bodies and the social body, adjusting them to normalizing standards, and thus rendered governable as citizens.

Among the schemes of knowledge/power regulating individual and social bodies, modern medicine is the prime-mover, defining and promoting concepts, categories, and authoritative pronouncements on hygiene, health, sexuality, and life and death. According to Foucault, the anatomical-clinical method is based on the pervasive medical gaze seeking out truths embedded in the human body.[8] Thus the medical gaze becomes a disciplining mechanism that, by defining human life as facts or the body, establishes the normative identity and behavior of individuals, and populations. Scholars influenced by the Foucauldian perspective have elaborated this argument further, claiming that the health profession has a disciplining influence beyond the clinic in shaping the social needs, rights and norms deemed appropriate for members of a modern civil society.[9] Thus while biomedicine is attending to the health of their bodies, it is also constitutive of the social, economic, and juridical practices that socialize biopolitical subjects of the modern welfare state.[10]

But these observations of how biomedicine works to define and reproduce biopolitical subjects cannot be left unchallenged. Foucault notes that in social regulation, subtle coercion takes hold upon the body at the levels of movements, gestures and attitudes,[11] but he barely explores how the subjects of regulation themselves draw the medical gaze in the first place, nor how their resistances to biomedical intervention both invite and deflect control. Using the encounters between refugee medicine and Cambodian patients, this paper problematizes biomedicine as a mix of good intentions, desire to control "diseased" and "deviant" populations, and the exigencies of limited resources that often compel medicalization. In California, many clinicians, themselves the children of immigrants, often display a deep faith in the efficacy of modern medical cure and practices for patients from third world countries so that they can function in the new country. Khmer refugees, in contrast, seek rather specific resources while wishing to elude the control over body and mind that goes with medical care. Thus the biomedical gaze is not such a diffused hegemonic power but is itself generated by the complex contestation of refugee/immigrant subjects pursuing their own goals and needs, but within the bureaucratic maze of American health and welfare providers. Clinicians and patients are equally caught up in webs of power involving control and subterfuge, appropriation and resistance, negotiation and learning that constitute biopolitical lessons of what becoming American may entail for an underprivileged Asian minority.

I will begin by discussing how immigration authorities read the political and diseased bodies of Khmer refugees allowed into the United States. Their arrival stimulated the invention of a field called "Southeast Asian Mental Health" that through the systematic naming and ordering of refugee illnesses, has the effect of controlling and reproducing their minority status. Next I consider a series of clinic encounters whereby health workers and refugees are shown to be involved in overt and subtle struggles over medical knowledge, cultural beliefs, and patient objectives. I end by discussing the agency of Khmer patients, viewed as the medical model of the chaotic refugee body, and how it is related to the ways Khmers "work the system" in their everyday fight to survive in the United States.

Screening and Disciplining Bodies: The Making of Certified Refugees

Following the Vietnamese invasion of Cambodia in 1979, thousands of Khmers managed to escape to refugee camps near the Thai border. Many refugees were peasants, most illiterate in their own language, and the camps were the first places they encountered Westerners. From the beginning, the encounters with American service agencies, church groups, and immigration officials produced a portrait of the refugees that viewed them as threats, both ideological and medical, to the American body politic where many would be settled. The goals of refugee recruitment, processing and resettlement programs were to socialize refugees to a category of newcomers defined as both contagious to and dependent upon the civil society.

Officials from the U.S. Immigration and Naturalization Service (INS) used a system called "Khmer Rouge screening process" in selecting Khmers in Thailand refugee camps for resettlement in the United States. Although there was overwhelming evidence that only a tiny percentage of refugees were Khmer Rouge members, thousands were rejected on unsubstantiated grounds of participating in Khmer Rouge brutality or Khmer Rouge affiliation.[12] At the Khao-I-Dang camp, the most circumstantial evidence, like working involuntarily under the Khmer Rouge authorities, or recounting stories that did not fit an assumed pattern of life in Khmer Rouge collective farms, was used to reject applicants.[13] In addition to translation problems, the refugees' body language, or smiling under stress, and reporting the deaths of relatives with a dispassionate face, made them Khmer Rouge suspects in the eyes of INS officers.[14] A scholar reported that the "INS tends to perceive Khmer Rouge affiliation where it does not exist."[15] Although the INS interviewers had a great fear of accepting the "Red" Other into the United States, they lacked cultural and political knowledge to accurately assess the applicants' stories, and many people who were part of the Khmer Rouge organization got through the screening process, along with thousands of others who were not. Between 1983 and 1985, the United States accepted 50,000 Khmer refugees from Cambodia.[16]

Khmers who cleared the INS screening were channeled to transit camps where they were subjected to language and cultural orientation classes aimed at "transforming them" for the country of resettlement. In the Philippine Refugee Processing Center (PRPC), signs in the administrative buildings proclaimed:

> Refugee transformation, the primary goal of the PRPC operations, is achieved through a psycho-social recuperative process involving the "critical phases of adaptation, capability building, and disengagement" which result in changing a "displaced person" into an "Individual Well-Equipped for Life in His Country of final destination."[17]

The transforming myth of the Overseas Refugee Training Program (ORTP) was to instruct refugees to "speak good English, be employable, be unwilling to accept welfare, and be happy" in America.[18] However, according to James Toffelson, the ORTP was an ideologically motivated strategy to instruct refugees in subservient behavior in order to prepare them for limited occupational categories in the American labor market.[19] In Carol A. Mortland's view,[13] the institutional transformation of refugees as an underclass went further, in the everyday regulation of camp relationships that reinforced the powerlessness of the refugees and their structural dependence on American patrons for their daily needs, movements and behavior. The effects of these programs—in food distribution, health, educational classes, social activities—were to intensify the liminal experiences of the refugees, as they learned their place in the intercultural status hierarchy that foreshadowed their future positioning within American society.

For liminal refugees, this process of social debasement[20] includes their construction as the contagious Other to American public health. The Centers for Disease Control (CDC) organized a transnational system whereby American public health advisors were stationed in asylum countries (Thailand, Malaysia, the Philippines) to monitor the health screening of U.S.-bound refugees. All refugees were given age-specific immunizations like DPT, polio, and measles for infants. Persons over two years old were X-rayed to screen for infectious tuberculosis. Those with active or suspected active TB were placed in quarantine, and not allowed to leave for the United States until deemed cleared. For many, refugee camps functioned as quarantine camps. In U.S.-arrival sites, CDC officers would notify local health agencies of each refugee's arrival, especially those with active or suspected active tuberculosis, within twenty-four hours of entering. In 1986 alone, the U.S. Health Services administered $6 million for local refugee resettlement agencies to conduct health assessments.[21] Upon arrival, refugees were given cash assistance and health care for up to eighteen months. Such extraordinary efficiency and expense ensured that although over seven hundred thousand Southeast Asian refugees have settled in the United States since 1975, they have not become a major threat to public health.

Nevertheless, Southeast Asian refugees were constructed as carriers of exotic and mysterious diseases. Not only were they typecast as having high rates of TB and hepatitis, but some were susceptible to what is referred to as "the Sudden Unexplained Nocturnal Death" (SUND) syndrome. Reports of sudden deaths, especially among the Hmong, have given rise to speculations about causes ranging from diet to the defoliant Agent Orange. Even before the refugees streamed into the United States, health workers had constructed Khmers as a people carrying exotic diseases as well as suffering from "mental illness" who must be treated,[22] and "transformed." The stamping of Cambodians as "certified refugees" and their medicalization as "diseased and sick" conditioned their reception in the United States.[23] The process of "transformation," now passed into the hands of the Voluntary Agencies (Volags) and health clinics, continue the focus on the problematized (interior and exterior, political and social) body of Cambodians.

Between 1989 and 1991, I conducted research on the relations between Khmer refugees and social agencies in the San Francisco Bay Area as part of a larger project on cultural citizenship. My survey sample included sixty Cambodian refugees in two lower-class communities. In East Oakland, I collected stories of war, escape, and illness, mainly from Khmer women in their homes, while in San Francisco, I participated in a Cambodian self-help group (with both male and female members). In addition, I interviewed professionals working with refugees in community clinics, mental health clinics, county medical offices, voluntary organizations, and social welfare agencies. Since I was not permitted to observe actual doctor-patient interactions, my following account is based on the interpretations both sides make of clinic encounters. Doctors and nurses were interviewed in the workplaces, while Khmers were interviewed in their own homes.

The Bay Area is a major destination for Khmer refugees, those coming directly from Asia or reuniting with their families and friends from other parts of the United States in the early 1980s.[24] As a first step in their resettlement, voluntary agencies handed out a guide called "Facts of Life in the United States," issued with the approval of the U.S. Congress and Department of State. The booklet is available in 13 languages, from Amharic to Khmer. After dealing with the legal status of refugees, the rest of the pamphlet covers hygiene and safety at home and in public. The introductory statement on sponsoring families is immediately followed by instructions to learn American ways of promoting healthy living. Interestingly, the focus on inadvertently offensive bodies dwells on smells. It notes that

Americans are very sensitive to personal body odors. Because of this, it is a good idea for people to bathe or shower and put on clean clothing every day, and to wash their hair and clothes often. . . . Our dentists tell us to brush our teeth at least twice a day. . . . Americans use many products to hide their natural body odors. Most of us use deodorants and mouthwashes. People do these things to prevent unpleasant body odors that may offend other people. . . .[25]

Other instructions include ventilating the home so that strong cooking smells would not offend the neighbors. Lindsay French maintains that compared to Americans, Khmers are much more sensitive to the subtle distinctions and meanings of odors (personal communication), and yet in this refugee handout, they are warned against offending American noses. Perhaps, smells, like viruses and diseases associated with refugees, are experienced by refugee workers as invisible but potentially offensive things that refugees bring with them, inadvertently invading the American sense of "place." While bodies can be physically contained, smells cannot. The focus on offensive smells, those "invasive" and invisible forces, highlights anxiety over regulating refugee bodies in space.

Refugee parents are urged to use diapers on babies. Other suggestions include not spitting or urinating in public because "Americans prefer clean public places." (Ironically, most poor refugees are resettled in low-cost, garbage-strewn neighborhoods). They are also warned about sexually-transmitted diseases. Refugees are thus immediately stigmatized at a very intimate level—the odors of their bodies and homes as likely to offend clean-living Americans. By giving prominence to sanitary measures, the *Facts of Life in the United States* booklet constructs cultural citizenship as attending to good hygiene, and its expression a sign of democratic sensibility. Refugees have to erase the smells of their humanity, their suffering, their culture, in order to become like "normal" Americans. I remember being greeted at a poor Khmer home with a woman spraying scent from an aerosol can. When I inquired why she was doing it, she said she had just been cooking Cambodian food, which, she had learned, "smelled bad to Americans." She had learned the lessons of stigmatized home and the necessity for buying good status. The normalization of the refugee body and home for the body politic has mainly fallen to the responsibility of the health system, whereas biomedical concepts and regimes determine what counts as healthy and culturally correct subjects.

The Emergence of Southeast Asian Mental Health

This section examines the ways biomedical hegemony defines the terms and practices whereby Khmer refugees become a particular kind of American minority. It focuses on the truth effects of naming and classifying illnesses among an immigrant minority as relations of power between American academic and medical "experts" and refugees from Southeast Asia. The control of the terms and practices that produce various "subjectivities" in the target population is itself a source of social power.[26]

Immigration scholars maintain that something called "immigrant psychology" depends to a great extent on the immigrants' "contexts of reception" in the United States.[27] They suggest that when lower-class newcomers like Khmer refugees have access to governmental aid and services, their rate of "mental health distress" is less than would be the case in the absence of state assistance.[28] This linear model of "immigrant psychology" assumes that the sufferings of diverse populations follow generic patterns, and that "mental health" constructs are universally applicable, while ignoring the complex micropolitics and consequences of encounters with the health profession. "Immigrant psychology" is taken to be a thing that exists among (non-European) immigrants who enter this country. No attention is paid to how the biomedicine plays a role in defining the nature and form of extent of this condition.

The arrival of Southeast Asian immigrants actually spawned medical terms creating a concept called "Southeast Asian Mental Health" that is unevenly applied to Cambodians, Hmongs, and Vietnamese.[29] Since the early 1980s, American medical workers have used a range of universal diagnostic tools as the lens through which refugees from Southeast Asia are viewed, represented, and treated. "Post-Traumatic Stress Disorder" (PTSD), a symptom associated with survivors of the First World War, and later generalized as an illness of survivors of concentration camps, became the health model for typecasting the problems of Khmer refugees.[30] Sometimes recast as "the boat people's anxiety," PTSD symptomatology includes: recurrent nightmares; feelings of sadness; social withdrawal; restricted affect; hyperalertness and startle reflex; sleep disorders; loss of memory; guilt; avoidance of activities that prompt recall of stressful events.[31] Another assessment tool freely applied to Khmer patients is a "Depression Rating Scale" that has been slightly modified for assessing "cross-cultural psychiatric disorder" among Southeast Asians. Claiming that Asian immigrants have a "private style . . . that suppresses expressions of dysphoric complaints," J. D. Kinzie and colleagues developed the Vietnamese Depression Scale.[32] This scale is sometimes used as the instrument for assessing other Southeast Asia groups like the Khmers, who have a rather different set of cultural beliefs and practices.[33] Another diagnostic tool, the "Children's Global Assessment Scale" (CGAS) has also been applied to Southeast Asian immigrants. In one study, Khmer school children in Oregon were rated on a scale of behavioral deviance, and the doctors claimed that the CGAS was a better predictor of the children's distress than their own teachers.[34] By these codes, Southeast Asian immigrants are medically defined as socially and culturally handicapped. The discourses touch on Khmers' cultural and intellectual competence and their need for medical intervention. Khmer patients have been described as "passive, obedient" as well as "noncompliant."[35] This characterization is explained as "the unique avoidance of thoughts or activities that reminded these patients of the past. The patients often refused to tell their story in any detail, and many have never told it to anyone else before. There was a conscious effort to deny events of the past."[36] Furthermore, "Many Southeast Asians have an unwillingness or an inability to differentiate between psychological, physiological and supernatural causes of illness."[37] These statements seem to suggest that Khmers are "difficult" patients whose noncompliance stems from cultural passivity, the traumas they had experienced in war-torn Cambodia, and their imputed intellectual limitations.

Mental health experts claim that Southeast Asians are disproportionately afflicted with "depression," "overdependency," "isolation," "psychosomatic illness," "somatization" and PTSD, compared to other groups in American society.[38] In a report to the California Department of Health, an Oakland clinic claims that 16 percent of Khmers suffer from PTSD; the condition was less prevalent among other Southeast Asians in the sample.[39] Khmers were said to be six to seven times more likely to be in severe need than the general population. Over 40 percent were in moderate or high need categories, and should be "targeted for dramatically increased services."[40] Although the intention to help new immigrants is genuine, the report interpreting Khmer refugees' needs was released in time to buttress appeals by the mental health industry for more federal funds, which had been severely cut back under the Reagan administration. Getting the money is tied to the official designation or Cambodians as a "depressed" minority.

Attempts to teach refugees medical concepts to understand their experiences have inspired more costly and technologically-based innovations by health researchers. A wife-husband psychologist-psychiatrist team produced a videotaped "educational drama about PTSD."[41] The PTSD videotape is distributed to selected groups of Khmer refugees for viewing, in the hope or sparking a catharsis of their (assumed) suppressed experiences. It is however a rather poor version of the Southeast Asian TV soaps avidly watched in Khmer households, and unlikely to elicit greater emotional release. After viewing the "educational drama," research assistants urge the participants to talk about their feelings and learn the new concepts. The professed aim was to "place PTSD symptoms within their unique sociocultural context and then to teach basic problem-solving skills dealing with major issues of daily living."[42] This videotaped medical drama has been hailed for "exorcising the evil that haunts Cambodians."[43]

By controlling the medical terms and practices, and seeking to instill them in patients, academic and medical workers are part of an overall scheme of power that defines the form and content or refugee illness and well-being, while producing the truth-effects that shape the subjectivities of Southeast Asian immigrants. Overworked and underfunded clinics, swamped with clients from all over the world, seek an efficient, though unsatisfactory, strategy to reduce the multicultural and personal details of patients' illnesses into diagnostic categories, so that they can dispense drug treatment. However, third world patients seldom make things easy: a doctor working with refugee patients notes, "Among the Southeast Asians, no one would come in and announce, 'I'm depressed.' "[44] As we shall see below, although health workers solicit refugee stories, they use clinical labels to typecast Khmers, who are urged to represent their experiences in universalizable terms, and to cram the riot of their suffering into little boxes on the psychiatrists' charts. In many cases, the effect of mental health treatment is to bypass or invalidate the patients' cultural understanding of their lives, as they are taken through a medical acculturation process that moves from the particular and cultural to the ethnic and the scientific American.

An Argentinian psychiatrist in San Francisco who has treated torture victims in his homeland criticizes local mental health practitioners for labeling Southeast Asian patients as "depressed," but rarely asking them about their war experiences.

> They don't tend to read about the killing fields. But with a little information, you know your patient went through hell, a hell that no human being understands or is able to think about, if they never went through this or something like the "mothers of the La Plaza de Mayo" went through. If you don't know what political repression is all about and you are not interested in asking the question, then you'll never know that the patient has something in his or her past that is horrible.

He notes a similar situation in the ways some doctors are ever ready to brand American veterans as suffering from PTSD, but almost never listen to their traumatic experiences or treat them with the attention they deserve. When I point out that Asian American health workers also readily label the suffering of Asian refugees as PTSD, he rather harshly observes that they are "victims of their own repression," meaning that despite possible common cultural experiences that can create more empathy between the clinician and the refugee patient, the band-aid approach of biomedicine takes precedence.

An important feature of Southeast Asian mental health is the significant number of Asian American health workers whose task include instructing refugees in the American medical nomenclature. While it is often claimed that their "Asian culture" and third world family origins make them more able to empathize with the cultural predicaments of refugees, Asian American doctors and nurses are at times even more insistent on the by-the-book definitions of what ails their patients. As we shall see, community clinics serving refugee populations are the sites in which medicine becomes a field of struggle over the cultural identity and subjectivities of the Khmers.

"Cultural Sensitivity" in Refugee Clinics

Northern California is the destination of refugees from all over the world, and local clinics are very proud of their "culturally sensitive" approach to health care. Many of the health workers are American-born Asians "who may have been raised in bilingual households and witnessed firsthand the collision of old Asian customs and new American ones." They understand concepts like *yin-yang* and the need to balance hot and cold food intake, while practices like visiting shamans are supported.[45] As the children or immigrants, refugees and holocaust-survivors, they are assumed to be especially sensitive to the cultural beliefs, practices, and immigrant experiences of war refugees and Asian newcomers. Cultural discourse is frequently deployed to implant rational thinking in patients who are culturally different.[46]

As first or second generation Americans, Asian (especially Chinese) health workers have earned professional degrees and moved out of Chinatown into suburban communities. Partly as a result of this transition into the American scientific world and into the middle class, they can be among the most ardent believers in rationality, and dismissive of premodern "superstitions" and practices. Perhaps because they are children of Asian immigrants who have suffered discrimination, some health workers consider it necessary to root out non-Western cultural beliefs as a strategy to gain acceptance and achieve assimilation. There is the suggestion that cultural loss is an unavoidable and necessary part of becoming American. But then rather ironically, some acculturated health providers express an underlying sense of Chinese cultural superiority towards Southeast Asians. Their location as a new category of health workers who are newly members of the middle class may also contribute to this faith in Western medicine, and occasional disdain for nonbiomedical forms of knowledge.

Furthermore, although the health providers are well-meaning and sympathetic, the pressure to "do something" with patients often means in practice that "cultural sensitivity" is used in a limited, strategic fashion to win patients' cooperation, facilitate diagnosis, and buttress the doctors' authority, rather than to give equal time or relativize biomedical knowledge.[47] Such health workers are often unable to take a critical view of their own professional role when clinic discourse defines them as ideal care providers for Asian immigrants. Indeed, stereotypical cultural concepts are deployed to construct an intersubjective reality that seeks to manipulate, incorporate, and supplant Khmer notions of healing, body-care, and knowledge. A main argument of this essay is that Khmer patients themselves learn to manipulate these expectations for their own ends.

Ronald Frankenberg[48] notes that sickness is a "cultural performance," a sequence of events in which disease narratives interact with patients' beliefs. For Khmer patients, refugee clinics become the sites in which a struggle ensues between biomedicine and their own understanding of their experiences, and the skirmishes and standoffs are the key elements in a dynamic learning process of cultural belonging/citizenship. However, the following cases of "talking medicine" and "refugee mental health" also reveal that while refugee medicine focuses on eliciting cultural talk that can be recast as symptoms recognizable to biomedical diagnosis, clinicians as well as patients are caught up in "webs of power"[49] that structure the domination of biomedicine over (inappropriate) cultural knowledge, and the conflicts within clinicians as they try to enlarge the meaning of care for Cambodian patients.

"Talking Medicine": Regulating and Subverting Drug Therapy

At one refugee clinic, culturally sensitive health care is defined as an "appropriate use of Western psychiatric methodology in non-Western population."[50] The approach is inspired by Arthur Kleinman's distinction between disease, which is caused by objective biological processes, and illness, or the cultural experience and understanding of affliction.[51] Other scholars have theorized cultural sensitivity as a "synthesis" between "psychiatry's biopsychosocial model and an often different socio-cultural model or human cognition" in the "acculturating group."[52] However, in practice, the two perspectives, biological and cultural, are not held in dialectical tension, but the effect has been to subsume and invalidate the cultural beliefs of the minority group under the biomedical framework. Although doctors and nurses make a show of collecting cultural data and talking cultural beliefs, their medical knowledge is seldom questioned, revised, or relativized; it is in fact strengthened by the gap between the patients' cultural understanding and the doctors' scientific (not viewed as cultural) interpretations. By constructing the cultural descriptions of patients as "somatic complaints," the main treatment is "rigorous symptomatic therapy (drugs)."[53]

There are two aspects to what the clinic calls "talking medicine." One is to get patients to talk about their experiences and beliefs in order to provide information that can facilitate diagnosis and the patients' acceptance of medical authority. Doctors and nurses seek to elicit migration histories from reluctant Khmer patients, who have unpleasant memories of interrogations by the Khmer Rouge and the INS. "Talking medicine" is viewed as a way to put nervous patients at ease, and by "validating the patients' feelings about life events" doctors hope to carry on an ongoing assessment of symptoms and treatment. The health givers, as much as the patients, are caught up in the regulatory effects of biomedicine, and cultural material is appropriated only to be incorporated within the medical framework. Khmer health aides use Khmer terms like "hotness in the body, pressure on the heart, and total body weakness" as substitute "native" terms for what doctors consider as symptoms of clinical depression. Furthermore, Chinese concepts like yin-yang are assumed to be omnipresent in Southeast Asian cultures, and doctors invoke yin-yang to explain "that chemicals in the brain can be out of balance and that this can be the cause or their symptoms and sad feelings. . . . Antidepressant drugs will restore this balance."[54]

Thus "talking medicine" in fact buttresses a disease narrative whereby stereotypical Asian patients' beliefs are integrated and transformed within the medical paradigm. In practice then, "cultural sensitivity" becomes a strategy that uses cultural difference not so much to understand particular experiences or illness as to read symptoms that confirm universalized states of biomedicine.[55] A doctor acclaimed for having dealt extensively with Khmer patients notes that "Depression is depression in all cultures. It has the same vegetative symptoms."[56] Although the intentions of health workers are genuinely to respect patients' pain, their cultural difference is viewed as a distorting screen that will, with difficulty, yield the symptoms that can be identified in biomedical terms so that appropriate drugs can be prescribed. The good intentions of the clinicians notwithstanding, the regulatory force of biomedicine absorbs cultural ideas and transforms them into code words that buttress medical authority.

At the same time "talking medicine" also becomes a strategy whereby health workers eager to provide more than drug therapy use the diagnosis process as a way to talk about the patients' past and current experiences in order to provide a sympathetic ear. A nurse discusses how health workers deal with Post Traumatic Stress Disorder:

We do a couple of things. We make sure that we work the person up medically so that we are not missing some physiological problem that can contribute to depression or somatization and that can actually be treated. . . . When the workups start coming back all negative, which is often what happens, I will say to the people that it is very common for pain in life to cause pain in the body.[57] And now we are going to do something different. Now we are going to have talking medicine. I frame talking about what has happened in terms of medicine because it makes it a lot safer for people. So we talked about your thyroid when you came in, we talked about your pelvic examination and now we are going to do another kind of talking medicine about these complaints you are having. Usually I start with the present and what is happening in your current life. "How many people are living in your house? Who did you bring over here with you? What is your community like?" And then, "Are you on welfare?" "What kinds of financial concerns do you have?" And then go back: "What was it like in the refugee camp? How was the transition?" Then back to the actual flight experience.

She calls these "mini-therapy" sessions because the nurses are not trained psy-chotherapists. By stressing their less strictly biomedical role, she reveals the staff's attempts to go beyond the dispensing of drugs to ask questions that deal with the im-mediate human and social problems of the patients. "Talking medicine" in this sense seeks to provide, along with the aspirins, emotional comfort and perhaps referrals for patients who appear suicidal. Clearly, the clinic staff see themselves as trying to give the best possible care to the multicultural refugee population, within the bounds set by biomedicine and clinic resources. While cultural sensitivity and talking medicine as strategies to elicit information to aid diagnosis may reinforce biomedical control, they can at the same time be subversive of biomedical treatment, and provide the spaces for attending to sick hearts and souls. The dual and conflicting aspects of clinic treatment describe a terrain wherein limited negotiation and empathy is possible, thus attenuating the cold and regulatory nature of modern medicine. Indeed, some refugees feel grateful to receive sympathy for their less tangible afflictions without having to go to the "crazy house" (mental health clinic). In practice then, the biopolitics of refugee medicine—mediated by the strategies of cultural sensitivity and talking medicine—can only be accomplished and reproduced through a daily cross-cultural negotiative and learning process on the part of patients as well as clinicians.

"Refugee Mental Health":
Silence, Telling, and Appropriate(d) Memories

The mental health clinic may unintentionally engender distress in immigrant clients through the enforcement of rules regarding appropriate memories to fit diagnostic categories, while the patient, once medicalized, is urged to resist "bad" memories. In an Asian mental health clinic, cultural sensitivity describes an approach that elicits cultural information in order to be invalidated or erased so that self-discipline can begin the work of helping refugee minds made chaotic and confused by war and displacement. Mr. Eam (a pseudonym) is a Khmer war refugee who is being trained as a bilingual therapist. He finds it an especially frustrating job to mediate between Khmer patients, many of whom are middle-age and older women, and the criteria of mental health. His job is to interview Khmer women referred to his clinic, and using the Diagnostic and Statistical Manual for Mental Disorders III (DSM III) as the measurement, sort the patients according to DSM III categories or "major depression," "schizophrenia," "conduct disorder," and "bipolar disorder." He then presents the cases to Asian American psychologists and psychiatrists, who make the final decision of "which category fits which patient," and prescribe drugs accordingly. Eam notes that although his current job is not that of a policeman, he must find the truth of his patients' lives:

> There is nothing inside their minds thinking that "Oh, I have this thing called "depression," this thing called "adjustment disorder," or whatever. . . . Not only do they not know how to tell their problems, but many do not want to tell the truth!

Despite his own harrowing experiences as a war refugee, in his current job, he can only subscribe to the biomedical "truth."[58]

In his view, patients lie because of shame over seeking help at a mental health clinic that many Khmers consider as synonymous with "a place for crazy people." Often, the shame comes from disclosing the collapse of family life and self-respect. He told a story of a Khmer man whose wife had run away with another man. He got into a street fight with African Americans and was sent to a hospital that referred him to the clinic.

> He didn't tell what his problem was, he had been drinking! He did not want to tell the truth because it's so shameful. . . . So my job is to find out exactly. In this country we expect clients to tell us what's going on. It's the client's willingness to tell us what the problem is if they want us to help. But with the Cambodian, we have to dig it up . . . to go deeper.

Like his counterparts in other clinics, Eam's major battle is simply to get Khmer refugees to talk. "Mental health" treatment becomes a struggle between silences and truths, appropriate memories and diagnosis according to psychiatric categories. Khmer refugees have survived war, labor camps, and flight by becoming masters in the contest between self-willed silence and forced confession. Under Pol Pot, there was a saying: "People would be saved if they plant the kapok tree (kor)." The word kor also means mute. A prophecy of doom noted that only by playing dumb would people survive: "only the deaf-mutes would be saved during this period of misfortune."[59] Silence and opacity become a shield of defense in the face of authority.

The mental health quest for hidden "truths" is made more difficult when Eam tries to get older women to submit to the regime of confession. Many refugees have great faith in Western medicine because they saw relatives and friends die from lack of proper medical treatment during the war.[60] Now they desire the medical magic bullet that they think can ease their pains, but they detest the "talking" part of the clinic culture. Some say to him, "I want to cooperate with you, but the method you use is so difficult, it involves discussion. . . . I feel dizzy, feel so exhausted." Furthermore, given their difference in age and female modesty, female patients find it too humiliating and painful to share stories of war deprivations and current health problems with a younger man.

In any case, Eam sees his job as getting them to say things that suggest symptoms identified in the DSM III chart. The next step is to prescribe medication, which though desired, is carefully administered by the patients. They complain that the drugs may be too powerful, and have the effect of blurring memories they may wish to retain, no matter how painful. This effect seems to concur with Eam's understanding of the goal of mental health treatment:

> Our medicine is to knock you down in order not to think, not to think about what's going on, about the family . . . just to knock you down, to go to bed. We believe that the more the patients sleep, the better the chance they will feel better. So they forget whatever stuff that upset them.

Not only are memories deemed true or false, but they are then appropriated to medical knowledge. Mr. Eam, genuinely concerned with the suffering of his patients, is a cultural mediator who believes that becoming healthy requires a mind that lets go of painful memories.

However, Khmer "mental health" patients resist such losses and take their prescribed drugs according to their own judgement of what is appropriate. One of Eam's patients is a widow in her fifties who has had high blood pressure and stomach problems for a long time. She suffers from dizziness and feels weak most of the time. When we met, she was sitting on the mat in her living room, showing me a shoebox of medicine bottles, many filled with pills:

> The medicine I got from there is good and it sometimes relieves the headache. . . . He tries to make all the women who have mental problems happy. But I think I lot. He told me to forget about the past and not to think a lot. But how can I forget? My husband was taken away from me and he has never come back. Some of my children [five] died because of lack of food and medicine. In 1979, I was a single mother with four sick children. When the Vietnamese occupied my country, I carried all my sick children by turn, running from one place to another to find a place free from the Khmer Rouge. I needed to find money to support my children. My hands were full. I took my two older sons who were very sick to the Battambang Hospital. I had to leave them there. I escaped to the Thai border. . . . When I arrived, all my energy was almost gone, and the two children who were with me were very sick too. We were sent to the Khao-I-Dang Hospital in Thailand. We stayed at that hospital for several months. When I felt better, I wanted to go back to Battambang Hospital to pick my two boys up. But I didn't know how to do this. . . . It had been very hard to escape to Thailand. I have felt sorrowful and sick since.

In the United States, she reconnected with one of the sons; the other had died at the hospital. Such memories are the connecting tissue to her past, and moral reasons for her current suffering. Her Buddhist faith may be defined as a "deathlife" philosophy in which consciousness of suffering and death is a moral condition of existence.[61]

This memory biomedical treatment seeks to blot out so that she can be freed from the shadow of death, and participate more fully in her adopted country. But although she needs medication, the old woman resists the medical dislodging of her past life, and what remains of her cultural self. Thus both the refugee clinic, with its conflicting goals of "talking medicine," and the mental health clinic, with its judgement of what is appropriate memory, provide very limited opportunities for the telling of stories in a full and uncensored manner. Overall, given the fact that American medical settings "constrain Khmers in expressing their own culture," the old woman seeks catharsis through talking of past traumas, not in the clinics, but in the presence of sympathetic relatives and friends who can share the pain.[62]

Medical Authority and Medical Regimes

In refugee clinics, daily encounters with health workers are lessons in new bodily regimes or "regularized modes of behavior"[63] relevant to the cultivation of behavioral traits like learning the routines of checkups, vaccination, family planning, and drug treatment, the temporal structuring of life that they were first subjected to in the transit camps. However, again and again, Khmer refugees are considered among the most problematic patients in learning medical routines. Their responses to medical orders are often found unsatisfactory, and labeled as irrational, passive and face-saving. Some Asian American health workers interpret Khmers polite smiles as expressions of their "fear of authority." Yet, there is also a recognition that the smiles stand for intransigence, and a subversive resistance to medical discipline. Khmer refugees deploy a range of tactics—silences, polite smiles, the resistant body, and faking illness—to subvert and circumvent clinic rules and control, and still retain the medical attention and resources they desire. Such cultural performances as patients are important lessons in citizenship through which Khmers figure out how to obtain resources controlled by experts.

A primary concern of Khmer immigrants is gaining access to prescription drugs. In the Bay Area, a majority of Khmers are on welfare, which also provides health benefits (Medi-Cal). A major reason for remaining on welfare programs is to safeguard their children's access to health care, which is very costly in California. In the refugee camps, Khmers, who had lost almost everything, learnt to attach themselves to someone who has power in order to gain access to goods and services,[64] thus adding a strongly instrumental cast to their traditional patron-clientelist orientation. This pattern of attaching themselves to institutionalized hierarchies of power was continued in the United States, where American service providers and experts often became the focus of such deference because they can provide access to important things like medicine.[65]

Of all Western medicines, Khmers are most interested in injectable drugs, intra-venous drips, and pills in which they have an incredible faith. It is based on the idea of putting good things into the body. An informant who was a pharmacist in Phnom Penh talks about Khmers going to the hospital regularly for injections if they did not feel too well. Pregnant women wanted injections to be strong and healthy. (However, as mentioned earlier, Khmer Rouge "medics" often injected injurious substances that badly harmed or killed patients during the war.) Lindsay French reports that in refugee camps, Khmers injected themselves with B vitamins and treated themselves with stolen antibiotic drips. She points out that Western medicine is viewed narrowly in this light as a magic bullet, while other aspects of Western healing are considered unnecessary and obstructionist.[66]

However, in clinic encounters, Khmer's respect for Western medicine is not matched by their respect for American doctors, whose techniques and interpretations they often find baffling and unable to heal their suffering. Tactics are required to bypass or subvert medical rules in order to get the medicine. Older Khmers expect healers (like the Khmer shaman or *kru Khmer*) to have special insights into illnesses without cross-examining the afflicted.[67] Yet in America, the doctors submit patients to an interrogation about many unrelated topics concerning themselves, their relatives, and migration history. A nurse in the refugee clinic reports:

> People sometimes doubt our abilities because we ask so many questions. "Well, what's the matter? Don't you know? If you have to ask these questions, then maybe you're not very good." In this culture, we think the more questions you know how to ask the more skilled you are. Oftentimes when I see patients I say, "You may not be used to this but I am going to be asking you a lot of questions. This is how we do medicine in this country. I know that in the country you come from, people didn't ask you so many questions." So we start from there.

Some doctors and nurses complain that Khmer patients seem to display skepticism when submitted to questioning. They wonder whether the doctors are tricksters, concealing their lack of knowledge by asking many questions and relying on many instruments, while failing to share the pain of their suffering.

Some Khmers resist the doctors' authority by not learning medication compliance. They complain that doctors prescribe too many drugs, giving them dosages that are "too hot." Even after clinic reassurances that their dosage is proportionate to their "smaller size" relative to Americans, Khmer patients routinely reduce their drug intake, or take their medicine irregularly, i.e., when they feel bad.[68] For instance, some take drugs in combinations determined by the color or size of capsules. To instill a sense of medical regime, the clinic gives each Khmer patient a card divided into columns represented by moon and sun symbols to indicate appropriate times in the day for taking medicine (Fig. 1). Some patients misread the linear representation of time and substitute their own schedule. Thinking that the diagram depicts the lunar cycle, they take their medicine according to the waxing or waning of the moon. Through controlling their own medication, Khmer patients hope to deflect the drug regime many are placed under, and ensure a continual source of medical attention and resources. One strategy is to stop taking drugs a few days before the next visit so that the doctor can see that "I am still ill." Instead of directly challenging doctors' advice, Khmer patients take the drugs while protesting that the illness lingers on, and that they remain unhealed.

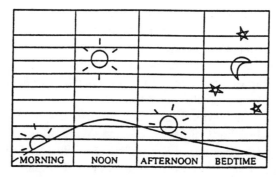

FIGURE 1. Card of daily schedule to take medicine.

Passivity of Women, Body of Resistance

In Cambodia, women played a major role in the daily care of their families, but in the United States they find themselves dependent on the modern medical system in which they operate as ignorant recipients. Working with a Chinese-influenced humoral theory, Khmers believe that hot and cold winds affect the health of the body. Bodily aches (including headaches) are often treated by pinching, cupping, and coining in order to relieve pain and bring toxic winds to the body surface, thus restoring balances among elements in the body, and between the body and the environment.[69] Hot and cold foods are variously prescribed to prevent imbalances in the body, or for restoring the sick body to health. Women's care of the body, through dietary and healing practices, together with their rituals commemorating dead ancestors, are social obligations to ensure the health and safety of the family. The link between physical well-being and nurturing one's social relations in this world and the next is clearly central to Khmer healing.

Perhaps not surprisingly, in the American clinic encounters, Khmer women are viewed as a special category of "difficult" patients, perceived as more "traditional and superstitious" than men. Furthermore, clinic workers characterize them as passive, silent, and fearful of authorities. Even Asian American nurses seldom talk to them in such a way as to break through their silences. Whereas the health workers saw Khmer women's passivity as simply a sign of their downtrodden cultural status, a passive posture can be read to mean a number of things, from tactics to deflect control while maintaining a relationship, to attempts to shield a vulnerable self. In Khmer culture, authority figures should not be questioned or otherwise embarrassed, so both Khmer men and women tend to display a passive obedience before authority.[70] This pose of passivity was further honed during the Pol Pot years, when, as mentioned earlier, by playing the deaf-mute, Khmers avoided disclosures and exposures that could result in terrible consequences to oneself and one's loved ones. In refugee camps and in American institutions, Khmers find that by being passive with powerful authority figures, they can dissemble about what they want to do and the reasons for doing so, while still maintaining the patron-client relationship that would grant them access to scarce resources. Often, the customary passive obedience is "compounded by fear and ignorance of our legal system"[71] as Khmer patients worry that by yielding up information about themselves to an American official, or deliberately disregarding rules, they may be threatened with deportation.

For instance, a Japanese American nurse who makes home visits says her instructions about reading body signs for pregnancy are often met by silence: "They don't say anything. They feel we're some kind of authority." Using a maternal and teasing manner, she urges Khmers to family plan. After the birth of a sixth baby in a Khmer family, she said to the father, "Papa, no more babies." "No one ever challenges or refuses you," but the next time she visited, there was a new baby. Harking back to her childhood in Hawaii, she compares Khmers to native Hawaiians as a gentle people who love babies. In this case, the nurse accepts that her good intentions will be subverted, by a people whom she sees as grateful to America for accepting them as refugees, and yet determined to follow their own desires about having babies. The nurse continued to visit them. Through their passive pose as clients of the state, this Khmer family has subtly negotiated a space for making their own decisions and yet still maintain official connections that do not threaten their family security.

Even more powerless than the men, Khmer women learned that they had no right to personal opinions and open disagreements with authority figures in Khmer communities and in American agencies. Furthermore, the women's passivity may mask the loss of self-respect, motivation, and suicidal tendencies among the survivors of war traumas.[72] One is never sure how many have been tortured in their flight from Cambodia, raped by Thai soldiers "guarding" the refugee camps, or what kinds of compromises they made to survive and care for their children, and how deep their sense of dishonor. A Khmer woman told me that young girls arriving in Los Angeles were traumatized by the physical examination required of all refugees. Even if they had escaped rapes, Khmer girls have never been seen naked by anyone, except perhaps their mothers.[73] (p. 436). They were thus horrified to be told to strip and lie under bright lights, with open legs raised up in stirrups. Thus pelvic examination by male physicians, even with a female nurse standing by, becomes a painful rite of passage into the modern medical system.

Refugee clinics have learnt of Khmer women's great sensitivity about exposing their lower bodies to the medical gaze. At the Northern California clinic:

> We have a policy here that we don't do pelvic exams on single women or women who are not sexually active because there is so much cultural stuff that is attached to virginity and an intact hymen.

Only female health workers do pelvic exams on married women or those whom they suspect have had sex or been raped. They are told the medical reasons for gynecological examinations. Whenever possible, young women who are examined are told that they are "still virgins." In preventive medicine, Khmer women are also taught to explore their own bodies, something they are not used to doing:

> I also teach women how to do their own breast exams which is kind of radical for them because they are not used to touching themselves in a specific way.

However, the nurse is not able to persuade Khmer women to go so far as to learn to use a diaphragm. They have to depend on patient coaching and are perceived as being used to "having things done for them."

While Khmer women learn medical manipulation of the body, they sometimes draw the line at surgery. In Khmer Theravada Buddhism, the physical body is viewed in unity with the social self and the soul; all three are closely interrelated. A sacred essence resides in the head of each individual, and the head must be treated with special respect. After death, the soul separates from the body and continues its existence, hopefully in a higher reincarnated form. In her research among Khmer amputees in refugee camps, Lindsay French[74] observes that to be born able-bodied and then lose a limb is a sudden downturn in one's fortune. It is a sign of bad karma, which represents not only a fall in status but also does not bode well for the future. Furthermore, for Khmer patients, surgery may unintentionally invoke torture during the war years. Soldiers on both sides routinely cut open the bodies of fallen soldiers to eat the livers or mutilate them further.[75] Many Khmers saw family members killed under torture and dismemberment, or injected with fatal substances.[76] As patients in clinics, Khmers are compelled to rethink the relationship between bodily integrity, social status, and war memories on the one hand, and biomedical forms of domination on the other.

Preventive medicine, for instance, requires medical interventions into hidden bodily processes to control the spread of cancer or regulate pregnancy. A nurse reports that a Khmer woman, when told that she had a breast mass, refused any medical procedure. Even after seeing five specialists and shown the X-ray image, she even resisted having a biopsy. She could not see a connection between her current feeling of health and the image of the diseased body. And the idea of being under general anesthetic frightened her. Her sense of well-being could not accept the connection between the X-ray image and a disease that she could neither see nor feel. The X-ray, an invisible penetration of one's insides, will lead to unnecessary surgery, a procedure that may lead to dismemberment and mutilation of the body. By following medical instructions, one will consign oneself to a karmic bad fortune, which will reduce one's status and social capacity to be effective in everyday life. Furthermore, she was asked to sign over the custody of her body for the operation. Surgery thus recalls situations under the Khmer Rouge, when being interviewed and signing forms often resulted in one's torture, dismemberment, and death. Her fears were so great that the clinic could do nothing, but worry about the possibility of whether the patient's resistance to preventive surgery will also dissuade her from pursuing a lawsuit further down the line.

Medical regimes thus not only socialize people to expected norms of patient behavior[77] but also instruct patients about the rules and rights that constitute the proper medical and juridical subject. Refugee women, especially those from Southeast Asia, become the paradigmatic clinical pictures of disorder. In California, Khmers are perceived as large welfare families who are becoming part of the underclass.[78] They epitomize the fecund premodern woman who must learn self-discipline and new knowledge to fit into modern civil society.

Since sex is such a culturally sensitive subject, Asian American nurses play a major role in reproductive health education. A Chinese American nurse sees her role as promoting "patient participation in the decision . . . to empower them as parents." Collecting groups of refugee and immigrant women in her clinic, she discusses the whole idea that one can plan pregnancies, and the different methods of contraception, and prenatal care. When her instructions are received in silence by Khmer women, she takes it to mean their "not wanting to lose face by asking an authority figure questions":

> And I say, wait a minute, you have a right to ask questions, you have a right to refuse, you have a right to another opinion. They say "yes," but do not comply with my orders. . . . Even though they are passive, they are even more demanding (than other patients) because we don't know what they are questioning, or what issues are there for them.

In her estimation, Khmer women are more passive than Chinese or Russian refugees. After her presentations, Chinese women would ask questions. In one meeting, "the Russians ask, 'Can I have a sonogram?' "[79] Instead of seeking the latest medical technology, Khmer women "turn their bodies over to authority figures. They will say yes to everything, leave and then come back pregnant . . . they're just saying it at times to placate us." As the nurse recognizes, the "passivity" of Khmer women constitutes an unspoken resistance to medical regulation of their pregnancies and family life.

Khmer patients are thus engaged in a complex type of contestation that both invites medical attention and yet repels it. Khmer women display polite smiles, stony silences, and pregnant bodies. Their sense of self refuses a clinical, detached attitude towards their bodies. They appear uninterested in lessons on birth spacing, the stages of pregnancy and phases in the birth-process intending to teach the cultivation of a modern attitude towards their bodies/selves. They are apparently impervious to medical interpretations of their problems, needs, and goals. Thus the medical gaze can be said to be reproduced by such passive resistance, which compels further medical instruction and resources to make them "better patients."[80] Because the unregulated fecund Khmer body seems both premodern and undisciplined, it confirms the image of a new (Asian) American underclass already stigmatized for its unwed, pregnant teenagers.[81] Furthermore, family planning is presented as an individualized decision to treat one's body as a manipulable machine, apart from its emotional, social, and political contexts. Nurses try to "empower" the women in decision making about having children, but cannot influence domestic patriarchal power that also claims control over the female body.[82]

The loss of children to starvation and disease during the Khmer Rouge years has increased the desire to have more children. Furthermore, family planning was an unknown concept and the women never talk to their husbands about sex, an area that is viewed as the husband's prerogative.[83] There is the stark reality that having more children in the United States will ensure greater government aid, in a context where few husbands have the skills to be employed. Thus although pregnant women attempt to deflect medical discipline, they wish to retain their claims on health care, and through their babies, on the wider welfare support system that will ensure the survival of their families.

Working around the Medical System

Resistance is seldom articulated, due to language problems, and an aversion to disagree with Americans who are all viewed as having provided safe refuge to Khmer refugees, and who continue to be providers of everything from over-the-counter pills to a living income. Instead, the locus of resistance is in their bodies, and its refusal and subversion of medical discipline. However, despite their wish to remain unappropriated by medical regimes, Khmer refugees hang on to government subsidized clinics because it is a key institution that helps secure their other needs. Because they feel the need to repel the perception that they are "living off the system," Khmers use nonverbal strategies to negotiate their specific goals with the medical authorities.

Khmers in different age groups and family situations are eligible for different combinations of health, food, and welfare supports, and strategies to secure these benefits have become a daily obsession.[84] Women with children under eighteen have access to Medi-Cal (federal and state health benefits) together with the Aid to Families with Dependent Children (AFDC) program. They also receive food stamps. Clinics are the gateway to other forms or supplementary support. Pregnant women are asked to get a clinic clearance in order to qualify for a supplementary food program (Women, Infants and Children), which will provide food and diaper vouchers for a child up to five years. Older refugees, or those with no young children, hope to receive the Social Supplemental Income (SSI), including food stamps, which are granted to people who are disabled, blind or sixty-five years old or more. Many Khmers I met have tried to get doctors to exam their eyes, ears, limbs, and even mental condition in order to qualify for SSI. Young and old Khmers make repeated visits to clinics to get drugs and a health certificate qualifying them for additional support. In some cases, Khmers fearful of a life on the streets, fake blindness and madness in their clinic examinations, creating dysfunctioning bodies/minds that mime their lack of sufficient social support. Thus, while medical agents try to enhance the disciplinary utility of the refugee body, Khmers manipulate their own bodies in order to circumvent control, while desperately seeking welfare rights to greater social benefits. Thus they do not entirely refute the trope of the "depressed Cambodians" because of its utility for ensuring their access to medicine, continuing health care, and additional social support.

Encounters in clinics then involve social contestations that go beyond skirmishes over medical discipline. Although doctors and health workers are in a sense socializing agents, the refugees are not "normalized" in quite the ways intended: as better patients. Instead, through their own perception of their own limited rights and security in America, Khmer patients are negotiating, with and through their health providers, for resources that will ensure their survival in this country. The wider network of welfare bureaucracy, of which community clinics are a part, is the training ground in which refugees learn what cultural citizenship entails for the poor.

Conclusion: Refugee Medicine

I have argued that the work of biomedicine goes beyond providing health care to shaping, in both intended and unintended ways, the cultural citizenship of different categories of patients. The biopolitics of medical production include institutions like refugee clinics that attend to sick newcomers and through the disciplining of everyday behavior, socialize them as governable citizens. However, I pointed to the limitations of a Foucauldian analysis for understanding the micropolitics of clinic encounters since Foucault's concern was with the generalized effects of biomedicine, and he did not extend his analysis to the complex intentions and manipulations of medicalized subjects who in their everyday life must operate in different webs of power. The above discussion reveals that the disciplining mechanisms of biomedicine, while linked to the bureaucratic apparatuses of Western democracies, are less powerful and all-pervasive than we have given them credit for. The clinicians themselves appear to be both agents and objects of biomedical regulation. They seek to reduce patients' cultural beliefs to biomedical terms, but at other times subvert medical procedures in order to provide emotional support; they instruct patients in the norms of medical regimes and yet must sometimes adjust to patients' insistence on "deviant" behavior. Perhaps the overwhelming sufferings of refugees daily remind doctors and nurses about the limits of biomedical care, even when they believe in it as the best medicine for life in modern society.

One finding of the clinic encounters between Khmer refugees and American clinics is that the subtle subterfuges of the cultural Other both frustrate and compel the medical gaze. They reveal that biomedical management and control are achieved and reproduced only through a process of negotiative, cross-cultural learning on the part of doctors and nurses as well as refugee patients. The Khmer patients, a largely illiterate peasant population, show themselves to be masters of inscrutability, skills that have helped them survive wars, and that continue to be relevant for their everyday survival as the most disadvantaged newcomers in American society. Encounters with clinics are a necessary part of their lives, but biomedicine, although part of the everyday relations of domination, cannot offer the deep healing that is sought. The following example reveals the complex intentions at work in dealings with clinics.

An elderly Khmer widow, Mrs. Yem, goes to a mental health clinic for her headaches, and to a private Vietnamese doctor, hoping that he will sign a medical certificate qualifying her for additional welfare aid. The clinic gives her shots and drugs. "The more I take them, the more trouble they give me. Like here [tapping on her temple], it feels like someone is drilling away and it hurts so much that I black out." Rejecting her medication, she sought out the *kru Khmer* who had foretold her husband's death on the voyage over. Now he advised her that she may have offended ancestral spirits. "Yes, I might have said something wrong. It is possible that I didn't think of the spirits, that we arrived in the America and we didn't make any offerings." The *kru Khmer* instructed her to set up an altar in her bedroom to appease the angry spirits. Praying to her ancestral spirits appeared to give her the kind of relief from suffering that the clinic could not.

While Khmers desperately need and seek modern health care, they continue their search for older, and more satisfying forms of healing. Nevertheless, biomedicine continues to be very powerful as an institution in the work of producing some-what normalized patients in modern civil society. Health workers find themselves as much caught up in the regulatory processes of refugee medicine as are the refugees themselves. These critical lessons in citizenship reinforce the Khmers' construction as underclass subjects in society, while doctors and nurses find that their sense of themselves as good caregivers is defined in part by their unwitting role as socializing agents of the state.

Notes

This paper is based on a larger research project funded by the Rockefeller Gender Roles Program. In the field, I was ably and patiently assisted by Maeley Kim, Vannary Orn, and Karharya Um, who introduced me to many subjects in Oakland and transcribed reams of interviews. This project would not have been possible without their help. I am especially grateful for valuable comments on this paper by Lindsay French, Lawrence Cohen, and anonymous reviewers. Early versions benefitted from comments by Donna Haraway, Kathryn Poethig, Vincanne Adams, and Anna L. Tsing.

1. In this paper, Cambodians and Khmers are used interchangeably. For the most reliable account of the Pot regime and its devastating effects on Khmers, see B. Kiernan and B. Chanthou (eds.), *Peasants and Politics in Kampuchea 1942–1981*, Armonk, N.Y.: M. E. Sharpe Inc., 1982. For the situation in the camps, see B. S. Levy and D. C. Susott (eds.), *Years of Honor, Days of Hope: Responding to the Cambodian Refugee Crisis*, Millwood, N.Y.: Associated Faculty Press Inc., 1986.

2. A brief comparison between the Khmer Rouge in Cambodia and the Red Guards in China can be found in E. Becker, *When the War Was Over: The Voices of Cambodia's Revolution and Its People*, New York: Simon and Schuster, 1986, p. 260. For an ethnographic account of how the Cultural Revolution gave vent to extensive surveillance and terrorization of ordinary civilians, see A. Chan, R. Madsen, and J. Unger, *Chen Village under Mao and Deng* (expanded and revised ed.), Berkeley: University of California Press, 1992.

3. M. Foucault, *The History of Sexuality*, Vol. 1: An Introduction, New York: Vintage, 1979, p. 145.

4. The Declaration of Independence, read in the United States Congress on 4 July 1776, stated in part: "We hold these truths to be self-evident, that all men are created equal, that they are endowed by their Creator with certain inalienable rights, that among these are life, liberty, and the pursuit of happiness. That to secure these rights, governments are instituted among men, rendering their just power for the consent of the governed. . . ."

5. M. Foucault, Governmentality. In *The Foucault Effect* (edited by G. Burchell, C. Gordon, and P. Miller), Chicago: University of Chicago Press, 1991, pp. 87–104.

6. Foucault, *The History of Sexuality*, p. 139.

7. A. Ong, The production of possession: Spirits and the multinational corporation in Malaysia, *Am. Ethnolog.*, 1988, pp. 15, 28.

8. M. Foucault, *The Birth of the Clinic: An Archaeology of Medical Perception* (translated by Sheridan Smith, A.M.), New York: Vintage, 1973, pp. 196, 198.

9. J. Donzelot, *The Policing of Families*, London: Hutchinson, 1980.

10. M. Hewitt, Biopolitics and social policy: Foucault's account of welfare. In *The Body* (edited by M. Featherstone, M. Hepworth, and B. S. Turner), London: Sage Publications, 1991, pp. 225–55.

11. M. Foucault, *Discipline and Punish: The Birth of the Prison*, New York: Vintage, 1979, p. 138.

12. Most Khmer refugees coming to the United States are of peasant origin, and their culture is a combination of pre-Buddhist animistic elements interwoven with and inseparable from Theravada Buddhism. They arrived in large numbers in the period 1980 to 1985. After 1987, the resettlement program was halted. Later arrivals, in small numbers, entered through the family reunification program or for special health or humanitarian reasons.

13. S. Golub, *Looking for Phantoms: Flaws in the Khmer Rouge Screening Process*, Washington, D.C.: U.S. Committee for Refugees, 1986, 11. See also A. Zito and T. E. Barlow, Introduction: Body, subject, and power in China. In *Body, Subject, and Power in China* (edited by A. Zito and T. E. Barlow), Chicago: University of Chicago Press, 1994, p. 7.

14. Ibid., p. 19.

15. Ibid., p. 8.

16. U.S. Committee for Refugees (USCR), *Cambodians in Thailand: People on the Edge*, Washington, D.C.: American Council for Nationalities Service, 1985, p. 11.

17. C. A. Mortland, Transforming refugees in refugee camps, *Urban Anthrop.*, 1987, pp. 385.

18. Ibid., p.85.

19. J. W. Toffelson, Response to Ranard and Gilzow: The economics and ideology of overseas refugee education, *TESOL Q.*, 1991, p. 543, 546, 549.

20. Mortland, pp. 389–90.

21. P. Q. Dan, Health issues of concern to the Asian immigrant population: Epidemiological issues. In *The Asian Woman*, New York: Cicatelli Associates, Region II Family Planning Training Center (sponsored by The Asia Society), 1986, pp. 8.

22. Ibid., pp. 5–11.

23. Many Americans think that the country is now under threat from the inexorable influx or immigrants from all over the world. The medical construction of immigrant subjects is not unprecedented in U.S. history. Since the late nineteenth century, Asian immigrants have been viewed as inferior racial bodies who should be excluded from the body politic. See R. Horsman, *Race and Manifest Destiny*, Cambridge, Mass.: Harvard University Press, 1981. The reception of immigrants was also framed by the larger long-term American view that newcomers of all kinds were the source of "germs and genes of an inferior sort." See A. M. Kraut, *Silent Travelers:*

Germs, Genes, and the "Immigrant Menace," New York: Basic Books, 1994. Today, this view is mainly reserved for refugees who are medicalized as polluting/flawed bodies that must be sanitized and reordered for the civil society.

24. See note 12.

25. *Facts of Life in the United States: Information for Refugees Who Come to the United States,* Lutheran Immigration and Refugee Services (LIRS), and Migration and Refugee Services/U.S. Catholic Services (MRS/USCC), Oakland, 1987.

26. Zito and Barlow, p. 7.

27. A. Portes and R. G. Rumbaut, *Immigrant America: A Portrait,* Berkeley: University of California Press, 1990, p. 175.

28. Ibid., pp. 175–77.

29. Even though there are other populations from Southeast Asia, like Filipinos, Indonesians, Malaysians, Thais, Burmese, and Singaporeans living in California, the term "Southeast Asian" is normally not used to refer to or include them. They are called Asians or Pacific Islanders. "Southeast Asian" is reserved for populations from those countries directly involved in the "Vietnam" War, 1962–1975.

30. J. D. Kinzie, R. H. Fredrickson, and J. Fleck, Post Traumatic Stress Disorder among survivors of Cambodian concentration camps, *Am. J. Psychiat.,* 1984, pp. 141, 645; and J. K. Boehnlein, J. D. Kinzie, B. Rath, and J. Fleck, One-year follow-up study of Post Traumatic Stress Disorder among survivors of Cambodian concentration camps, *Am. J. Psychiat.,* 1985, pp. 142, 956.

31. J. D. Kinzie, Overview of clinical issues in the treatment of Southeast Asian refugees. In *Southeast Asian Mental Health: Treatment, Prevention, Services, Training and Research,* (edited by T. C. Owen), Washington, D.C.: U.S. Department of Mental Health, 1985, pp. 113–35.

32. J. D. Kinzie, S. M. Manson, D. T. Vinh, N. T. Tolan, B. Anh, and T. N. Pho, Development and validation of a Vietnamese-language Depression Rating Scale, *Am. J. Psychiat.,* 1982, pp. 139, 1276.

33. E. Gong-Guy, *The California Southeast Asian Mental Health Needs Assessment,* Oakland: Asian Mental Health Services, 1987.

34. W. H. Sack, R. Angell, J. D. Kinzie, S. Manson, and B. Rath, The psychiatric effects of massive trauma on Cambodian children. II. The family and school, *J. Am. Aced. Child Psychiat.,* 1986, pp. 25, 377.

35. M. A. Muecke, Caring for Southeast Asian refugee patient in the USA, *Am. J. Pub. Hlth.,* 1983, pp. 73, 431. See also note 31, pp. 123, 125.

36. Kinsie. P. 127.

37. Ibid., p. 116.

38. Ibid., p. 113–35. See also Gong-Guy.

39. Gong-Guy, pp. 2–3. See also Kinsie, p. 126.

40. Ibid., p. 9.

41. J. White-Baughan, P. M. Nicassio, and D. M. Baughan, Educational drama and problem solving training for symptoms of PTSD in Cambodian refugees. Talk and videotape presented at the *Refugee Information Exchange Conference,* Sacramento, August 22–24, 1990.

42. Ibid.

43. B. Abramson, Exorcising evil that haunts Cambodians, *San Diego Tribune,* June 22, 1991, pp. A1, A6.

44. J. Krich, Culture crash, *Mother Jones,* October 24–27, 1989, pp. 24–27, 52–53.

45. *The New York Times*, 28 June 1992, p. 10. While lauding the "cultural sensitivity" of these clinics, the article ends by mentioning a Chinese doctor who dissents from the approach. He said, "What we have to do as providers is to be curious. We have to ask again and then again. This is not about these individual (cultural) things. It is about caring, and out of caring searching out what we need to know."

46. See note 7 for a discussion of how cultural discourse is used to control "irrational" incidents like "mass hysteria" among female workers in Malaysian factories.

47. See also S. W. Foster, The Pragmatics of culture: The rhetoric of difference in inpatient psychiatry. Presented at the American Anthropological Association Annual Meetings, Chicago, November, 1987.

48. R. Frankenberg, "Your time or mine?": An anthropological view of the tragic temporal contradictions of biomedical practice. *Int. J. Hlth Serv.*, 18 (1988): 11.

49. L. A. Rhodes, *Emptying Beds: The Work of an Emergency Psychiatric Unit*, Berkeley: University of California Press, 1991.

50. P. Delay and S. Faust, Depression in Southeast Asian refugees, *Am. Family Physician*, 36 (1986): 179.

51. A. Kleinman, *Patients and Healers in the Context of Culture*, Berkeley: University of California Press, 1980.

52. J. K. Boehnlein, Clinical relevance of grief and mourning among Cambodian refugees, *Soc. Sci. Med.*, 25 (1987): 376.

53. Delay and Faust, pp. 180–81.

54. Ibid., pp. 182–83.

55. See also M. Taussig, Reification and the consciousness of the patient. *Soc. Sci. Med.*, 14B (1980): 3.

56. Krich, p. 52.

57. There is irony in the nurse telling Khmers that "It is very common that pain in life causes pain in the body" since the Khmers themselves consider health as an inseparable part of maintaining one's relationships with family, both alive and dead. For Khmers, illness is seldom a discrete physical phenomenon apart from the social identity of the afflicted. For instance, a Khmer peasant often attributes illness or misfortune to angry ancestral spirits, which can deprive one of the vital life-sustaining essence. See M. Ebihara, Interactions between Buddhism and social systems in Cambodian peasant culture. In *Anthropological Studies in Theravada Buddhism* (edited by M. Nash et al.), New Haven: Yale University Southeast Asian Studies, Cultural Report Series no. 13, 1966; M. T. Chou, Peasant Women in Northeastern Thailand: A Study of Class and Gender Divisions among the Ethnic Khmer Loeu, Ph.D. dissertation, Department of Anthropology and Sociology, University of Queensland, pp. 194, 216–17, 1985; and J.-P. Hiegel, Introduction to Khmer traditional medicine based on experience in refugee camps in Thailand. In *The Asian Woman*, New York: Cicatelli Associates, Region II Family Planning Training Center (Sponsored by The Asia Society), pp. 78–88, 1986.

58. Before the Khmer Rouge took over, Eam was a policeman in Phnom Penh. In the subsequent slaughter of members of the Lon Nol regime, he was the only member of his squad to survive.

59. Becker, p. 204.

60. Not only were people deprived of modern medical care under the Khmer Rouge regime, untrained "medics" injected toxic and poisonous substances called "ach tunsiy," or rabbit's secretions, into the sick, thus causing their death. See N. Haini, *Haing Ngor: A Cambodian Odyssey*,

New York: Macmillan, 1986; and *The Tenderloin Times*, September 2, 1991.

61. Frankenberg notes that Western biomedicine is overly-focused on "lifedeath," that part of life in which death is not yet consciousness, if not denied; see note 48, p. 18.

62. J. Marcucci, Sharing the pain: Critical values and behaviors in Khmer culture. In *Cambodian Culture Since 1975: Homeland and Exile*, (edited by M. Ebihara, C. A. Mortland, and J. Ledgerwood), Ithaca: Cornell University Press, 1994, pp. 138–39.

63. A. Giddens, *Modernity and Self-Identity*, Stanford: Stanford University Press, 1991, p. 244.

64. See note 61.

65. J. Ledgerwood, Portrait of a conflict: Exploring changing Khmer American social and political relations, *J. Refugee Stud.*, 3 (1990): 135.

66. Personal communication.

67. In Cambodia, shamans (*kru Khmer*), both female and male, heal the sick by prescribing herbs and setting bones, but their primary work is in divining the cause of a person's illness and mediating with spirits to hell illnesses and remove misfortune. See note 40. In refugee communities, the *kru Khmer* continues to do a flourishing trade attending to the sick who are also seeking Western drug therapy.

68. Many consider Western medicine too "hot" for Khmers, and should be taken only in small doses; see note 35, p. 436. See also J. D. Kinzie, The establishment of outpatient mental health services for Southeast Asian refugees. In *Refugee Mental Health in Resettlement Countries*, (edited by C. L. Williams and J. Westermeyer), Washington, D.C.: Hemisphere Publishing Corporation, pp. 217–31, 1986. Self-regulation of health is common in the peasant society many refugees came from. In Cambodia, women deal with everyday health and birth-related issues as part of their domestic repertoire.

69. Muecke, p. 437.

70. Ibid., p. 435.

71. Ibid.

72. See, for example, *Boston Globe*, June 8, 1986. In fact, the notion of Khmers being a "passive," "less aggressive" people (their recent violent history not withstanding) than other Asians derives in part from writings that attribute their "less disciplined" culture to Theravada Buddhism, the main religion of Khmers. See R. G. Rumbaut and I. Kenji, *The Adaptation of Southeast Asian Refugee Youth*, Washington, D.C.: Department of Health and Human Services, Family Support Administration, and Office of Refugee Resettlement, pp. 75–77, 1988.

73. Ibid., p. 436.

74. L. French, Amputees on the Thai-Cambodian border: The political economy of injury and compassion. In *The Body as Existential Ground: Studies in Culture, Self, and Experience*, (edited by T. J. Csordas), Cambridge, U.K.: Cambridge University Press (forthcoming).

75. Becker, p. 21–22.

76. See note 60.

77. T. Parsons, Illness and the role of the physician: A sociological perspective. In *Mass Psychogenic Illness: A Social Psychological Analysis*, (edited by M. Colligan, J. Pennebaker, and L. Murphy), Hillsdale, N.J.: Lawrence Erlbaum Associates, pp. 21–31, 1985.

78. J. Desbarats, Cambodian and Laotian refugees: An underclass. Presented at the *Population Association of America Annual Meeting*, San Francisco, April 4, 1986.

79. Mentioned in a report on the clinic in *The New York Times*, 28 June 1992, p. A10.

80. See E. Martin, *The Woman in the Body*, Boston: Beacon Press, 1989, for a critique of obstetrics as a medical control over women's bodies, and the birthing process, so that the doctor, not the

mother, "produces" the baby.

81. Social workers complain about the increasing number of Khmer girls becoming pregnant and dropping out of school. Workers in the *Women, Infant and Child* (WIC) program also note the increasing number of pregnant Khmer teenagers among their clients.

82. A. Ong, Refugee love and Khmer families: The cultural work of citizenship in California. Presented at the *Am. Anthrop. Assn. Meetings*, November 1993.

83. Older peasant Khmer women believe that the number of children they have is predestined, as a reward or punishment for their past lives. A woman becomes pregnant after dreaming about a man who presents her with a gift, signifying the sex of the children. The bodies of partners having sexual intercourse must be "cool" or in balance to facilitate conception. See J. C. Kulig, Conception and birth control use: Cambodian refugee women's beliefs and practices, *J. Commun. Hlth. Nurs.*, 5 (1988): 235. Though these ideas indicate a moral or religious system of self- regulation, they radically differ from the medical model being taught in the hospitals.

84. In the late 1970s and early 1980s, refugees from Southeast Asia were supported by the federal government for the first two years. Thereafter, their support was transferred to social welfare programs that are funded by a combination of federal and state resources, the amount varying by the state. Many people argue that Southeast Asian refugees have migrated from state to state in pursuit of getting better welfare aid packages. Informants maintain that movements into California, where the benefits are among the highest in the country, were mainly prompted by family reunification, the large Southeast Asian communities, the weather, and the social and political climate.

Gina Masequesmay

---

6   Everyday Identity Work at an Asian
     Pacific AIDS Organization

Introduction

In the words of sociologist W. I. Thomas, "What is perceived as real becomes real in its consequences." A power dimension, however, must be added to this statement for fuller understanding of how some human groups are better equipped to realize their ideas and impose their sense of world order on others with less power to negotiate. This paper incorporates a critical approach[1] to the study of race construction and/or reification. I apply Michael Burawoy's proposed "extended case method"[2] to my ethnographic data in order to explore the link between everyday "identity work"[3] at an Asian Pacific AIDS organization and the larger racialized and gendered political economy. Thus, this paper addresses a critical concern of reifying race in racial politics as well as in studies of race and racism, or race relations. For such purpose, the concept of "racial formation"[4] as proposed by Michael Omi and Howard Winant is most helpful in framing this issue. Using data[5] from my participation- observation, I explore how everyday "identity work" at an Asian Pacific AIDS organization can reify race. This concept of racial "identity work" draws a parallel between works of social scientists[6] and social service providers in reifying and/or deconstructing "race." Thus, I would also argue that the attempt to separate academic work of "constructing" race from the political sphere is ideological. "Identity work" whether by academics or social service providers consists of racial projects that, for the most part, reinforce the racial (as well as gender, class, and sexuality) order in which we all partake.

In what is now the United States, a racialization project[7] resulted from the differentiation Christian European colonists made as they encountered the non-European stocks of heathens. Different racial categories for social groups emerged and later modified as these non-European "Others" competed or posed threats to the material and symbolic resources that "American" settlers had entitled as their destiny in this westward expansion to civilize the wild frontier. The notion of a "white race" emerged along with creations of nonwhite races as opposites.[8] This necessary distinction between whites and nonwhites became more sophisticated as it transformed into a system of hierarchical distinction that is based on a combination of phenotypic features, particularly skin color, and, in more subtlety, class and gender/sexual positionings (Takaki 1979; Almaguer 1994). This system that apparently uses physical criteria to socially define and allocate people to different positions in society came to be known as racism (van den Berghe 1978). This historical process from a notion of differences to a system that continues to make differences is an example of how a practical as well as ideologically-based distinction that was perceived by people in power could be realized into a continuous system of processes of not only making distinctions but also ensuring differences. These processes are what Omi and Winant (1994) would refer to as "racial projects."

In academia, this process of issuing differences disguised itself as studies on race relations. According to Prager (1982) in "American Racial Ideology as Collective Representation," the original racist framework of presupposing differences between groups and homogeneity within groups remains unquestioned while more sophisticated explanations are given to reify the project of racialization. What is seen here is not just the manifestation of racism in the social science but how racism is also constituted in the production of knowledge. For scholars interested in race and ethnic relations, the question of the role of the researcher in reifying race and ethnicity often incapacitates them from such works and derails researchers from the more significant focus—the processes of racism. In other words, one must not forget that race reification is the result of responding to a larger system of "racism." "Race" must be seen in the context of processes that facilitate its construction and of actors who are conscious or not conscious of its political consequences.

As indicated before, the result in academic pursuit of "scientific knowledge" on race relations is a fetishizing of racial differences. Of course, there are few examples of exceptional works that try to move beyond the original autonomous race paradigm and suggest an interlocking systems of oppression, exploitation, and domination based on gender, class, sexuality, etc., not just race (Collins 1990; Lather 1991). For the most part, works on racial relations reify race by imposing the researcher's definition of race or emphasizing the subject's understanding of race after the researcher has problematized race to the researched. Although the methods proposed are different, what is in common in both traditions is exploring the effects of racism. Put it another way, their focuses are on race rather than racism. Consequently, both traditions are engaged in racial projects.

Until the researcher consciously admits to be engaging in a racial project, the political consequences of such work of theorizing are glossed over and overshadowed by the celebration of contributing to the scientific enterprise of producing truths. Both micro and macro traditions often neglect the political nature of their research and in effect reify race by producing works that would generate more works to arrive at the best definition/understanding of race. Both traditions often compete to present a "truer truth," as the macro would critique the micro on relativism and the micro would critique the macro on abstracting reality. In sum, by engaging in a contest to find truths and to argue for the best tools to be used, both macro and micro traditions overlook their roles in the hegemonic process that depoliticizes scientific inquiries on race as political, racial projects. This oversight, in effect, reifies race rather than giving insights into the analytically distinct macro and micro processes of racism.

Method

Given this concern about the reification of race, a critical ethnography that requires a power-reflexive approach on the very issue of constructing race can shed insights into the micro-processes of race construction in the context of a larger racialized social structure by not just lay people but also social scientists, the legitimate agent of knowledge production. This essay examines the social construction of race by staff and volunteers of an Asian Pacific AIDS organization and includes a discussion of how my presence and self-consciousness as a researcher and volunteer effect my findings and analysis.

This analysis is one level removed from the original research of describing the data and summarizing findings of possible or deemed significant theoretical insights. I consider this a second-level analysis in that a power dimension is added to the original data analysis. Thus, I will examine the power relationship between myself—the researcher—and the research subjects that effects the recording of certain information as data. This power-reflexive approach requires that background information about the researcher and not just about the researched be discussed in the data analysis. First, though, I shall give some background about the Asian Pacific AIDS organization.

APAIT: History, Organization, People

The Racial Funding Politics of Social Services

In my first visit to the Asian Pacific AIDS Intervention Team (APAIT),[9] I asked the staff how was it that they came together to have this "API (Asian and Pacific Islander)[10] program." One of the staff responded that "white people in power could not understand us otherwise." He motioned with his hands as if trying to grasp something amorphous above us and continued, "This is the only way they know how to see us." Underlying this statement of annoyance in regard to white ignorance is a critical acknowledgment of the need for APAIT staff to work within the confines imposed by "white people in power" in order to deliver AIDS services to the "underserved API population."

APAIT's Volunteer Training and Orientation Manual, dated October 29, 1994, contains an article by Deborah A. Lee and Kevin Fong that originally appeared in the

SIECUS Report in February/March 1990 and recounted how mainstream American society reacted to the issue of AIDS and people of API heritage (Lee and Fong 1990). In one of the first public AIDS conferences, held in 1983 in San Francisco at the University of California Medical Center, an epidemiologist stated that Asians were believed to be immune to the deadly virus. At the time, there were no reported cases of AIDS among either Asian (or Italian) men, and the medical community was hopeful that studying this group would reveal important clues about the mysterious disease. Perhaps fueled by myths, stereotypes, and misinformation about Asian male immunity and clean lifestyles (free of drug and alcohol abuse), there was a substantial increase in personal ads between 1982 and 1984 soliciting Asian men for relationships; Asian men may have also endangered themselves because of the popular opinion that they were immune to AIDS.

Three weeks after the AIDS conference in San Francisco, the first case of AIDS in an Asian person was diagnosed in California. From 1983 to 1987, statistics were kept only for white, blacks, Hispanics, and "Others" (lumping together Asian and Pacific Islanders, Native Americans, etc.). No national record of Asian and Pacific Islander AIDS cases existed until 1988. The "Asian/Pacific Islander" category—as well as the separate category for Native Americans—came about because of nationwide advocacy efforts by many different groups. Lee and Fong's article further provided statistics[11] of the increasing rate of AIDS in the API population. Statistics were possible because data available when the API population became a separate category from the "Others" category. As one speaker at the Los Angeles County Women and HIV Conference puts it, to be identified as a "target population" means receiving direct funding allocation from the government.

APAIT is an API-staffed organization that was funded in 1991 to specifically provide AIDS intervention and prevention services to the "API community." Since that time, it has gone through tremendous expansion (thanks to statistics to prove needs) from a strictly volunteer-run program in a gay API organization to a primarily government-funded organization. Coming out of the gay API movement,[12] APAIT originally served only the API gay community. However, activists began to realize that "the problem was larger than any could imagine. They needed to educate the Asian community at large because no one was doing it. None of the mainstream agencies were bringing resources to the Asian community because the number was so low. And, the number was so low because people were not getting tested. It was a Catch-22."[13]

There was also a concern that the "Western models" of AIDS education, support, and outreach were "culturally inappropriate" and therefore ineffective for prevention and intervention work in the API community. Consequently, APAIT became the pioneering agency to meet the needs of the API community. Because it is the first API AIDS agency of its kind and because there were no "culturally sensitive" models available, the staff have had to learn through trial and error what will work for their clients and develop "culturally sensitive programs." As staff members Nathan and George see it: "It's better to do something, even if you make a mistake, than nothing at all because there is nothing out there now." Thus, the work that the staff plan out is based on their best calculation (their knowledge about the target population) and will be evaluated and modified after implementation. In this process of trial and error and the sharing of information and experiences by staff, the work for specific outreach activity is modified and standardized. As a result, the staff become "experts" in their pioneering work because it does not rely on mainstream models.

Setting themselves in opposition to "Western models" that are "culturally insensitive," APAIT members in effect reinforce the boundary between themselves and the ignorant or insensitive "white people in power." Yet, within the API group, the motto of "cultural sensitivity" helps delineate the different ethnic, gender, and sexually-oriented groups. Hence, new programs are being created to provide particular needs for particular groups. These programs, however, are not born out of thin air. They are the result of staff recognition of needs within a particular community and staff advocacy for a specified program to meet those needs. A process of grant-writing to justify funding begins, and a new program is born when funding institutions approve the grant. During the time in which I visited, APAIT was very successful in implementing new programs to serve a "larger arena" of APIs.

Organizational Growth and a Need to Stabilize

In light of staff diversity and continuous growth in programs, APAIT staff admitted being "overwhelmed" and "confused" about the "overall process" of the "hectic" environment. Probably because of APAIT's origin in opposition to "white" responses, APAIT staff find themselves constantly in a "reactive" or "crisis" mode. They only have enough time to respond to practical issues as they arise and do not have the luxury of planning far ahead. Because of the rapid change within the organization, efforts have been undertaken to make it "more established." Based on evaluation by staff and clients of "what works and what doesn't," the staff began a process of standardizing APAIT's program activities. Also, "mid-level" positions were created to better coordinate programs. This attempt to stabilize the "chaos" is an organizational necessity. However, I will show later that a fixation on normalizing can impede the progressive objectives of its radical members. As a practical organizational concern, the "grounding" effort in the midst of chaotic possibilities entrenches the staff to define and therefore limit what should be considered "API AIDS work." In addition, the bureaucratization of APAIT changes the organization structurally, from a "family atmosphere" of peer support to a "more impersonal" bureaucratic organizational pyramid.

The People Involved with APAIT

All APAIT staff are of API descent and are college educated. The majority (at least 80 percent) of staff are in their mid-twenties to early-thirties. For volunteers, the age range is wider, from high-school age to forty-something. The racial composition is also not strictly API. Two members are Caucasian while the rest are of API descent. In both groups of staff and volunteers, the majority of the people are gay men. There are fewer women than men, and their sexual orientations range from lesbian to bisexual to straight. All the people I met and talked to have a vested interest in the "empowerment of the API community." They became involved with APAIT through friends who are staff or volunteers with APAIT.

I became involved with APAIT out of academic and personal interest and entrée convenience. I was taking an ethnography class and needed a site for my fieldwork. Given my intellectual interest in identity issues because of my Vietnamese ethnicity, past involvement with the API social service community, and curiosity about my possible lesbian inclination, APAIT was a promising site for my exploration of sexual, ethnic, and racial identities.

Politically, I was hoping to contribute something to the API social service community. Because of my past network in the API social service community, I was able to ask a former coworker (who was then director of APAIT's counseling unit) if I could research his organization. After many exchanges with him and the main director, I was granted permission to do participation-observation at APAIT in the hope that I could lend an "outsider's perspective" to the organization that was "growing too fast" for its members. The documentation of the staff and organizational changes sounded beneficial to the overwhelmed members.[14]

Although never articulated explicitly, another reason for granting me entrée was that I seemed to be on APAIT's side by showing my interest in working to "empower the Asian American community." In many conversations with members, I exhibited knowledge and understanding of the problems API social service providers face, which along with my API status facilitated my connection to the staff.

Based on my past work experience, I was aware of a perception in the social service community about academic researchers going into the community to "suck out information" and never giving back anything. In general, researchers are perceived as aloof and part of the elite who are indifferent to the struggle of disenfranchised communities. They are the evaluators sent by the government to enforce administrative guidelines that are irrelevant to the work of "front-line staff." Thus, I was very conscious of how that perception might hinder me from establishing trust with the staff. My apprehension that the staff would be suspicious of my role was confirmed in my first visit.

> Ron . . . joked about me being a spy from the government. . . . I told Ron that I would die before becoming a spy, or be a pawn for the government. . . . Someone half seriously and half jokingly asked if I wanted to check up on them to see if they were doing their jobs.[15]

My irregular visits, due to a tight school schedule, also did not help to assure the staff of my reliability and therefore my trustworthiness. I found myself continuously trying to establish and reestablish connection with the staff. Consequently, I became very sensitive to the issue of "connecting" or "establishing commonalities" in social interactions among staff and volunteers. This special attention to the process of connecting became one of my ethnographic focuses, even though suspicion faded once I became more integrated into APAIT as a volunteer. In retrospect, my profile fit well into the general profile of staff and volunteers.

The Significance of API Identity Work

"Identity work" refers to the attempt to connect with people by evoking certain categorical identities such as race, ethnicity, gender, and sexual orientation. As indicated earlier, in my efforts to connect and establish rapport with APAIT members, I noticed a common pattern of everyday interaction between people. In an effort to communicate and establish rapport, people try to discover shared commonalities to further their understanding of each other. By knowing that they share similar experiences, they infer that they might share similar views of such experiences and therefore some aspects of life, thus creating a bond. When people evoke similarities of race, ethnicity, or sexual orientation, the bond is not based on a particular shared incident but rather on a host of assumed events that they might have shared. Such assumptions are commonplace in the United States because its history has been and continues to be organized around race, ethnicity, class, and sexuality. For example, bonding by race is more discursive and at the same time more deeply rooted than bonding because of a particular experience. Even when people do not share all the experiences that are indirectly evoked, an imaginary community is nevertheless conjured and the actors become bounded in this process called "identity work."

In educating about AIDS, the staff and volunteers use this method (connecting based on race, ethnicity, gender, sexuality) to evoke a common community for themselves and the audience. This connection with the audience smoothly lays in the message that AIDS does affect their shared "community."

Because AIDS is still a relatively new issue for many Asian ethnic groups, the Asian connection is the first practical step before addressing all the different ethnic groups. As illustrated in a meeting among AIDS service providers, a Vietnamese AIDS educator commented that

> because the people don't see [AIDS in their community] they don't think it affects them. What [he] would like to see happening is a panel of API with HIV broadcast by the ethnic media so that the people [can identify with Asian faces and therefore] can see AIDS does affect their community.

Here, the speaker did not focus on a specific ethnic panel but an API panel. His assumption was that people of API descent will make connection with other Asian-looking people. Racial connection will suffice and ethnic connection may help but is not necessary. In the case of targeting the API community, having a specific ethnic panel would alienate some audience members who were not of that ethnicity.

Establishing Racial Commonality in Delivering API AIDS Services

According to *The American Heritage Dictionary of the English Language* (1981), "to identify" is to associate or affiliate oneself closely with a person or group; to ascertain the origin, nature, or definitive characteristics of someone or something; or to equate and determine as identical. The signaling of a common categorical identity (racial, gay, ethnic, etc.) evokes the involved actors to identify with one another. The signaling is a step to connect to strangers and to develop further rapport. When the connection is based on race, this process of connecting is what I refer to as "API identity work."

At a planning meeting for an HIV/AIDS education outreach program to decide whether to have an HIV+ API speaker in the presentation, the staff agreed the speaker would "leave a chilling effect" on the audience. In disagreement was whether the "HIV+ speaker" needed to be straight. The intended speaker was gay, and some staff thought it would be better to find a straight HIV+ person for the presumably straight sorority and fraternity members in the audience. Others insisted that an API guest speaker with the "API visual cue" would be "enough" for the "Asian" audience to link and identify with. The speaker's status as gay need not be identified for the audience to connect and, in fact, such identification as gay may cause disconnection. Thus, the API identification with the audience was appropriate and sufficient to connect to every audience member. The majority are straight, and the gay issue is rendered unimportant. This issue of competing identity works will be elaborated more later.

Defining "API Problems" and Reinforcing Stereotypes in Doing AIDS Work

In an organization where the majority of the people are Japanese American and Pilipino American gay men (despite the growing ethnic and sexual diversity), how do people who do not share these dominant characteristics connect? "Doing API identity" is *practical* in the concerted effort to fight AIDS. The imposed "API" category that brings together a diverse group of people is, in this "expanding" and "confused" environment, the only commonality among people of different political and cultural persuasions.

In rejecting "Western models" that are not culturally relevant, the staff reassert certain stereotypes about people of Asian descent. For example, sand-therapy is a model one APAIT staff member preferred over the formal group therapy because

> it was an effective way for Asians to express themselves nonverbally since Asians "don't want to talk. It's very hard because we don't want to deal with our feelings so a formal support group may not be what they want." Thus, she believed sand playing may be a better forum for self-expression.

Other assertions I witnessed were that "Asians usually don't talk about drugs or sex"; Asians are "polite on the outside because it is a typical Asian thing to do"[16]; sex-taboos are a common value among Asian communities[17]; Asians care about stigma and saving face[18]; and HIV+ Asians fear shaming the family and do not come out as being HIV+ or being gay.[19] These assertions distinguish the problems that APIs face from problems of other racial groups, help to resignify the common experiences of APIs, and reinforce the understanding of for why there is a need for a special program specifically for APIs.

In other instances, assertions such as "Asians like to gather over a meal"[20] or "Asians are into group [kinds of] things"[21] are pass-on "knowledge and experience" to help staff plan activities that would be appropriate and effective to their population clientele.

Similar to defining problems within the "API" community, staff also point to problems outside the community. Receiving little funding to serve the diverse API community is the result of a racist government and a culturally insensitive funding bureaucracy. One problem that the staff highlight is the "racist assumption" that "Asians are not affected by [AIDS]."[22] This common assumption is reinforced by Asian invisibility in mainstream AIDS talk and the low number from the epidemiology data. Staff as well as some experienced volunteers explain that the low numbers are because people do not know about available HIV-test sites and the importance of getting tested. The low statistics on APIs unfortunately result in little or no funding for APAIT. This, in turn, hinders the necessary outreach to advocate HIV-testing for people who are involved in "risky behavior."

Adding up these challenges from within and outside the API community, the staff have a catch-22 dilemma to explain their limited situation: Asians have this "defensive thinking that it's people over there"[23] and until they see Asian faces in AIDS/HIV discussions, "they don't think it affects them"[24] and would not take precautions such as safer-sex practices and HIV testing. Even with the increasing number of HIV+ API clients who have been tested, APAIT staff still have to struggle to get new faces "out there" for county public hearings and local, state, and national conferences. Cultural barriers limit their ability to have HIV+ API speakers.

The fear of being alienated by one's family and community is illustrated by a Thai woman who would only speak at conferences not in the Thai community. "Clients don't want to go into an API setting because they don't want to increase their chances of meeting someone they know." Hence, "cultural issues" hinder them from freely adopting "Western models" or playing the rules of statistics advocacy.[25] An activist since day one of the API AIDS movement explains at an AIDS conference workshop on API and AIDS that

> in order to talk about services, we need to talk about politics, and before we can talk about politics, we need to talk about cultural values. If we in the API community cannot admit the existence of GLB [gays, lesbians, bisexuals], drug users, etcetera, we cannot deal with the issues of AIDS. Many APIs are reluctant to seek services because they perceive the mainstream agencies won't understand and the API agency will judge them. . . . Asians are into group things and care about stigma and saving-face.

The problem with HIV is that people have this defensive thinking that "it's people over there." So, as this activist saw it, one preventive approach is to have someone whom the community respects talk about AIDS and education the community in an effort to foster a change of thinking.

The examples above show the political implication of staff's generalizations and explanations of the challenges in the API community. In talking with other APIs, they inevitably engage in API identity work to make connection. This work creates and evokes a common experience that inadvertently define "API problems." In other words, identity work stressing commonalities would unite people with common obstacles to advance their common interests. By confirming their values and beliefs, their understanding of their circumstances, and the challenges they must face together, the diverse staff and volunteers could join hands under the "API banner" to provide API AIDS services. As Yen Le Espiritu (1992) argued in *Asian American Panethnicity*, AIDS caregivers have united to construct and reinforce this Asian and Pacific Islander identity because it is politically and, consequently, economically advantageous to do so.

Recognizing the Importance of API Identity Work

How APAIT organizes itself is based on the politics involved in funding minority groups. Because of the small number of reported AIDS cases for Asian ethnic groups, Asian minority groups banded together for political visibility, voice, and representation.

People involved with APAIT are very much aware of the issue of representation. To have outsiders (non-Asians) see an Asian face is important in the AIDS circle because APIs are usually underrepresented or invisible. To have an Asian workshop or a representative in mainstream organizations and meetings is crucial given the history of marginalization. It is usually understood by outsiders that this Asian-looking person will represent the interests of APIs. On the other hand, among insiders (Asians) the issue of representation focuses more on the specific ethnic groups. The dominance of certain Asian ethnic group undermines the idea of a full spectrum of Asian ethnics. For example, one member described an API workshop at a Washington, D.C., conference as "being too Japanese" as opposed to being "API."

APAIT, as an HIV/AIDS organization that specifically serves the Asian and Pacific Islander population, inherits the problems of diversity within the API community. As an organization that has taken on the task of doing HIV/AIDS services to the API diverse population, APAIT has assumed the role of bridging the gap between the API community and the larger society, positioning itself as the API representative. "To be out there" is important in terms of educating the larger society (especially with regard to funding services) about the similar cultural challenges of people of Asian and Pacific Islander descent. APAIT staff have also stressed differences in an attempt to obtain funding for different API groups. The expanding programs, such as the new "South Asian" program, reflect this move to include more API groups.

Language barrier is another reason and justification for more funding in order to hire staff who can serve as interpreters to the monolingual APIs. The staff for these new positions need to be culturally sensitive as well as linguistically proficient.

APAIT also acts as a bridge between the diverse ethnic communities by drawing out similarities to connect and coalesce. Differences are recognized and acknowledged, but only to validate each other's uniqueness. Diversity is usually not the focus in coalition building. It is only used as an argument for more funding to serve the linguistically and culturally different API communities. Given APAIT's role, the arrangement of APAIT makes establishing similarities and recognizing differences on racial terms a conscious action of staff in their everyday work.

Besides the organizational benefit to stress the uniqueness of being API, performing API identity work is a matter of everyday practicality. Among the players, the API identity is the only common denominator for connection in interaction. It is also an identity that evokes a racial structure by reinforcing certain stereotypes.

The creation and maintenance of the uniqueness of being API and the hypotheses of the "API problems" are negotiated and reaffirmed every day in interactions between actors. In speaking with one of the staff, I realized that as another API person, I was expected to affirm what was said about APIs and that not doing so would be a breach of our API connection:

> David began to explain that Asians with HIV or AIDS would rather go to the mainstream organization because they are afraid they may run the risk of running into someone they know in the Asian community. It's this whole notion of saving face, he said. [I wanted to make sure I knew what he meant by "saving face" but I] felt that [the explanation should be self-evident and should not require] me to ask David to spell it out for me. . . . [I realized later that what made me hesitant to ask was] this assumed bond and expected knowledge background that [David and I] had created at the beginning based on our common past— we were employed under the same agency although in very different lines of work.

Our "same agency" was an Asian Pacific drug prevention and intervention organization where both David and I were exposed to "the cultural barriers" for APIs. The issue of saving face is not new to us, and for me to ask David what he meant by "saving face" would have been a breach to our bond and connection as APIs.

The practical everyday work of connecting by race can be extended beyond analysis of the immediate situation. The larger racial funding system is behind the importance of doing API identity work, and the actors are politically conscious of their roles in reifying race and empowering the API community.

Negotiating "Relevant" Issues and Forging a Common Agenda

Occasionally, politically conscious actors challenge the popular meanings of "Asian" by raising issues of differences, but in doing so they do not intend to undermine the agenda of coalition building that takes precedence over issues of differences.

Challenging Sameness of APIs

In AIDS work, the lumping together of people with diverse cultures and languages has created programs and organizations like APAIT that subsist on such diversity and constructed "sameness." Beyond the API labeling, most people identify themselves more specifically in terms of ethnicity and/or cultural upbringing. Yet the label has served as a point of rally and mobilization to demand representation and "API visibility" in the mainstream discourse. The following is an example of how the notion of sameness of APIs is challenged.

In an exercise to sensitize social service providers to the issues of API lesbian/gay/bisexual youth, a participant was asked to arrange people in a line from "Least Asian" to "Most Asian." The person having to do the lineup became apologetic in the process. He explained that he arranged people based on his stereotypes of the "typical Asian." When the facilitator asked how the other participants felt being where they were in the line, they said that they "did not mind" too much the position they were placed in because "we're all the same." Moreover, the person who arranged the lineup said:

> If it were up to him, he would arrange us in a circle because we are all the same. I wanted to play devil's advocate and asked him what he meant by the same. As soon as I asked, I realized I was disrupting the cohesive bond of the group. He told me that he didn't think we were all the same but that, "you know, we are all API." I shook my head to indicate I did not understand what he meant. He told me that he did not know how to explain this and say it but that we are all Asian and therefore are similar. [It seems that the rubric "Asian" is what we orient our thoughts and actions to when we think of ourselves in the U.S. racial dimension.] I thought I saw others nodding their heads as he turned to them to reconfirm this sameness that we supposedly share and understand. I felt I was becoming a troublemaker and decided to drop it by saying okay. He again apologized to people for having placed them as he did. A different man came and shook his hand to say it's okay.

The illustration here demonstrates the idea of the power of language to bond people. Just by evoking the word "Asian," the participants perceived "sameness" among a culturally diverse group of individuals. My challenge to the notion of being the "same" temporarily disrupted the group's assumed cohesiveness. In building a movement or in raising consciousness, evoking a group identity is a crucial step in rallying people to action. We focus on our similar experiences of being oppressed so that we can unite and fight against the powers that be. Thus, my questioning of our sameness undermines this effort of coalition building.

For purposes of coalition building, we stress the similar fate of being categorized together. We seek cultural similarities. Eating rice, having taboos about sex, and not being comfortable with self-expressions are examples of how the staff established a link between different groups. Fundamental to this work is that we begin to identify ourselves as "Asian," "API," or "Asian American." In this process, we position ourselves and bond with each other around these related labels. Those who challenge this notion of sameness are seen as making trouble and disrupting the cohesiveness of the group.

More Than "A Clash of Styles": Constructive vs. Deconstructive Politics

Deconstructive politics[26] stresses differences, which are seen as inherent in group politics. To empower the marginalized, disenfranchised, and stigmatized, differences in opinions and experiences must be heard. In this sense, deconstructive politics unites people based on differences rather than on commonalities. It challenges the common method of forging a consensus through seeking commonalities. According to Ron, it takes things apart before putting them together. It assumes the traditional ways of doing things as inherently biased towards reinforcing the dominant power structure and shutting down dissenting voices. Thus, deconstructive politics stresses differences as a way of challenging the status quo.

The following is an illustration of the different perspectives and styles (constructive vs. deconstructive) of the staff as played out at a volunteer training meeting:

> [We] started half an hour late and Miyeong did not want the volunteers to have to stay longer than what was scheduled. Nathan was not as time-oriented and was more concerned with the process—what the volunteers were getting out of this discussion and how they feel about the process. So, I saw Miyeong's and Nathan's styles clashed. Nathan was outspoken about what he saw and felt. Miyeong seemed not to want to display their contrasting views in front of the volunteers. . . . After the role-play, we went around the room to ask how people felt. Again, Miyeong and Nathan seemed to clash over how they wanted to facilitate the meeting. Nathan demonstrated that he felt he was being silenced by Miyeong. "I want to wrap this up so I can get in my [say]," Nathan said to Miyeong when he felt she was shutting him out of the conversation. . . . There was another finer point that I can't remember, but Miyeong thought it was going to go off on a tangent and tried to steer the discussion elsewhere by saying, "I thought we were going to wrap this up." Nathan responded that if this was going to be an evaluation and we were going to go in a circle to do this, we need to discuss things that arise and include everyone in the circle. Earlier, he also showed that he was upset at how Miyeong (and Trang) had wanted to move the agenda along and did not fully address his suggestion on the structure of the training. . . . When it was Nathan's turn, he expressed that he wanted more interaction and he thought the outline and note-taking that Miyeong was doing hindered the dynamic of the group. Everyone was looking at the notepad instead of each other. He wanted to do away with the note-taking. He suggested that the information on the different programs could be given out later on. He also thought that the information might be overwhelming for the volunteers. He wanted things to be informal, and he felt Miyeong's note-taking made the atmosphere too much like a classroom. Miyeong [simply] said that they were wasting precious time evaluating the structure and they needed to move along. Nathan demonstrated this malcontent by talking to George loudly about taking things apart to put them back together, and that was not done here. Miyeong did not allow the time for that but moved on with the discussion.

Nathan's style of taking things apart and putting them back together was not Miyeong's style. She, in fact, stated clearly that she had always done things the same way and that it had worked for her. For Nathan to suggest new ways was in a sense undermining Miyeong's newly established method. In an organization where things are changing rapidly, establishing, normalizing, and standardizing activities and methodologies are necessary and practical solutions. Deconstructive politics, however, is not about approaching the majority's consensus when it might mean negating dissenting voices. Its intent is processing through differences to arrive at a newfound identity and understanding (Elbaz 1992). Given the different strategies and the present situation at APAIT, the normative praxis of building commonality takes precedence over the more radical deconstructive practice of queer politics as well as "third world" politics.[27]

Thus, there are two different aspects into this phenomenon of identity work.[28] One aspect focuses on unity based on constructed common characteristics; the other follows the line of deconstructive politics that focuses on differences and challenges the normative praxis (Gamson 1991; Elbaz 1992). The above example shows how normative praxis can have political impact in dismissing dissenting voices. I observed the incident, at the start, as "a clash in styles." Upon reconsidering the politics of some of the queer API staff and volunteers, however, I realized that this "embarrassing" moment was a rare moment in which dissenting voices were heard. Unfortunately, it was dismissed in the larger effort to move along the agenda of "doing API AIDS work."

Undervisibility of Marginalized Issues in API AIDS Prevention Work

Given the funding structure that categorizes people into "high risk" groups, APAIT AIDS services is comprised of programs targeting specific groups such as women and "men who have sex with men." There is no overarching program to target all APIs, but rather a compilation of specified (ghettoized) programs that hopefully would cover as many APIs as possible. The responsibility of the coordinators for each program is to raise issues that represent their "target populations." The following examples demonstrate how such funding structure and other situational factors limit the ability of APAIT to fully address feminist, gay, and HIV/AIDS-related issues in its AIDS prevention work.

Women and AIDS

For a long time, the story of women living with HIV was untold. Concerns related to women are often overlooked by men, the dominant decision-makers of the majority of movements and organizations. Indeed, for some women, the saying is that "women don't get AIDS but they die from it" (The ACT UP/New York Women and AIDS Book Group 1990). In the beginning of the AIDS movement, research was done only on (white) gay and bisexual men. Little was discussed about symptoms occurring in women. This neglect in research on and the lack of education outreach to women made it difficult to for women to receive early intervention services. Many women died before they ever found out about the intervention measures (The ACT UP/New York Women and AIDS Book Group 1990). It was only through women advocacy groups that research has begun to address women's concerns.

Similarly, APAIT started out as a service to gay and bisexual men. It was only through the conscious efforts of a lesbian member to raise awareness of women's issues that funding was requested for a Women's Program. At that time, the larger society also began to acknowledge[29] the lack of services to women so that funding allocation for women became possible.

In the early years of the AIDS movement (late 1980s to mid-1990s), the composition of many AIDS service organizations had (white) men as paid employers and employees and women as nonpaid volunteers/helpers (Patton 1990; Morales and Bok 1992). A similar structure was seen at APAIT. The Women's Program was coordinated by a one-woman staff. Although she received help and support from other staff members, she was the only paid staff involved in this program. There was a women's committee to help her, but it was a volunteer group. Half of this group was comprised of APAIT women staff who were volunteering their time. On the other hand, the programs geared toward "men who have sex with men" have about four and a half full-time paid staff positions. Although this may be a result of the funding system, in some way it was also a reproduction of the larger patriarchal system. The members were not immune to sexism.[30] Given the sexist funding system and the underrepresentation of women at APAIT, efforts to include women's issues or to raise feminist concerns were activities of feminist members. These attempts, however, may be a challenge to the male-dominated, male-centered way of running APAIT. Feminist concerns interfered with the smooth operation of building consensus by challenging the dominant (male-oriented) way of doing things. At a planning meeting for a safer-sex social event, feminist issues were raised but were dropped due to practical considerations and the praxis of building consensus and not dissension.

> When we went over the HIV/AIDS IQ questions, Karla remarked that one question should be revised with the following changes: "HIV+ Mother" to "HIV+ woman" and maybe from "unborn child" to "fetus." The question should also be reworded so that the focus is on the 75 percent chance of not transmitting instead of the 25 percent chance of the HIV+ woman transmitting to the fetus. We then got into discussing the AZT mandatory test in New York and some other technical issues. When we got back to the revised question the "unborn/newborn child" was left unchanged. I made a remark to Karla that we haven't changed "unborn child," and she agreed with regret. It was either a mess to change the wording and to still cover the scope that the original question had or an indication that I did not care too deeply to raise the issue of "fetus" versus "unborn child," [because I dropped the issue. I felt like it could be a divisive issue since the pro-life and pro-choice movements have constructed the debate. Although both Karla and I decided not to raise the issue again,] . . . Karla's suggestion raised our consciousness or at least mine to think of how women are portrayed in the politics of AIDS.

In another planning meeting, a staff member raised the issue of date rape in our discussion on safer-sex negotiations. This issue was dropped in the end because of the limited amount of time that the staff had to deliver the message about AIDS and thus a discussion on date rape would be "beyond [their] scope" and "pass [their] abilities" to adequately deal with the issue. It was settled that if the topic was raised by the audience, the staff could refer them to other service agencies. Their job, though, was to deal with AIDS/HIV education and AIDS/HIV alone.

Thus far, the examples demonstrate the daily negotiations of different political agendas by politically conscious actors. The strategy of building consensus overrides other efforts (e.g., raising feminist issues) that challenge or question the unity and bond of the group as well as the practical limitation of the organization. At APAIT, it is the API identity that prevails. When acts that counter this normative commonality-building praxis occur, we witness something of a breach in the interaction. The everyday practices of connecting thus have political consequences and meaning.[31] Sometimes, the practice is a deliberate and conscious act to connect and evoke a social project to destigmatize and demarginalize oppressed groups. At other times, actors are not as aware of the political implications of their everyday praxis of building a consensus and end up reinforcing the normative identity structure. The evidence thus far supports Omi and Winant's (1994) concept of a "racial project" and highlight Espiritu's (1992) micro-level panethnicity processes. In an environment where there is this overarching theme to stabilize and build coalition amidst increasing diversity, the deconstructive style of identity work (focusing on differences) is a rare occasion. When explicitly employed, this style of politics is considered a problem to members of APAIT who are trying to build a coalition through sameness rather than differences.

Dissociating Gay Issues from AIDS

As an organization that tries to ground itself in doing API AIDS work, the connection with the API community is crucial. Given that the API community is either homophobic or reluctant to deal with the issue of homosexuality, APAIT staff tend to dissociate AIDS from homosexuality. This is not an easy task given the intertwining roads of the gay/lesbian movement and the AIDS movement (Elbaz 1992; Patton 1990).

It was the gay community that was hit hardest by AIDS. So, for any individual who considers himself gay, it is impossible not to have to deal with AIDS issues. Ron, who lost ten friends between 1993 and 1995 due to AIDS, terms it "the chronic grieving" of having to cross name after name out of one's phone book. Historically, it was the gay/lesbian/bisexual community who took on the issue of AIDS to empower themselves and demanded the government be more responsive to this epidemic (Elbaz 1992). So, AIDS issues are not limited to gay and bisexual men but also extend to lesbians and bisexual women who have gay and bisexual men as friends (The ACT UP/New York Women and AIDS Book Group 1990). Moreover, it was the rise of the queer movement that gave the AIDS movement its edge. The gay model of "coming out" was used to talk about the individual process of destigmatization by "coming out HIV+." The original movement was to empower individuals through education. As the AIDS issue became more incorporated into mainstream discourse, activities of educating and supporting HIV-affected and HIV-infected individuals became professionalized. The goals changed from self-empowerment to services as the AIDS industry emerged (Patton 1990). As the epidemic began to take its toll in the straight community, services and involvement were no longer only gay/lesbian/bisexual although they are still predominantly queer.

Despite APAIT's derivation in the queer API movement, the following examples show that API issues prevail over queer issues at APAIT. While API identity work is a bonding process, doing API queer identity work undermines the API unity created by evoking differences in sexual orientation among APIs. As an API organization, APAIT structure favors doing API identity work as a strategy of building commonality over doing queer identity work, which may raise divisive issues by focusing on differences of sexual orientations.

The bonding effect of doing API identity work is illustrated in the following exercise at an API GLB Youth sensitivity training workshop:

This time, Nick picked a woman to arrange us in a line from "most gay or lesbian" to "least gay/lesbian." There was almost a unanimous wail to this grueling exercise. . . . The woman arranged us. . . . The woman explained she did it according to her stereotypes that GLB people are more liberal so that she based it on looks and how we dressed. The woman on the straight end said that she didn't consider herself conservative but there she was at the conservative end. [She was wearing a business suit—skirt, blouse, blazer, and high heels—and make-up.] The next woman and I started focusing on the issue of being seen as conservative or liberal instead of being seen as straight. The people on the "most gay/lesbian" end said that it was okay with them (in terms of not being offended even though their placement was incorrect) [because] they knew who they were. . . . The people in the middle said that they felt more comfortable being in the middle because they are not at either extreme, [and because of their work as progressive social service providers and API advocates they] especially [did not want to be] perceived as conservative. [When another person did the lineup,] people said that it was fine for them to be seen as more gay/lesbian as long as they know who they are. . . . What was interesting about all of these comments was that no one said it was the same to be on either end of the spectrum or anywhere in between [as happened with the Asianness exercise]. There was no assumption of people with different sexual orientations having something in common. There was some implicit acknowledgment of differences. No one said that they would arrange us in a circle instead of a line because we are all sexual beings. . . . Statements such as "It's fine with me to be seen as gay/lesbian but I am not" underscore the assumption of the marked, categorical differences in sexual identity and expression. I thought this was an interesting contrast to the most/least Asian exercise where we agreed to be all the same.

Given the staff's conscious effort to develop a community to fight AIDS, they create or engage in activities and talks that would elicit common bonds between a group of culturally and linguistically diverse people. The API identity prevails over other identity issues such as gay/lesbian/bisexual (or gender) concerns because the latter evokes differences. Moreover, the idea of API was historically a social construction (imposed and reactive) to unite different groups to accomplish a goal. There is an implicit understanding of differences, but the focus is on unity and sameness. We are seen as the same (Oriental), and we face similar stigmas and discrimination.

In contrast, doing gay/lesbian/bisexual identity work would only unite people who identify themselves as such. API people would be divided into straight and queer. There would be no specific common goal or agenda besides, perhaps, in creating a society that would be more open to different sexual expressions and identities. Whereas *doing API identity work* unites groups of people who were similarly discriminated against, *doing API queer identity work* only unites APIs who see themselves as not straight. The larger straight API community within the API community does not experience sexual-orientation discrimination for being straight. Being straight is the norm. Doing API queer identity work would undermine that sense of commonness. Thus, in an API organization that is sensitive to issues of sexuality, whether sexual identity will come to the forefront is situational in that it depends on the participants' agenda. For staff, the goal at that moment might be to create unity or to expose different sexual orientations. If the audience is queer, then gay signaling would create bonds. If the audience is straight or mixed, however, gay signaling or hinting at queer sensitivity might or might not be necessary, depending on the actors' agenda. At times, it could be disadvantageous if the audience is homophobic.

In an organization that is predominantly queer (ten out of fifteen), one would think that the queer identity would be much more visible than in a "straight setting." However, this is not the case in staff representing the agency. At a volunteer orientation meeting, the staff asked the volunteers about their ethnicities and language abilities but did not ask about sexual orientation. It was important to know if the volunteers could speak different languages and whether they were culturally competent to deal with the specific ethnic groups. As important, I would think, would be to know how comfortable the volunteers were in regard to dealing with different sexual identified groups. The volunteers who were "gay-friendly" or "open-minded" would also be an asset to APAIT, especially since the dominant programs were to serve "men who have sex with men."[32] This "gay knowledge" or "gay friendliness" was, however, not asked about by the staff. Many of the volunteers who were gay did reveal their sexual orientation during lunch, a setting that was not part of APAIT's formal work environment. After lunch, there was a more playful atmosphere because of this bond of similarity and empathy. Yet, the staff deliberately did not ask about the sexual orientation of the volunteers out of respect for their privacy. The stigma within the API community about homosexuality made management difficult between normalizing nonstraight sexuality and at the same time respecting people's privacy. Besides sensitivity to the stigmatized label, most staff adhered to respecting individual's personal identification. Thus, the volunteers had to come out and connect with the staff. The staff would only go halfway in identifying themselves as gay or bisexual. They did not try to probe and label the volunteers because of the ubiquitous stigma on nonstraight behavior in the API community.

In short, a fostering of an "API community" evokes certain shared values. One such shared value happens to be a taboo on homosexuality. Thus, although all the staff and volunteers are "open" or "gay-friendly," there was still apprehension about evoking such issue in the API identity's framework. In other words, issues of stigmatization that threaten the API coalition are subsumed by the larger, practical agenda to coalesce.

HIV Infection and AIDS

Like gay identity, "HIV-infected" identity evokes stigmas and does not connect everyone, whereas "HIV-affected" would unite everyone working at APAIT. Hence, there is an undervisibility of HIV+ identity work. Maybe the talk on the disease and its effects is scarce because the activities I observed and participated in revolved around the issue of prevention. Had I studied the Client Services unit, I might have a different take on the morbid reality of AIDS.

This lack of talk on the morbid reality of AIDS reflects my focus on prevention issues. I have no understanding of what it must mean for staff and volunteers in Client Services to deal with issues of sickness and dying. I only had a glimpse of that reality when I interviewed Ron, who told me of "chronic grieving." This is the experience of many HIV-affected gay men who continuously have to cross friends' names out of their phone books. As this treatment advocate pointed out, though, the emphasis at APAIT is on staying healthy and "living long enough for the cure." This positive outlook orientation, however, has its disadvantage in that staff from the Education and Prevention unit have little exposure to sick and dying colleagues and clients and thus do not know how to handle such a "crisis." According to Ron, the staff needs bereavement training. Since some of the staff are HIV+, the time will come when all staff must confront on a "more personal" level (with coworkers rather than just clients) the issue of dying from AIDS. According to Karla, it was hard for everyone when one of the staff got sick. They have all been trained to deal with clients and to reinforce positive aspects of living with HIV, but they have yet to handle issue of a staff member's death. APAIT is a relatively new organization that emphasizes intervention and prevention, so it has not experienced the continuous tragic loss of lives that older organizations face or the deaths that AIDS hospices handle.

Structural constraints and everyday practicalities dictate that identity work focusing on commonalities must prevail over identity work that stresses or causes differences. For the survival of the organization, the API identity work is promoted over other identity issues that might threaten the cohesiveness of the group by evoking differences. Of the different types of identity works discussed, doing API identity work prevails at APAIT.

Conclusion

In my effort to establish rapport with APAIT staff, I began to notice a dominant pattern of interaction that involved finding commonalities and building consensus among staff, volunteers, and clients. When such identification is based on categorical identities (race, ethnicity, gender, sexual orientation), this form of interaction fits what I defined earlier as "identity work" because it reconstructs (usually reinforces) the meanings of the evoked identity or identities.

In an organization that originated out of queer API politics, these everyday identity works have political significance in redefining the meanings of those identities. Each identity work carries with it a "political" agenda. API identity work is parallel to Omi and Winant's (1994) "racial project" and is demonstrated in this paper as an everyday "panethnic" project. There are, as well, gay, ethnic, and gender projects that interplay with the project of pan-Asianism at APAIT every day.

Given the increasing diversity of staff and volunteers, there are constant nego- tiations of different political agendas or projects (ethnic, gay, feminist) in both the planning stage and the delivery of services. And, because the services are framed as AIDS services to the API community, the API political agenda comes to the forefront while queer and feminist issues are subsumed. In other words, the API identity work that stresses sameness prevails because the structure of the organization encourages it. Thus, besides the practical interactional strategy to connect that makes prevalent identity work stressing sameness, the funding system of APAIT reinforces API identity work. As APAIT expands in programs and staff, it needs to build a coalition to provide API AIDS services. For both interactional and structural reasons, API identity work prevails over other identity issues.

This prevalence of API identity work can be framed as examples of the micropro- cesses whereby "race" plays the "organizing principle" role of shaping daily interac- tions. These interactions, for the most part, reify "race." To focus on "race," however, is to miss the point that racism is the culprit behind these racialized interactions. Fortunately, for me, in doing ethnographic work, the field is open to more interactions than those that would fit perfectly within my hypothesized model of race reification. Identity work is not just an attempt to connect by building commonalities. There is another style of identity work that focuses on differences (deconstructive) rather than sameness.

Identity work that emphasizes differences is an interactive style of deconstructive politics. This style of identity work is rarer, however, because situational strategy to connect with others on commonalities is a practical everyday phenomenon, which most actors do not see as a normative act that reinforces the existing hegemonic order. In other words, the hegemonic racialization is constitutive of the "practical" everyday praxis of establishing commonalities. Conscious of this hegemonic effect, radical activists of APAIT focus on recognizing differences as a way of coalition building. To them, deconstructive politics is the way to challenge the normative practices that reproduce the existing social order.

The normative practice of establishing commonalities to connect with others at APAIT has political consequences in reifying the API identity. To challenge this im- posed identity requires the work of politically conscious actors to renegotiate its mean- ing in everyday identity work. By stressing differences rather than commonalities, these politically conscious actors deconstruct the normative praxis of establishing and assuming commonalities and bring to light the political consequences of such actions.

The political implication of this finding is that the radical intentions of the actors are constrained by government- regulated objectives so long as APAIT remains a government-defined service organization. Nonetheless, to see how work is negotiated each day by different actors with different identity projects is also to witness where issues can be raised and methods of doing API AIDS work can be renegotiated. Although room for change is limited, there is also conscious resistance every day.

As APAIT tries to stabilize itself, its open space for negotiating different political agendas is becoming narrow because the work is becoming more routinized and standardized.[33] By applying a common identity politics instead of deconstructive politics, APAIT becomes more and more of an organization of normalizing and bureaucratizing instead of a force that challenges the process of normalization, control, and domination.

As a field researcher, being a participant-observer allows me to see the parallel racialized structures that shape my academic work and APAIT members' AIDS work. Because of the racial funding politics, AIDS works at APAIT are racialized and everyday interpersonal interactions reinforce a common API culture. Likewise, because of the original race paradigm in studies of race relations (a racist project in that it imposed, assumed, and created racial differences), my attempt to understand group relations at APAIT becomes legitimized because I framed my concerns under the subject of race studies. Effectively, my findings further legitimize the importance of race studies by adding more insights to this topic.

Besides seeing the parallel works of scholars and social service providers, as a participant-observer I see the boundary between the academic world and the world of APAIT as blurrier than when I do pure observation. As a volunteer for APAIT, I, like other APAIT members, engage in API identity work that reifies race at that level of interaction at APAIT. As a researcher, I further reify race by recording my volunteerism into the academic world. In so doing, I add to the accumulation of knowledge about race and thus relegitimize the original racist project. Given the same effect of race reification, the two processes from the lay world and the academic world seem similar. When the distinction line between the two worlds is lifted, one can then see as ideological the constructed distinction between laypeople's racializing and social scientists' racializing. Participation-observation allows me to be an insider at and outsider of APAIT, but in the process of moving back and forth, I came to realize that there are not many differences between the two worlds. In fact, when this racialized process is contextualized in the larger historical process that Omi and Winant (1994) have termed "racial formation," it becomes clear that we all engage in large- and small-scale racial projects. In other words, in studying "race," the processes and methods we engage in to understand race must be examined in context of the larger system of racialization.

My ethnographic study of APAIT reveals the importance of employing a critical approach to studying race. The processes of racialization that make race real are the essential components in understanding both the subjective meanings of race for actors and objective results of reification or deconstruction of "race" in a racialized state.

Notes

1. I am loosely applying Stephen Pfohl's (1994) outline of a critical approach as consisting of situating the investigated phenomenon in a historical context of power relations. The researcher must also employ a power-reflexive methodology that links power to the production of knowledge. In this case, it is to question how my own work may reinforce the status quo.

2. According to Michael Burawoy in *Ethnography Unbound* (1991), the extended case examines how the microsocial situation is shaped by external forces. It attempts to elaborate the effects of the "macro" on the "micro" and requires that the researcher specify some particular feature of the social situation that requires explanation by reference to particular forces external to itself. The examination and linking of everyday interaction to the larger social structure allow the researcher to explore the different forms of resistance to systems of domination in a postindustrial, capitalist society.

3. I adopted this term from my advisor, Robert Emerson, to initially describe the interaction of establishing commonalities (based on race, gender, ethnicity, sexual orientation) and building consensus among APAIT staff and volunteers. This term took on more meaning as I continued the research. Identity work is not just signaling or establishing a categorical identity but involves negotiating on issues pertaining to the meaning of such identity/identities. There is also identity work that stresses differences rather than commonalities. I observed this from politically conscious actors who engage in deconstructive politics. This style of politics challenges actions that reproduce the normative order that activists claim is oppressive. For example, the model minority stereotype applied to APIs limits any discussion of needs and problems people within this category may face. Political activists are aware of the political consequences of such perception of a homogenous API group and thus make a conscious effort of stressing heterogeneity. Whether identity work stresses differences or similarities, the end result is politically significant. Hence, one may consider these types of identity works as "everyday identity politics."

4. Omi and Winant (1994) define "racial formation" as the sociohistorical process by which racial categories are created, inhabited, transformed, and destroyed.

5. For purpose of confidentiality, I have used pseudonyms in place of real names.

6. This conclusion is induced from my own experience in this fieldwork and deduced from the literature on critical, emancipatory works of feminists and scholars of color.

7. The term is as defined by Omi and Winant (1994) and summarized by Tomas Almaguer in *Racial Fault Lines*.

8. Besides larger institutions setting the agenda of racial categorization, David Roediger's (1991) *The Wages of Whiteness* shows how the European working class began to take advantage of this identity.

9. These are rough estimates because APAIT is continuously expanding, which results in changes in staff size and programs.

10. Throughout this paper I use the term "Asian Pacific" or "API" as interchangeable terms with "Asian American" because the actors also use them interchangeably. The new use of "Asian Pacific," or for short "API," instead of "Asian American" reflects a new thinking in the API social service community to expand their target population. For activists, it is a political tool in the racial politics of representation and a way to be more inclusive and sensitive to issues of historically underrepresented communities. Recently, these communities are the Pacific Islander communities. On the government bureaucracy side, it is convenient to throw

"Pacific Islanders" into the "Asian" category. Evidence of the imposed nature of this categorical identity is the term "Asian Pacific American" or "APA" that was also offered by activists but did not gain popular usage in the social service field.

When not quoting people, I use the term "API" to describe people who look Asian (based on popular understanding of Asiatic phenotypes) and events that are attended by Asian-looking people. Members of APAIT use "Asian" for short to mean "Asian American," a popular term that evolved out of the student movement during the late 1960s to "self-define" its community. The new term "API" or "Asian Pacific" as in the case of APAIT is a recent development and has been used to replace "Asian American" and "Asian" by people who are aware of the politics of representation.

11. There was a 77 percent jump in API AIDS cases between 1987 and 1988 according to the SIECUS Report. Another report that the volunteers received—"Asian and Pacific Islander AIDS Cases, Los Angeles County," with sources from the Epidemiology of AIDS in Asians and Pacific Islanders in Los Angeles, the Advanced HIV Disease Surveillance Summary, and the Los Angeles County Department of Health Services HIV Epidemiology Program—reported that during 1986–1987, the incidence of AIDS in APIs increased 63 percent while between during 1988–1989 the increase was 73 percent. As of June 30, 1994, 450 API AIDS cases were reported in Los Angeles County and 62 percent of the cases were Asian immigrants. Thirty-three of the cases were women. An average API AIDS rate from 1985 to 1993 was 40.9 percent. Among the API subgroups, the Thai population has the highest rate of 110.4 percent, followed by Samoans with 92.2 percent, Filipinos with 51.9 percent, Japanese with 40.6 percent, and Vietnamese with 35.1 percent. When I spoke with the staff, they did not seem to take the statistics as the only guide to their efforts. They often talked of underreported cases. The reasons given were that people are hiding due to the stigma and shame that the API community fosters. People were not getting tested because of ignorance and misinformation about HIV transmission.

12. A friend of the director and staff who died of AIDS "in silence" galvanized a circle of friends in an API queer organization to learn more about the issue and educate each others in the organization. They pinpointed cultural barriers as a key reason people in the API community are reluctant to talk about AIDS. They were also confronted by Eurocentric models of education and prevention that were "culturally inappropriate" for the API population.

13. Field note no. 1, interview with APAIT director.

14. In fact, I naively agreed to let the director, Dan, see my notes. He thought it might help to read over an outsider's perceptive of the organization that is in a state of flux. At the time, I thought it might be good to have Dan go over the notes in case I misinterpreted something. However, this became complicated as I found myself reassuring the staff that I would delete anything they do not want Dan to read. In addition, Dan also had asked me to not print out certain materials that are sensitive. I thus found myself in an awkward position many times trying to sort out my roles and purposes, which were not that clear to me as a novice ethnographer. Besides printing out and handing in censored notes to respect members' privacy, I excluded my preliminary assessment of my observation so that my interaction with the staff would not be affected too much by what I wrote. This effort to minimize my impact of my actions on the data was, however, a somewhat misdirected investment. My very presence as an "outsider" (not staff) created feelings of anxiety and self-consciousness for me, and there was also a sense of awkwardness—if not for staff then certainly for me. I will discuss later how that impacted my focus to build trust with the staff.

15. This and subsequent extracts are taken from my field notes.

16. Karla discussed her difficulty dealing with a Korean newspaper contact person to get APAIT ads in the Korean newspaper:

She would get verbal agreement from them but would not find any ads in the papers. . . . She speculated that it might be cultural reasons: "Maybe they think it doesn't affect Koreans. They're maybe homophobic or AIDS-phobic." . . . Karla said that Doug [a Korean APAIT staff member] was helping her "to understand why the Koreans were having such a hard time with this. Culturally, they just don't think AIDS has anything to do with them. And a lot of times they would just be polite on the outside because that's just the thing to do. But, if they don't agree with it, they would just do something differently. But to your face, they'd be polite to you. That seems to be a typical Asian thing to do anyway. . . . If they had a problem with it, I wish they could just tell me instead of letting me run around in circles thinking everything is fine, and then not getting anything done. So, it's difficult." (Field note no. 5)

17. I was talking to a new South Asian staff member and, since I had little knowledge of the South Asian culture, we were trying to define what were the commonalities among Asians. This was one of the commonalities he drew up for me. (Field note no. 13)

18. Field note nos. 3–6, 9, 10, 12–14.

19. Ibid.

20. Field notes nos. 3 and 14.

21. Field note no. 12, in an API workshop at the Fourth Annual Los Angeles Conference on Women and HIV.

22. Field note no. 4, interview with Karla and Pam on the challenges they face working on API AIDS issues.

23. Field note no. 12, comment from a panelist at the Women and HIV Conference's API workshop.

24. Field note no. 4.

25. The low rate of API AIDS cases and the difficulty of finding people to "come out" and do public testimony present challenges for APAIT staff to play politics of representation in the social services arena, where significant rates and new voices and faces matter in receiving funding or not.

26. The ideas presented here are from my interview with Ron, my observation of Nathan and Miyeong's clash in work styles, and my own readings on radical politics (queer, people of color, third world). Works by Elbaz (1992) and Gamson (1991) are two examples of the works I read.

27. According to Richard, a volunteer, third-world politics is another radical, liberation movement by nationalists to fight against capitalist colonialism.

28. Calhoun (1994) also discussed these two styles of identity politics in the new social movements.

29. Funding for women became available after much protest by women ACT UP members (and later men ACT UP members) as well as women in other AIDS organizations and movements.

30. At a planning meeting between staff and volunteers of the Women's Program and the program targeting "men who have sex with men," I witnessed how the female staff members dealt with a comment devaluing women's work that a male staff member made:

This is the first time they are planning a co-gender event. Hence, "Safer-Sex Social/Magnet Event," where the first is the women's version and the latter is the men's version. The staff apparently never talked in detail of their own events so that part of the beginning session was exchanging information of what the Women's Committee does in its Safer Sex Social and what the CHOWs [Community Health Outreach Workers, a program targeting men who have sex with men] do in their Magnet Event. There was a question to Nick on the differences between the Magnet Event and the Safer Sex Social. Nick said he was not sure of the difference between the two. Nick said that [the men's event] is "more ornate." Miyeong asked for him to explain what he meant by "ornate." [The men] usually have a dance, skits, and demos. Although the women did not have a dance, the women in the group articulated that it was not much different from the magnet. One of the men said that there was more planning that goes into the Magnet Event. The women protested to say that they also put a lot of planning into their events. In fact, they not only do skits and demos, but more. Unlike the Magnet Event where the primary event is the dance (to draw in crowds) and the education is a sub-event, the Safer Sex Social integrates education into the games. Trang said that the social is usually three hours long and the format that they have used works well, so she wanted to keep it for this two-hour, co-gender event. (Field note no. 1)

The above scenario not only illustrates how the women staff often have to bring attention to the sensitive issues of and about women, but also how Trang in the end asserted the effectiveness of the Women's Program and proposed that its format be used in the co-gender event.

31. The topic of "everyday identity politics" was something on which I originally wanted to focus the paper, but the dossier process persuaded me to "stick with identity work." Originally, I used a social movement framework to analyze APAIT. The negotiations of various identity issues were thus seen as everyday identity politics. I had wanted to explore at APAIT what Gilbert Elbaz (1992) called "the politicality of everyday life." This is a topic worth pursuing, especially if I bring in the data about the staff's attempt to define professional work versus personal activism. I plan to pursue this idea after the dossier process.

32. This term is the name of the program. Again, this is an example of the sensitivity of staff not to use the stigmatized term "gay or bisexual men."

33. In my latest visits to APAIT, I have noticed this effort to standardize and routinize activities. One of the staff, Aaron, expressed to me that the work had become more routinized and that he did not feel the excitement he once had.

References

Almaguer, Tomas. 1994. *Racial Fault Lines: The Historical Origins of White Supremacy in California.* Berkeley: University of California Press.

Burawoy, Michael et al. 1991. *Ethnography Unbound: Power and Resistance in the Modern Metropolis.* Berkeley: University of California Press.

Calhoun, Craig, ed. 1994. *Social Theory and the Politics of Identity.* Cambridge, U.K.: Blackwell.

Collins, Patricia Hill. 1990. *Black Feminist Thought.* New York: Routledge.

Elbaz, Gilbert. 1992. The Sociology of AIDS Activism: The Case of ACT UP/New York, 1987–1992. Ph.D. dissertation, CUNY.

Espiritu, Yen Le. 1992. *Asian American Panethnicity: Bridging Institutions and Identities.* Philadelphia: Temple University Press.

Gamson, Joshua. 1991. Silence, Death, and the Invisible Enemy: AIDS Activism and Social Movement "Newness." In *Ethnography Unbound: Power and Resistance in the Modern Metropolis.* Edited by Michael Burawoy. Berkeley: University of California Press, 35–57.

Lather, Patti. 1991. *Getting Smart.* New York: Routledge.

Morales, Julio, and Marcia Bok. 1992. *Multicultural Human Services for AIDS Treatment and Prevention.* New York: Harrington Park Press.

Omi, Michael, and Howard Winant. 1994. *Racial Formation in the United States from the 1960s to the 1990s* (2d ed.). New York: Routledge.

Patton, Cindy. 1990. *Inventing AIDS.* New York: Routledge.

Pfohl, Stephen. 1994. *Images of Deviance: A Sociological History* (2d ed.). New York: McGraw-Hill.

Prager, Jeffrey. 1982. American racial ideology as collective representation. *Ethnic and Racial Studies* 5:99–119.

Roediger, David. 1991. *The Wages of Whiteness: Race and the Making of the American Working Class.* New York: Verso.

Takaki, Ronald T. 1979. *Iron Cages: Race and Culture in Nineteenth-Century America.* New York: Alfred A. Knopf.

The ACT UP/New York Women and AIDS Book Group. 1990. *Women, AIDS, and Activism.* Boston: South End Press.

van den Berghe, Pierre L. 1978. *Race and Racism: A Comparative Perspective* (2d ed.). New York: John Wiley and Sons.

Benito M. Vergara Jr.

7   Betrayal, Class Fantasies, and the
     Filipino Nation in Daly City

> It's the only place in the world with more Filipinos than there are in Daly City,
> California.
> —Cesare Syjuco, *1001 Reasons to Stay in the Philippines*
>
> America's where the money is, baby!
> —Tina Paner, from the film *Sana Maulit Muli*

If you drive down California's Skyline Highway a little too fast, you might miss Daly City altogether. Bordering San Francisco to the north, Daly City, like much of suburban America, stretches its boundaries into the next town, in a diffuse mass of tract housing—varying in age, cost, architecture, and prestige—that extends from the Sunset District in San Francisco all the way down south to Foster City and beyond. What were once acres of cabbage patches and pig ranches became, in the late 1940s through the 1970s, seemingly endless rows upon rows of suburban dwellings crisscrossing the Colma hills. Its streets swathed with mist, Daly City—or as some locals called it, "Fog Gap"—was emblematic of what critics called in the 1960s "the West Coast housing mess" (Chandler 1973, 130).

This is where, in a city with a total population close to 95,000, about 25,000 Filipinos make their home. As the largest and fastest-growing ethnic minority in the city, Filipinos comprise 27 percent of the population. From a population count that stood at 14,400, the number of Filipinos in Daly City nearly doubled between 1980 and 1990 (Daly City/Colma Chamber of Commerce 1992, 3). In the 1990 census, those who identified themselves as "white" outnumbered Filipinos by only 10,000. In all, 45 percent of Daly City's residents are foreign-born. The large influx of Filipinos to the United States is traceable to the revised immigration laws of 1965, which produced a fivefold increase in the Filipino immigrant population in the succeeding five years. Since 1965, Filipinos have made up the highest number of Asian immigrants admitted annually. By 1990, there were 1.4 million Filipinos in the United States;

approximately 64 percent were born overseas (Querol Moreno 1994). This large proportion of Philippine-born Filipinos in the overall population resonates in the composition of the Filipino community in Daly City.

These large numbers are only part of the reason that enshrines Daly City—or "Dah-ly City," Filipinos say jokingly—in its peculiar place as "Little Manila," or "Manilatown," even though the appellations may not seem particularly applicable.[1] Certainly, with respect to the "-town" suffix, this is more "properly" applicable to areas within bigger spaces like cities, as in San Francisco, but not Daly City (or Monterey Park, California, for that matter). Moreover, there is no single grouping of areas or census tracts in Daly City where Filipinos reside. To begin with, Filipino populations in cities like Los Angeles, Honolulu, or Seattle are certainly larger, but there is a higher concentration in the obviously smaller Daly City. There are also towns in California like Delano, Stockton, or Union City with older, more historically established Filipino communities—former centers of Filipino agricultural migrants in the 1920s and 1930s—but Daly City retains its title as "the *adobo* capital of the U.S.A."

As a Filipino accountant told me, "I had heard of Daly City even before I arrived in the United States. There are lots of Filipinos there." Friends in the Philippines inquiring about my research would ask, upon hearing the name Daly City, "Aren't there lots of Filipinos there?" At the offices of the *Philippine News* in south San Francisco, a few persons were actually surprised when I told them that Filipinos comprised only about 30 percent of the city's population. "Is that all? I always thought that it was 60 percent. Eighty, even." Perhaps only Jersey City in New Jersey qualifies as Daly City's mythic East Coast counterpart.

As noted above, however, cognizance of this "concentration" is somewhat illusory, as one city's inhabitants and services spill over into the next. Indeed, Filipinos are spread out everywhere in the San Francisco Bay Area: with the exception of "whiter," wealthier communities like Atherton and Menlo Park, Filipinos live in large numbers down the Peninsula, all the way to South Bay cities like San Jose and Sunnyvale. In the East Bay, in towns like Hercules, Antioch, Pinole—whose public library contains an impressive Filipiniana collection—Filipinos have long been making their mark.

Riding on the SamTrans bus that weaves through the Daly City streets, one constantly hears snatches of conversations in Tagalog and Ilocano. The 20J passes through Daly City's St. Francis Heights and Serramonte districts—the latter about 44 percent Filipino—and stops in front of the Seton Medical Center, the largest employer in the city and responsible for the initial influx of Filipino medical technicians and nurses after it opened as St. Mary's Help Hospital in 1965. The center of all this Filipino activity is Serramonte Mall, where, amidst the McDonald's, the B. Dalton's, and the Mervyn's, Filipinos of practically every demographic background congregate. Every day, veterans and senior citizens—most are men, and many look formal in their coats and ties and slicked-back hair—sit on the mall benches reading newspapers, gossiping, and queuing up for lotto tickets. One informant in his twenties told me: "I can see myself looking like them in the future, man. Hanging out at Serramonte, wearing a baseball cap, eating a hotdog." Another generation is represented by

Filipino American teenagers in "hip-hop" attire who hang out at the mall like everyone else.

Filipino restaurants abound in Daly City, from the ritzier Tito Rey, with its dress code, to the more than a dozen *turo- turo*-style eating places where one can find anything from *kare- kare* to *sinigang na bangus*. Branches of the Filipino originals are everywhere in evidence: Max Fried Chicken, Barrio Fiesta, Goldilocks. Chips, crackers, and candy imported from the Philippines, as well as locally-made Filipino meat products, are widely found in Asian food stores, including the occasional Filipino market. There are video rental stores with movie posters featuring Richard Gomez and Sharon Cuneta pasted up on their windows. Through the Lopez-owned cable network, The Filipino Channel, residents can have Dolphy sitcoms and news from the Philippines beamed into their living rooms every day. A half-dozen Filipino newspapers circulating in the Bay Area keep the community informed about happenings affecting Filipinos worldwide.

Daly City is indeed an *"adobo* capital" of sorts, but this "identity" is based not only on its being in the United States, but also on its roots in the Philippines as well. Daly City's identity derives from what its city fathers call "the most ethnically diverse city in San Mateo County" (Daly City/Colma Chamber of Commerce 1992, 3) as well as from the imaginings and dreams of social mobility by Filipinos in the Philippines. It seems ironic to discuss identity—particularly where national identity is concerned—as being relational when, "on the ground," it is perceived as essentialized and timeless, despite efforts to uncover the hegemonic trickery engendering it. But, in the case of Daly City, distinctive identity formations are produced in the transnational intersections of conceptions of class and nation. As Arjun Appadurai observed, the mass media has enriched the formerly "residual practices" of "fantasy and imagination": now, fantasy is "a social practice; it enters . . . into the fabrication of social lives. . . ." (1991, 198). It is in this fantastic aspect, combined with the teleology of immigration, that Daly City constitutes an embodiment of potential within the Filipino's sphere of possibilities. Daly City, in a sense, represents a certain class ideal that is both product and component of Filipino middle-class imagining. It represents a kind of national belonging as well, but it is an ideal that is fraught with the potential loss of the very markers that indicate belonging to this particular class and nation.

The focus of this essay is on the post-1965 immigrants, most of whom arrived in the mid-1970s through the mid-1980s, and not their children, the second generation, who have been coming of age politically in the United States. I also do not focus here on the Filipino migrant laborers of the 1920s and their children, or the so-called second wave of immigrants in the 1950s and their American-born offspring. Though substantial historical work has been done on the first and second waves of Filipino immigrants, the post-1965 generation, composed primarily of politically fragmented and consistently underemployed professional and skilled workers, has been largely neglected by scholars. Though resistance comes from both fronts, Asian Studies and Asian American Studies are growing closer to each other, at least in terms of their subjects and the geography of their respective realms. Both academic fields, at least during their inceptions, were themselves created, in metonymic gestures not unlike those that gave birth to nation-states, over vast, seemingly unmanageable terrain. The undeniably large influx of Asian immigrants into the United States after 1965 alone demands the academic inclusion of histories claimed by well over half of those who call themselves Asian Americans. This essay seeks such a recovery, one that recognizes the necessity of Filipino American studies in Philippine studies and vice versa, and the ways in which the boundaries of both fields acutely affect analytical perspectives. One must be aware, however, of the political perils surrounding such a maneuver. The struggle for empowerment must be rooted in the local, but there must also be recognition of the common historical and economic structures that affect Filipinos both here and in the Philippines.

The scholarly consensus in the last decade or so is that new patterns of migration have been appearing, and that previous conceptualizations of migration, which included mechanistic push-and-pull paradigms, are now inadequate in describing the new phenomenon. Migrants are creating social spaces that bridge cultural, political, and even geographic borders, and forging loyalties that span national and familial boundaries. This "process by which immigrants build social fields that link together their country of origin and their country of settlement" has been called transnationalism (Glick-Schiller, Basch, and Blanc-Szanton 1992, 1). Changing notions of nation, place, culture, and identity have also led scholars to reconceptualize anthropological studies of migration. Previous metaphors of disconnection and uprooting have been questioned, portraying migrants' activities as constituting "a single field of social relations," as opposed to being "fragmented social and political experiences . . . spread across state boundaries" (Basch, Glick Schiller, and Szanton Blanc 1994, 5). In many cases, the everyday lives of migrants exist independently, or even in defiance, of state-constituted borders.[2]

In "looking" at both Daly City and the Philippines, I use as a guide George Marcus's (1986) observation that to represent the larger systemic context of one's subjects, it is necessary to examine different field sites and incorporate multiple locales in ethnographic writing. The growing interconnectedness among "cultures" worldwide—fostered by the movements of migrant peoples, but also by mass media—should be reflected in ethnographic method. By comparing the transnational aspects of these conceptions of class and nation, I show how they define and complement each other. Imagining is done in different directions, after all.

To begin to understand the post-1965 generation of Filipino migrants to Daly City, one must "go back" to where it all began— seven thousand miles away in the Philippines, where the dreams and anxieties of middle-class Filipinos in Manila affect Filipinos in both the United States and in the Philippines.

Departure as Betrayal of the Nation

In 1993, a book edited by Isagani Cruz and Lydia Echauz appeared in Manila bookstores. Titled *1001 Reasons to Stay in the Philippines*, the monograph, presented in a format admittedly cribbed from U.S. self-help guides like *Life's Little Instruction Book* and *The Portable Life 101*, manifests a particular class's fantasies, as well as their perspectives, concerning notions of Filipino identity. The book, according to the editors, was meant to be a collection of "positive thoughts about the Philippines," hoping to "make life more enjoyable for the millions of Filipinos who prefer to live in their home country rather than face isolation, alienation, and prejudice outside. . . ." (Cruz and Echauz 1993, preface).

Consisting of two or three pithy quotes on each page, the "1001 Reasons" are by turns droll, touching, and often surprisingly revealing. Most of the reasons given revolve around platitudes concerning the beauty of the country—"the implacable enchantment of its 7,100 islands," says poet Anthony Tan (p. 132). And having one's family and friends nearby—"I want to be able to bump into old friends and people I grew up with when I walk the streets," claims Glicerio Sicat, President, Interpacific Capital Philippines (p. 9). But a significant number evoke some form of nationalistic service to the country, as may be seen from the quotations below:

> Times call for every Filipino to think of self last and country first. This is not the time to desert our country for convenience of selves. Happiness, dignity, and recognition come first before material possessions. (Isidro Cariño, President, Asia Research and Management Corporation, p. 25)

> Each Filipino has the obligation to help improve and uplift the country economically, politically, and spiritually. I would like to fulfill my obligation in whatever way I might be able to, no matter how small and seemingly insignificant. (James E. Festejo, p. 183)

> There is a need to develop a critical mass of Filipinos who are willing to sacrifice personal interests for national good. (Roberto S. Sebastian, Secretary of Agriculture, p. 45)

> I'm trying to live up to my name—*nagpapakabayani* [being a hero]! (Bayani V. Evangelista, Publisher/Editor-in-Chief, *Mediawatch*, p. 136)

As these comments suggest—another interviewee says that those responsible for Philippine development are "silent heroes" (p. 158)—leaving the Philippines is tantamount to a betrayal of sorts, a nonfulfillment of an obligation to contribute to the nation. Departure is a betrayal of the nation to pursue what are seen as purely personal interests.

These comments further imply a binary opposition between money and nation.[3] Those who leave, ostensibly in pursuit of money, are seen as unwilling to sacrifice for the nation, as thinking only of themselves. In this interesting twist in the definition of "heroism"—for merely staying in one place!—nationalism is also tied up with the naturalization of the link between ethnicity and place, that is, that people of a certain ethnicity, and for that matter people of a certain nation, belong to one particular geographic place (Malkki 1992, 27).

Remaining home, in turn, is linked with the invocation, preservation, and consequent reification of "traditional" Filipino character traits depicted as nothing but positive:

Neighbors still care enough for each other to drive a sick child to the hospital. (Gloria S. Chavez, College of Business and Economics, De La Salle University, in Cruz and Echauz 1993, 18)

Strong extended family ties. Good formative years for children. Opportunity to help less privileged ones. (Roman F. S. Reyes, senior partner, SGV & Co., p. 143)

I am a first class citizen in my country. It is the only country where the people understand *utang na loob, pakikisama,* and *bayanihan* [debt of gratitude, companionship, and cooperation]. (Roberto Benares, Insular Investment and Trust Corp., p. 34)

Those who don't have reasons for staying should leave, so we can have this beautiful country all to ourselves. (Barry Ponce de Leon, civil engineer, Department of Public Works and Highways, p. 189)

A plant warehouse head working for the San Miguel Corporation puts it aptly when he likens "the Filipino tradition of togetherness and support" to being in a mother's womb, stressing the primal, essential character of tradition and, interestingly, its connection to place (Cruz and Echauz 1993, 29). The implication is that when one leaves the Philippines, one similarly leaves its protective environment, and one's sense of service, behind. It is as if the Filipinos who choose to stay deem the parameters of nationalism and national belonging as coinciding squarely with and within the state's own borders.

But this middle-class rhetoric of betrayal—something more akin to the loss of *pakikisama,* rather than an act of unpatriotism—flies in the face of apparently successful attempts by both the Aquino and Ramos administrations to crown overseas contract workers (OCWs) as new heroes. The OCWs were responsible for contributing more than $3.595 billion in the first nine months of 1995 alone, underscoring the government's parasitic dependence, in the form of the "Philippines 2000" economic program, on the export of cheap labor to countries where workers' rights are fraught with uncertainty.[4]

This suggests that the reference points of Cruz and Echauz's interviewees may really revolve around the difference between leaving and staying away. The title of their book—not to mention the very reality of its being written—already confirms a desperation of sorts to stem the hemorrhage of "deserters." But "staying" can only be the opposite of "leaving" as long as those who have "left" do not return for good. As Rey Ventura, writing about Japan, reminds us:

There is no Japanese Dream, and yet Japan, for the Filipino, has become a second America. There is no Statue of Liberty in Yokohama—and why should there be? A statue of the Yen would be more appropriate. We do not dream of becoming Japanese citizens. . . . We do not imagine that we will settle there for ever. (1992, 165)

What I am suggesting is that the interviewees may be defining themselves and their country specifically against the United States, and Filipinos in the United States. For Filipinos in Abu Dhabi, Jeddah, Singapore, Yokohama, Kuala Lumpur, Melbourne,

Madrid, Koln, London, and Hong Kong, staying away permanently is an idea that is not as viable—or a possibility that lodges itself as deeply in the national imagination—than the notion of eventually settling in Chicago, Hialeah, Houston, Baton Rouge, Kodiak, Fresno, Seattle, or West Covina. I am not discounting those Filipinos in the United States who do not intend to stay permanently, but the lines outside the U.S. embassy on Roxas Boulevard in Manila are an obvious manifestation of how deeply woven into the national fabric this possibility of relocating to America is. And, within this horizon of expectations, lies Daly City.

Betrayal vs. "Home Service at its Best"

The distinction between leaving and staying away can itself be subsumed underneath a more overarching opposition between Filipinos in the United States and in the Philippines: that of money and of the nation. As seen in the interviews above, the self is posed against the nation: the self, with its dreams of material success, is to be renounced in the service of the nation. E. San Juan, Jr., in his inimitable, overheated way, has characterized Filipinos in the United States as having "dutifully internalized the ethos of bureaucratic individualism, the ABC of vulgar utilitarianism, inculcated by the media and other ideological apparatuses in the Philippines and reproduced here in the doxa. . . ." (San Juan 1994, 7). Although he follows his pronouncement with a discussion of his frustrations concerning an appallingly apolitical Filipino community—"fragmented and inutile" are his words—his rhetoric similarly falls within the binary construction of money versus nation.

For the interviewees of Cruz and Echauz, the "pull" of money is seen to go against the strictures of nationhood and an untainted Filipinoness. One of my informants from Daly City makes the same distinction between Filipinos in the Philippines and Filipinos in the United States through his reference to a conflict between "*matiryalismo*" and "*nasyonalismo*." In the course of our conversation, he tells me that Filipinos in the United States can certainly be "nationalistic," too, if they contribute to relief programs in the Philippines and the like. After a pause, he corrects himself by adding, "I guess that's not much." The paradox here is that it is precisely money, thought to be antithetical to loyalty to the nation, that itself provides the catalyst for heroism, undertaken for the nation's sake. The quest for money, amidst the privations of other lands, can make heroes of OCWs. The acquisition of money, then, does not taint equally. Its corrupting power lies in the seeming singularity of the United States to evoke such betrayed feelings among the "nationalistic" middle classes who have been left behind.

This partially explains the odd erasure of the figure of the overseas contract worker from the nostalgic sweep of the interviewees' answers reported by Cruz and Echauz (1993). Again, the contrast between leaving and staying is rhetorically employed. In the case of OCWs, the circulation of money is controlled and kept mostly within the confines of the nation's borders. It is money, earned and circulated outside by green-carded immigrants in the relative luxury of the United States, that is detestable. Nowhere is it discussed that some people may seek their fortunes overseas because they must, in order to support their siblings and children.

The irony is further stretched when compared with other "reasons" given for staying:

> I detest housework. I need someone to keep house for me, cook meals, wash and iron clothes, so I can pour my energies into development work, helping the poor and making this country a better place. (Victoria Garchitorena, Executive Director, Ayala Foundation, Cruz and Eschau 1993, 19)

> The orchids I have grown. Efficient maids to prepare meals while I rest from the day's work. (Edna Formilleza, former Undersecretary of Education, p. 31)

> Maids, *yayas*, and drivers—home service at its best! Boracay, Dakak, and Palawan—heaven next door! (Isabel Yotoko, writer, p. 83)

> I don't have to do house chores. I have four maids and a driver doing everything for me. I'm a queen at home. (Mariela Corpus Torres, housewife, p. 113)

> I don't need a weather report to help me decide on my wardrobe for the day. My housemaids give me freedom and leisure time for a job and entertainment outside the home. At present, in terms of the inflated-peso value of my old house, I can call myself a millionaire. (Sylvia Ventura, p. 133)

> I can wake up in the morning and not bother making my bed, knowing somebody else will do it. (Antonio Concepcion, Senior Vice-President and Chief Marketing Officer, La Tondeña Distillers, p. 191)

"Home service at its best," indeed: the irony of this class blindness is not lost on the reader, who will remember the hundreds of lower- and lower middle-class Filipino women working as maids and babysitters overseas. (Note that the interviewees' credentials—schools, occupations—are easily interpretable as shorthand for "middle class" and "upper middle class.") The convenience of having maids not only affirms one's class standing, but gives one a reason—or indeed, *the* reason, as some interviewees admitted—to stay in the Philippines. The maids are seen as better off working for Filipinos and earning paltry wages, as opposed to working abroad and being able to stretch the riyal further.

My position contrasts with Rey Ventura's rather simplistic assertion that "the richer you are in the Philippines, the more likely you are to go abroad and to settle there for good" (1992, 164). This is true perhaps only to the extent that the Philippine incomes of those who have left for good have been able to support partially, but not fully, the requirements of one's class habitus—hence, the departure in pursuit of the fundamental embellishments of middle-classness already attained by those who can "afford to stay" in the Philippines.

The interviewees of Cruz and Echauz (1993) also suggest a link between class and nation: that one's class perquisites allow one to grow more fully as a Filipino. Their maids not only purchase more time for the job, but also more opportunities to pursue and gain cultural capital. The paradox, of course, is that most of the cultural capital to be acquired in Manila comes in the forms engendered by American media, particularly film and television (with cuisine and, to a lesser degree, fashion as possible exceptions). Ironically, it is the immigrants who tentatively put themselves in a better position to consume these more legitimized products that shores up class standing. But, from the perspective of Manila, to live in the United States inhibits the possibility of leisure that the middle class requires: "Here we are real people, not shadows holding two to three jobs to survive," says a deputy manager of the Lufthansa office in the Philippines (p. 191). As Pierre Bourdieu writes, ease "represents the most visible assertion of freedom from the constraints which dominate ordinary people, the most indisputable affirmation of capital" (1979, 255). And, as we have seen, the "efficiency of maids"— which includes the removal of the burden of making one's bed—makes the middle-class Filipinos "real people" and frees them up for "more efficient service" to the nation, to make it "a better place."

To be maidless in America (and losing that particular class marker) constitutes a fear enough, in this sense, to keep the upper middle class in its place.[5] They can therefore be "silent heroes," in contrast to those who have left the homeland in an act of betrayal. Perceptions of this betrayal are parlayed into interesting stereotypes—not really perpetrated through social power, but through their numbing repetition—that, at many times, seem completely contradictory to each other. Filipinos in the United States can both be praised for their financial successes and condemned for their seeming abandonment of the sinking ship that is the Philippine state. Only those deemed to have been extraordinarily successful (and therefore worthy of a certain worldwide acclaim)—actress Lea Salonga, businesswomen Loida Nicolas-Lewis and Lilia Clemente, for instance—are seen to escape the clutches of cash and its taintedness, and are embraced by national belonging once more. The contradictions in these stereotypes are even more clearly seen through the relatively uncomplicated prism of Philippine film.

Material Success and Filipino Authenticity

A movie produced in 1994 called *Home Sic Home,* starring the Filipino comedian Dolphy, paints the same sort of portrait of life in America. The widowed Dolphy leaves his son's family behind in the Philippines after being petitioned by his other son, who resides in the United States. (Both visa and plane tickets even arrive in the same envelope.) The son, of course, has "changed" and become irretrievably yuppie: he and his Filipina American wife drive a flashy car and live in a comfortable home in the suburbs of Los Angeles. After the obligatory traveling to San Francisco, Hollywood, and Las Vegas, Dolphy soon realizes that life in America isn't what he expected. His son leaves him at home on weekdays, and he is afraid of using the phone to call long-distance without his son knowing. Things get worse, for he is essentially left home to take care of his grandson, who is bratty, thinks his grandfather is odd, and, worse, does not understand or speak Tagalog. The film follows Dolphy's misadventures in looking for a job with his friend, played by the late Panchito: they find employment as hospital attendants very easily. The bad guys come in the form of two Immigration and Naturalization Service (INS) agents who investigate Dolphy's green-card marriage to another Filipina, played by the much younger Dina Bonnevie. (They eventually fall in love with each other.) But Dolphy gets into a car accident and, at his hospital bed, the grandson, blinking away tears, promises to learn Tagalog. Dolphy recovers and decides to return to his less well-off son in the Philippines.

The 1995 film *Sana Maulit Muli* illustrates the same conflicts, but the pressure of money in this example is most strongly contrasted against romantic ties. Aga Muhlach plays Jerry, an advertising executive in Manila who refuses to give up his career to be with his fiancee Agnes, played by Lea Salonga, who has just been petitioned to come to the United States by her mother, who had abandoned her at a young age. Agnes grows more despondent each day: she is shown getting terribly lost in San Francisco, her mother treats her as a servant, and her bratty younger siblings dislike her. "I don't belong here," she says, and thinks of returning, but realizes, "*Ang daming halos magpakamatay na makarating dito* [There are so many who would almost give their lives trying to get here]." Despite her pleas for Jerry to join her, he decides to wait instead for his promotion, telling Agnes that he is not ready to marry.

Now deserted by Jerry, Agnes finds a job doing difficult, menial work in a seniors' home. The film fast-forwards a year and a half later: Agnes has now become a successful real estate agent (after working first as a receptionist, then as a secretary) in Foster City, California, and has already bought a beautiful A-frame house in Half Moon Bay. But Jerry suddenly reappears and finds a completely different Agnes: harried, consumed by work—but also self-confident, aggressive, her voice without a trace of her old Tagalog accent. Jerry finds a series of odd jobs as an illegal alien—chopping up logs at a lumberyard, cleaning cars on a lot, and washing dishes at a Filipino restaurant in Milpitas. But their occupations are not the only tables that have turned. Agnes is now unwilling to commit: "*inagaw ka nang ambisyon sa akin* [ambition grabbed you away from me]," she tells Jerry. After quitting his job (where he is cheated out of his wages by the Filipino manager), he asks Agnes to marry him now or go back to Manila with him. Agnes refuses him twice. "It's not true that everyone wants to live here," Jerry says before he leaves for the Philippines. The film ends improbably with the woman (of course) leaving her career and the couple reuniting on the streets of Manila.

These films reflect and distill the image of the Filipino in the United States according to beliefs held by people I have spoken to in the United States, and by Cruz and Echauz's interviewees in the Philippines. The films work with tropes easily recognizable to their audiences in Manila, alluding to a familiarity of sorts with images and situations of the Filipino immigrant life. The long, backbreaking hours of work, victimization by fellow Filipinos and, most importantly, the personal transformation of immigrants upon their arrival (however "accurate" these perceptions may be) are images the two films produce and affirm. Dolphy's son has seemingly earned his money at the expense of his soul and is only redeemed later by his belated profession of allegiance to family. Evoked in these films are transnationally shared standards of class—the house, the car—signs recognized in a transnational language of wealth. Similarly, the naturalized, mythic trajectory of upper middle-class wealth is reaffirmed, although the films upset this by (of course) making romantic and/or familial love triumph over a lucrative career, or the possibility of one.[6]

Another stereotype affirmed in these films is the widely-held notion that Filipino children raised in America are spoiled and rude to their elders, something often attributed to their upbringing in a different environment. But more integral to *Home Sic Home*'s theme, which is echoed in *Sana Maulit Muli*, is its obsessing over language. Language becomes more potent a national symbol in a foreign context and is used to patrol the perimeter of national belonging. In interviews and in social settings, one often hears such comments from first-generation immigrants when referring to Filipinos (especially youths) raised in the United States: "But she's not Filipino, she doesn't speak Tagalog anymore." Conversely, Filipino Americans in a symposium held at Skyline College (whose student population is predominantly Filipino) in San Bruno, California, complained about how recent immigrants, upon finding out that they do not speak any Philippine languages, would say, "*Sayang* [Too bad]. You should learn"—thereby, in their words, questioning their identities as Filipinos.

Another complaint that I often is "*nakakainis sa lahat* [most annoying of all]," says an informant who works at a social service agency in reference to Filipinos who "pretend" they do not speak Tagalog. "*Lalo na kung halata mong marunong magsalita* [Especially if you can tell that they know how to speak]," the informant adds. Language is at issue in another criterion of Filipinoness. A politically prominent woman who lives near Daly City tells me that, for many Filipinos, "*ayaw nilang masabi na meron silang accent. Sabi ko, pag nawalan kayo nang accent, hindi kayo Pilipino* [They don't want it said that they have an accent. I say, when you lose your accent, you are not a Filipino]." Certainly, distinctions are tricky; Tagalog is by no means understood by every immigrant. But the regular irritation displayed by those who cling to Filipinoness is reflective of the seeming artificiality of English when spoken by a Filipino, who, regardless of location, *must* speak a Philippine language. English and an American accent are also connected, as in the Philippines, to class: "*anong klaseng pataasan nang ihi iyan?*" an informant colorfully commented, in a scatological reference to one-upmanship. The borders of the nation are constantly defended in the minutiae of everyday life.

The movie protagonists' easy ascent into the reaches of the upper middle class, and its price, also ties in with other stereotypes as well. In 1974, in the early days of Marcos's *balikbayan* program, Letty Jimenez-Magsanoc wrote a rather malicious essay in the *Philippine Panorama Magazine* derisively describing the persons referred to by the newly-coined term:[7]

> . . . she gushed forth with all the Americanese adjectives she'd picked up . . . that indicate beyond a doubt to her friends . . . that their *Balikbayan* really knows her English. She even pronounced Tondo with a long O.
>
> . . . this particular *Balikbayan's* name used to be Patsy but since she migrated to the Land of the Free and the Land of the Brave, she's become Pat.
>
> When interviewed, a *Balikbayan* [with no green card, the writer stresses] blurted out: "I'm so glad to be back in your country . . . er . . . I mean, our country."
>
> When the *Balikbayan* goes shopping (bless his darling dollars), he strains his arithmetic, multiplying and dividing dollars by *"paysus"* whenever applicable. If the figures add up right, he goes on a buying spree. (Jimenez-Magsanoc 1974)

Throughout the essay, Jimenez-Magsanoc's pointed remarks revolve around either the *balikbayan's* increased capacity to spend or the horror of how expensive imported goods are: "The prices of goods imported from the States dismay the *Balikbayan* . . . shaking his head feeling sorry for his brother Filipinos who will go to their grave without ever having sunk their teeth into the luscious softness of Three Musketeers or *Playboy's* Playmate of the Month." Again, she refers to the immigrant's relationship with money, coinciding with the shedding of qualities of Filipinoness.[8] Interestingly, her irritation also registers on a linguistic level, from pronunciation, vocabulary, the changing of names, and slips of the tongue. The implication is that the betrayal of the nation seems to be perceived and played out not only on an everyday level, but on a practically unconscious plane—or it may even be, as Jimenez-Magsanoc seems to imply, a deliberate linguistic affectation. This general loathesomeness accorded to the upper middle-class Filipino immigrant, whether in the United States or back in the Philippines—she calls them *"Balikyabang"* (*"yabang"* means to boast)—is played out on both class and national levels.

Filipino Class Divisions in Daly City

It is, however, the very obvious class differences within the Filipino immigrant population of the last thirty years that complicate the usually homogenized image of Filipinos in America as successful and upper middle class. This image of Daly City as suburb triumphant, coupled with the "model minority" myth that some Filipinos seem to gleefully celebrate, also obscures a significant amount of declassed laborers. As noted earlier, the years following 1965 comprised the migration of mostly middle-class medical and scientific professionals. Today, many Filipinos have ended up employed well beneath their educational attainments: as babysitters, parking attendants, security guards, clerks, navy cooks, waiters, janitors—all members of the so-called service industries. Stories abound of nurses and physical therapists being underpaid and forced to work only night shifts as well as handling the shifts alone.

These occupational woes, in turn, allow for the formation of class-based epithets like *"mga patapon sa atin* [trash back home]" and *"halatang biglang yaman* [obviously nouveau riche]," descriptions uttered by some of my informants. Certain Filipino restaurants in the Bay Area, for instance, are said to be frequented by the *"sosyal* [higher class]," while others are said to be *"bakya"*—despite the fact that the main difference in the restaurants' clientele more often has to do with age than with perceived economic standing.[9]

Daly City reflects these class differences behind a screen of upper middle class homogeneity. Helen Toribio, a counselor with the Pilipino Bayanihan Resource Center based in Daly City, describes the city as having a "kind of superficial image like it's very upper middle class," citing its "projection overseas in the Philippines." She stresses how Daly City is seen abroad: "They don't show this side of Daly City," she says, referring to the Top of the Hill district bordering the Ingleside section of San Francisco. "These are poor neighborhoods of Daly City," Toribio explains to me; this older, somewhat rundown neighborhood is inhabited by about two thousand Filipinos, comprising almost 31 percent of the population in that census tract. It is mostly in the Philippines, and in crafted images like films, that Filipino immigrant life takes on the glow of the successful bourgeoisie. This coexists uneasily with often-recited stories of immigrant sacrifice, of being "shadows holding two to three jobs just to survive," which are ultimately blurred into the soft glaze of upper middle class prosperity. It is, in effect, a similar kind of class blindness that glosses over the countless nannies and gas station attendants of Filipino origin.

For instance, a statistic often cited by Filipinos ranging from community leaders to magazine publishers is that the annual median household income of a Filipino family is about $14,000 higher than the United States average, according to the 1992 Census Bureau Current Population Report. (In fact, average Filipino household income, at $43,780, is even higher than the comparable white household income calculated at $38,909.) But these numbers are misleading: Filipinos have a higher number of persons per household, which certainly inflates total household income. Among Asian families, Filipinos have the highest proportion of families with three or more income earners. Such households constitute 30 percent of all Filipino households; for the whole United States, the comparable figure is only 13 percent.[10]

Being in the United States does seem to make it easier for declassed workers to acquire certain markers of the middle-class life even as they lose others. An informant marvels, for instance, at how easily one can put a down payment on a new car in America. All this is in contrast, the informant says, to the conditions in the Philippines: how he pays his taxes, "and nothing ever happens; look at our roads," he adds. In the United States, a car and a house in the suburbs are, for apparently many Filipinos, not far out of reach, thanks to the magic of credit and thirty-year mortgages. It is, ultimately, indicative of how money in America suddenly gains a kind of elasticity not seen in the Philippines. Money suddenly goes a longer way, allowing the consumer to choose from a wider variety of products.

I want to pose what newspaper columnist Hermie Rotea called, as early as 1972, "the six-times mentality in relation to the dollar-peso exchange rate" (1972, 4) as a contrast to the reasons given earlier—typified by an atmosphere of so-called traditional Filipino values—for staying in the Philippines. Corruption and inefficiency of the government are often cited by my informants as reasons for leaving the Philippines. But it is clear that frustration concerning money and the diminishing purchasing power of the peso is what primarily spurs the immigrant to leave. But, standards of living in the United States are deceptive, San Juan claims; he writes about the "mutable exchange rate of dollars to pesos" and how, "ignoring cost-of-living disparities," this becomes the true "opium [sic] of the masses" (1994, 4). Actively computing the exchange rate, particularly before purchases, is an act described as something tourists and very recently-arrived immigrants do. This mathematical slippage, an operation revealing a primary orientation towards the homeland, conceals the class disparity behind the monthly paychecks. The differences in cost of living are glossed over; it is the sum that counts—and the car and the house that go with it.

This frustration with money matters is related to another seemingly paradoxical "state," in opposition to the affluent veneer: that of "second-class citizenship"—an often-cited condition of Filipino immigrants in the United States that suggests, as one of the interviewees above puts it, a "first-class" citizenship in the country of one's birth and, by extension, of belonging. ("Second-class citizen? Serbisyong-bayan muna [Service to the nation first]," Aga Muhlach says in the movie Sana Maulit Muli, once again evoking the binary opposition.) Though the concept of second-class citizenship also implies a certain political awareness—a denial of rights to minorities, for instance, or the daily experience of racism—it also revolves around, depending on who says it, "class" rather than "citizenship," and, once again, the absence of maids. Living first class in the Philippines, as a Filipino should, and according to the dictates of one's class, primarily entails the capacity to consume; it also means not having to work two or three jobs, or working at a job commensurate to one's education. Once again, this highlights the importance of money, which brings one a step closer to tainted money from overseas. Those without the wherewithal to live as they "should," or "could," leave and stay away, and are in turn branded as outside the ambit of Filipinoness.

"Citizenship," however, earns equal weight (or lightness) in the phrase "second-class citizenship" when one considers its significance. The near-mythic rituals of obtaining a green card and taking the oath of citizenship is combined, but less strenuously, with assertions that one is still Filipino. The category of "U.S. citizen" does not diminish this sense of national belonging, so an indignant immigrant might say. Indeed, it may be more correct to say that, for the immigrant, exertions toward the affirmation of one's nationhood become largely unnecessary—or, even truer, unnoticed—unless questioned. And this is not just because the mantle of political citizenship can easily be shucked off; it is probably also because the terms of its problematics do not come to the surface of everyday life as often. But the malleability of citizenship seems to exist only for the new citizen, for doubtless the community back home may be poised to inscribe difference at each juncture.

The argument advanced here must be qualified, however, for it seems tangentially related to the assertion that the middle class bears the burden of nationhood more heavily than the so-called masses. And this is partly right in the sense that the problematics of nationalism may be seen as a mostly middle-class concept, but the instilling of nationalistic concepts through public education, both formal and informal, has long placed the weight of the nation fairly equal on everyone's shoulders. The creeping in of class cleavages alone, to point out the obvious, attests to the failure of this nationalist project to transcend "internal" differences. Questions of national belonging certainly erupt into public discourse among Filipino immigrants, but they similarly manifest themselves, at fitting times, in choices made every day.

Transnational TV and the Consumption of Filipinoness

I had initially approached studying Daly City in terms of what I saw as the nostalgic impulse, a force that could be considered socially generative. But I was later struck by a comment made by Jose Ramon Olives, managing director of ABS-CBN International, who remarked to reporters that, through The Filipino Channel (TFC), he was "in the business of selling emotions" (Gutierrez 1995, B1). Olives adds that "TFC's primordial role is to help scuttle the Filipino's crustacean mind-set so they can feel, think and move *up* as one, instead of pulling each other down." (John Silva of *Filipinas Magazine* would also say of his former publication: "We sell nostalgia, we sell emotions.") Another article about the channel also quotes a radio broadcaster from Vallejo, California, who says that TFC "brought back memories of when I was growing up in Quezon City."

Their comments are interesting precisely because nostalgia is certainly not the operative social force in this case: nostalgia deals more "properly" with temporal, not spatial, distance, as Phillips writes (1985, 65). Temporal distance hardly character- izes TFC's up-to-the-minute programming from the Philippines. Unlike other ethnic television stations, there are no locally-produced Filipino TV shows on the channel; in contrast, TFC is expanding rapidly, with 24-hour programming of "Ang TV," "The Sharon Cuneta Show," and a whole slew of Filipino movies. An article in *Filipinas Magazine* cites marketing manager Manuel Lopez, Jr., as attributing TFC's popularity to "the desire of Filipino Americans to maintain their cultural identity and heritage." The article adds that Lopez has received "hundreds of letters" from pleased viewers, particularly parents who "tell [him] it's the best thing that's ever happened to their kids" (Salido 1995, 26–27).

Television may be creating this transnational link, but the viewers' seeking-out of current showbiz gossip is by no means nostalgic. The popularity of a television station that broadcasts programs so seemingly far removed from the everyday lives of Filipino Americans is remarkable. With its utter lack of coverage of Filipino American issues, the world of The Filipino Channel is an oddly myopic one, regaling its twenty-five thousand subscribers with the immediacy of life, without satellite feed delay, in the Philippines. "Except for the commercials," Lopez tells the reporter, "you'd think you were watching TV in Manila." As a complete replica of Manila's ABS-CBN Channel 2, TFC fills the need to assuage a certain sort of homesickness, one based more on bridging spatial distance rather than time.

Looking at Daly City from this perspective suggests that the Filipino community in this city may be involved in something more profound than merely maintaining ties to the homeland. It is of course an eager response to the call of savvy marketing, but also, as with many other things in Daly City, a collective assertion of Filipinoness. One can see this in the annual *Santacruzans*, with costumes rendered authentic to the last glittering detail; the newspapers that seamlessly combine the scandals from hometowns both in the Philippines and abroad; the easily rentable videos that bring into living rooms the latest from Manila's film studios; the countless Filipino restaurants mostly indistinguishable from each other. One can perhaps read these manifestations as efforts to keep the nation closer, as part of a passively concerted longing to demonstrate national belonging. They are, in effect, a claiming of a reified heritage that would be denied them back home, a production and consumption of things Filipino (which potentially fends off accusations of betrayal) in order to live perhaps as much as possible as if they were in the Philippines. Perhaps branding The Filipino Channel as being completely removed from immigrant life is wrong; perhaps the homeland has everything to do with Filipinos' everyday life in America.

It is a paradoxical situation, one that seems to repudiate the assertions that Filipino immigrants possess a remarkable ability to assimilate. In Jimenez-Magsanoc's view, "No immigrant or alien resident absorbs America's attributes faster than the Filipino. That all comes from the Filipino's tried and tested ability to adjust to most any situation. . . . The Filipino automatically recasts his image after that of his adopted land" (1974, 9). Abdul JanMohamed similarly states, too easily, that immigrant status "implies a voluntary desire to become a full-fledged subject of the new society. Thus the immigrant is often eager to discard with deliberate speed the formative influences of his or her own culture and to take on the values of the new culture. . . ." (1992, 101). The post-1965 Filipino immigrants to the United States do not readily fit such a portrait. Are we, then, speaking here of a redefinition of the immigrant, in terms of the retention of ties to a "homeland"?

Class desires prevent the endowment of a complete authenticity on these trappings of Filipinoness and the occasions for their manifestations, however, for a true bridging of the distance embedded in these material reminders would entail a return to the homeland. Indeed, it is not precisely a striving for the "original" that is the locus of desire. The desire perhaps remains only for the striving itself, and not the referent, which is why this kind of consumption feeds off the luxury of distance: the humidity, rampant crime, and traffic jams can only be felt through, and warded off by, the printed page and the glow of the television screen. "The Filipino Channel," Olives tells me in an interview for the *Philippine News*, "is to make them realize that the country they've left behind is not as bad as how they think it is."

Daly City, therefore, acts as an imperfect mirror, one that erases the reality of the lower middle class but simultaneously reflects its residents' class and national anxieties and longings. This image can be seen as a product of the cultivation of class dispositions—which include migration and *a* Daly City itself, as the act of leaving becomes more and more concrete a possibility in the breadth of Filipino middle-class imaginings. But it is, at the same time, an image both resented and envied back home for how it goes precisely against the same class and national standards. The spatial connections may be delineated as such: one can say that Daly City is, in a sense, a Quezon City where the buses run on time; a Laoag City where every house has a two-car garage; a Davao City where its middle-class residents can acquire their wide-screen TVs and minivans, as transnationally shared symbols of middle-classness, in a manner impossible for them to achieve back home.

Notes

1. A real Manilatown, with barbershops, hotels, restaurants, and clubs, did exist just south of San Francisco's Chinatown until it was swallowed up by the financial district. One of the last structures to remain was the International Hotel; the defense against the eviction of its tenants became a rallying cry for the Asian American civil rights movement in 1977. Today, the area south of Market Street—or what has not been made into convention centers—contains primarily Filipino residents. Described in 1979 as "perhaps the largest Filipino ghetto in the U.S.," the Filipino tenement houses, "sandwiched in alleys," are located next to warehouses and whorehouses (Luna 1979, S2). Many Filipino veterans also make their home in the low-income hotels in the Tenderloin district.

2. To what degree is transnationalism a reaction to actual, changing empirical phenomena? Forms of cultural dialogue and social fields linking different places have existed ever since precolonial eras; migrants ever since the rise of wage labor-based capitalism could also be called transmigrants. Are the changes of the late twentieth century sufficient to declare the emergence of a new process, or is transnationalism merely the product of revisionist migration studies? One cannot deny that global connections have intensified, as evidenced by the immense circulation of people and capital all over the world, the growing political involvement of migrants with their homelands, the influence of mass media, and the developments in communication technology. However, one cannot help but be wary about the concept of transnationalism: that the difference it describes, that the newness it claims to articulate, may only really revolve around a matter of degrees.

3. The silence about the burden of the colonial and neocolonial relationship is quite interesting to note, and is somewhat beyond the scope of this paper—or, indeed, may have everything to do with it, at the very least in terms of fantasy as social practice. The trope of betrayal is hardly ever couched within the framework of a "return" to the former metropole.

4. As Rosario Ballescas writes, the government is "utilizing the young women of the Philippines in exchange for immediate but temporal and artificial financial alleviation; utilizing the . . . women to try to resolve poverty, a role which should rightly be borne primarily by the government. . . ." (1992, 114). In fact, Filipinos in the United States sent $2.79 billion as remittances in the first nine months of 1995—transnational financial links that contribute to the maintenance of familial ties strained by the calls of global capitalism (*Philippine Daily Inquirer* 1996, 4).

5. A few may remain undaunted by the problem of maidlessness, such as wealthier Filipino immigrant families with their own *yayas* in tow, allegedly paid well below minimum wage. But, for most, the need for a maid is usually met by petitioning for one's parents who, if already retired, end up staying at home to take care of the grandchildren.

6. Indeed, as can be seen from newspaper columns, films, and television talk shows, the biggest toll exacted by the circulation of migrant labor worldwide has been on the family, regardless of which form it may have. I intend to explore the relationship between family and the nation further in my dissertation.

7. The *balikbayan* program was, in essence, a massive public relations campaign for Marcos, to show those in the United States that his *Bagong Lipunan*—or New Society, a phrase that did not outlive his regime—was for the good of the country. *Balikbayan* season officially began on September 1, 1973, reaching out to about seven hundred thousand Filipino "residents and their descendants" in the United States. Marcos rolled out every come-on he could think of: a temporary tax holiday from the Department of Foreign Affairs; the creation of a special military tribunal focusing on crimes committed against tourists, to try and decide cases within twenty-four hours; a National Hospitality Committee, headed by his wife Imelda, to ensure that "government officials will see to it . . . that guests at all times will enjoy courtesy, honesty, convenience, safety and security"; that the generosity of the guests is not abused, even by their own relatives, through a public education program; "discounts on airline fare, hotel and food rates, and shops selling 'native handicrafts' "; and free medical and legal services, in case "some of these Filipinos may have legal problems about property or inheritance cases" (Alvarez-Bihis 1973, 15). One could seriously interpret this as paving the way for a future reconfiguration of state and national borders, but it was still primarily a campaign to drum up positive publicity to conceal the terrors of martial law. The program also paved the way toward the institutionalization of the OCWs' monetary role, beginning with the early temporary migration to Saudi Arabia in the mid-1970s.

8. The quaintness of the "Three Musketeers" aspect of Jimenez-Magsanoc's observation is due to the fact that extremely liberal import laws in the mid-1980s have allowed the huge influx of imported candy bars and such into local *sari-sari* stores. A recent visit to a supermarket in Manila confirmed this: less and less locally-made products were on the shelves, and much of the commodities—from milk and paper napkins to potato chips and cookies—were imported, usually from Australia and the United States.

9. To return to maids: Raul Pertierra astutely observes that "much of the media outrage about Filipinos working overseas is directed as much to the fact that they are working as maids than that they are potentially exploitable. The growing image overseas of the Filipino as maid is what is objected to. This low view . . . undoubtedly reflects the views of the Philippine elite who resent that the country's image is shaped by their social and cultural inferiors" (1992, xv). A class-based blurring again occurs when one considers that many domestic workers are college graduates and/or former professional employees.

10. John Silva, former associate publisher of the San Francisco-based *Filipinas Magazine*, bemoans the lack of "consumer strength" in the Filipino community in the United States. "We buy cars, we have twenty billion dollars' spending power," he says in an April 1995 conference at the University of California at Berkeley on the future of ethnic publications. Citing a study that their subscribers' second car is a Mercedes-Benz, Silva goes on to say, "I get so upset that up to now, there is no recognition of Filipinos as consumers." *Philippine News* (1995, 2, 4) similarly cites "a reliable 1991 marketing study" that estimates Filipino buying power at $52 billion annually.

References

Alvarez-Bihis, Ressie. 1973. Operation homecoming. *Philippine Panorama* (Oct. 17): 15, 21.

Appadurai, Arjun. 1991. Global Ethnoscapes: Notes and Queries for a Transnational Anthropology. In *Recapturing Anthropology: Working in the Present.* Edited by Richard G. Fox. Santa Fe: School of American Research Press.

Ballescas, Ma Rosario P. 1992. *Filipino Entertainers in Japan: An Introduction.* Quezon City: The Foundation for Nationalist Studies, Inc.

Basch, Linda, Nina Glick Schiller, and Cristina Szanton Blanc. 1994. *Nations Unbound: Transnational Projects, Postcolonial Predicaments and Deterritorialized Nation-States.* Langhorne, Penn.: Gordon and Breach.

Bourdieu, Pierre. 1979. *Distinction: A Social Critique of the Judgement of Taste.* Cambridge, Mass.: Harvard University Press.

Chandler, Samuel. 1973. *Gateway to the Peninsula: A History of the City of Daly City.* Daly City, Calif.: City of Daly City.

Cruz, Isagani R., and Lydia B. Echauz. 1993. *1001 Reasons to Stay in the Philippines.* Manila: Aklat Peskador.

Daly City/Colma Chamber of Commerce. 1992. *1992–93 Business Directory.* Daly City, Calif.: Daly City/Colma Chamber of Commerce.

Glick-Schiller, Nina, Linda Basch, and Cristina Blanc-Szanton. 1992. Towards a Definition of Transnationalism: Introductory Remarks and Research Questions. In *Towards a Transnational Perspective on Migration: Race, Class, Ethnicity, and Nationalism Reconsidered.* Edited by Nina Glick Schiller, Linda Basch, and Cristina Blanc-Szanton. New York: New York Academy of Sciences.

Gutierrez, Lito C. 1995. Network aims to reach all Filipinos anywhere. *Philippine News* (June 28—July 4): 1, 12.

JanMohamed, Abdul R. 1992. Worldliness-without-World, Homelessness-as-Home: Toward a Definition of the Specular Border Intellectual. In *Edward Said: A Critical Reader.* Edited by Michael Sprinker. London: Basil Blackwell.

Jimenez-Magsanoc, Letty. 1974. The "Darling *Balikbayan*." *Philippine Panorama* (Jan. 20): 9.

Luna, Victoria. 1979. "When we get to America, life will be . . ." *Ang Katipunan* (June 16–30): S1—S2.

Malkki, Liisa. 1992. National Geographic: The Rooting of Peoples and the Territorialization of National Identity among Scholars and Refugees. *Cultural Anthropology* 7(1): 24–44.

Marcus, George E. 1986. Contemporary Problems of Ethnography in the Modern World System. In *Writing Culture: The Poetics and Politics of Ethnography.* Edited by James Clifford and George E. Marcus. Berkeley, Calif.: University of California Press.

Pertierra, Raul, ed. 1992. *Remittances and Returnees: The Cultural Economy of Migration in Ilocos.* Quezon City: New Day Publishers.

Philippine Daily Inquirer. 1996. Workers' remittances shoot up by 67 percent. *Philippine Daily Inquirer* (January 14): 4.

Philippine News. 1995. Your strongest link to the $52 billion Filipino market (pamphlet). South San Francisco: Philippine News Incorporated.

Phillips, James. 1985. Distance, Absence and Nostalgia. In *Descriptions.* Edited by Don Ihde and Hugh J. Silverman. Albany, N.Y.: State University of New York Press.

Querol Moreno, Cherie M. 1994. FilAms 2nd highest income producers among AsianPacs.

Philippine News (January 26—February 1): 1, 15.

Rotea, Hermie. 1972. U.S. Statehood for R.P.? *Philippine News* (June 1–7): 4, 5.

Salido, Sheila C. 1995. Beamers. *Filipinas* (September): 26–28.

San Juan, E., Jr. 1994. Toward the Twenty-First Century: Where Are You From? When Are You Going Back? In *Allegories of Resistance: The Philippines at the Threshold of the Twenty-First Century*. Quezon City: University of the Philippines Press.

Ventura, Rey. 1992. *Underground in Japan*. London: Jonathan Cape.

Kyeyoung Park

8   Sudden and Subtle Challenge: Disparity in Conceptions of Marriage and Gender in the Korean American Community

> The ceremony of marriage is intended to be a bond of love between two surnames, with a view, in its retrospective character, to securing the services in the ancestral temple, and in its prospective character, to securing the continuance of the family line.
> —from the *Li Chi* (Book of Rites)

The traditional view of marriage in Korean culture has influenced the formation of the Korean immigrant family. For instance, in the 1980 census data, 89.4 percent of all Korean children under age eighteen lived in households with two parents present, the second highest figure recorded for any American ethnic group. According to 1992 United Nations statistics, only 14.7 percent of Korean families are female-headed households in contrast to the more than one-third of U.S. households (*Korea Times* 1/8/1994).

Just as Edward Said eloquently critiqued Western writings about the Orient in his book *Orientalism* (1979), standard representations of the Korean immigrant family tend to perpetuate an orientalist fallacy. According to the standard representation, the Korean immigrant is spared social problems such as incest and family violence because of Confucianism tradition. The stereotypes of Korean immigrant women are of pitiable and downtrodden women. Laura Nader has critiqued similar Western viewpoints of Arab women.[1]

Since the 1970s, there have been increasing cases of domestic violence among Korean Americans, due largely to the "husbands' inferiority complex" developed as a response to women's increasing economic contribution to the family economy (*Korea Times* 10/26/1993). In 1990, a Korean American theology student in California battered his wife and killed their three-month-old baby. This violence shocked the community (*Korea Times* 9/90). It was reported that the wife, as the breadwinner of the family, had adjusted well to the United States, while the husband had not adjusted and, hence, could not accept his wife's increased status. This violent incident raises questions about definitions of marriage and gender relations among new Korean immigrants in America.

The contradiction between history as we live it and history as we are represented asks us to reconsider the biased representation of the Korean immigrant family and the role of women. An increasing number of Korean American men and women do not feel comfortable with marriage in the conventional sense, as described above.[2] They are in the process of reinterpreting and transforming marriage within a newly defined context of immigrant life, *"imin saenghwal."* Here, marriage often becomes a socially contested field in that "the marriage process mirrors wider social realities but also . . . contributes to a reordering of social relationships."[3]

In exploring how Korean American men and women interpret and transform marriage, I focus here on the dynamics of gender relationships by presenting this redefinition of marriage and gender in four related areas: (1) forms of marriage; (2) marital expectations among unmarried Korean Americans; (3) roots of marital and gender conflict; and finally, (4) emergence of marital incompatibility, leading to withdrawal, separation, divorce, and other problems. I use the term "gender" as "a way of referring to the social organization of the relationship between the sexes."[4] In comparing men's concept of marriage with that of women and analyzing the sociocultural implications of this disparity in the Korean American community, I emphasize the point of view that "marriage must be understood as part of a wider system of sexual and political relations, both heterosexual and homosexual, which are the outcome of historically specific social processes."[5]

While I do not present women's viewpoints as overturning gender relations, I maintain that Korean American women, instead of remaining silent, are now voicing their feelings and ideas. Their perspectives will eventually have significant impact on community life.

I conducted research during 1984–1985 in the Korean community in New York City and collected supplementary data in 1990 in Los Angeles and New York City, the largest and second largest Korean communities in America. My main sources of data were interviews conducted with fourteen women and sixteen men.[6] All were Korean immigrants; seven were *ilchŏmose* (one-point-five generation, or those who came to America as teenagers). Men's and women's ages and marital status distributions were similar. The occupational and educational levels of women interviewees were slightly higher than their male counterparts.[7] Just as "the active participants in the Asian American feminist organizations are mostly middle-class Asian women, college students, professionals, political activists, and a few working-class women," I anticipate that middle-class and professional women will play an important role in the Korean American feminist movement.[8]

More important, I present immigrant stories as attempts to radically unsettle gender relations and politics in the Korean American community. By presenting these stories, I am not seeking to create a general typology but to expose the tip of the iceberg of changing gender relations. In the future, gender and marital conflicts are likely to increase, aggravated by Korean immigrants' lack of cultural tools to deal with these problems and also by their limited access to the mainstream social service network.

Forms of Marriage in the Korean American Community

In Korea, traditionally, the arranged marriage has been the predominant pattern of mate selection. "Although the mode of mate selection has undergone significant changes over the last two or three decades, a great majority of marriages are still arranged or semi-arranged."[9] The contemporary arranged marriage usually involves parental permission for an "introduction" by a matchmaker, who carefully appraises the backgrounds of the prospective bride and bridegroom, leading to a so-called "love" period before marriage.[10] Even love marriage has not corresponded with the Western form of love marriage. For most Koreans, love marriage means that a young couple met and had a dating courtship period without the formal intervention of the parents and relatives.[11]

Kendall identifies a small but significant shift of emphasis in Korean perceptions of the roles of wife and daughter-in-law. For example, in her study of Korean *Pyebaek* wedding ritual, she observes that the groom bows with the bride, and the bride's kowtows are rewarded with cash—token gifts that sanction a secluded honeymoon and presage the bride's new role as mistress of her home. Following upon more frugal procedures, ritual silks and kowtow money also transform a traditional rite of incorporation into a celebration of affinity, a self-consciously costly affirmation of kinship in an increasingly diffuse and mobile society.[12]

Unlike urban Korea, Korean American marriage involves the syncretism of American and Korean culture. Wedding ceremonies are predominantly held at Christian churches. The *Pyebaek* ceremony described by Kendall is often omitted, although it has been recently revived. Interestingly enough, American customs of the bride throwing her bouquet and the bridegroom removing her garter belt, and the Korean custom of bridegroom teasing/beating, are sometimes held right at the wedding ceremony.

Although researchers have studied changes in marriage in contemporary Korea, there are few studies involving Korean Americans. Koreans in the United States are confronted with new social conditions: larger numbers of young people remaining single than in Korea, cohabitation without legal marriage, an increase in separations and divorces, homosexual relations, new patterns of domestic organization, and international and interracial marriages.

In the United States, in addition to arranged, "semi-arranged," and love marriages, Korean Americans also follow three other routes to marriage. The first of these is "parcel marriage," *sop'o kyŏrhon*, a major form of marriage in the Korean

American community. Parcel marriage is similar to the "picture bride" marriages in which turn-of-the century Korean and Japanese immigrant men married women in Korea and Japan by first exchanging photos.[13] In a parcel marriage, men—and occasionally women in America—look for spouses in Korea with their relatives' help. This leads to continuous exchange of parcels until the new spouse joins her or his mate in America. A second route to marriage is called "bogus marriage," *wijang kyŏrhon*. A bogus marriage is arranged to secure legal immigrant status.[14] This often involves monetary transactions, and may or may not lead to cohabitation. Many Koreans call these first and second routes "thunder marriage," *pŏngae kyŏrhon*, because in both cases, a couple often marries in haste. A third marital route is the "international marriage," *kukche kyŏrhon*, a union between a Korean woman and an American soldier.[15]

Marital Expectations among Unmarried Korean Americans

In addition to developing new routes to marriage, Koreans in America also have redefined the concept of marriage itself. Richard, in his thirties, came to America when he was thirteen years old. He considers himself "flexible" in that he is not going to marry for the sake of marriage. In this sense, he and other young Korean Americans claim, they are different from and a bit more progressive than their first-generation parents:

> I am not going to marry until I find a good person. I think that a husband should treat his wife almost as he would his own brother, roommate, or best friend, not to mention he should love her.[16]

However, as he describes the ideals for his future wife, he emphasizes his need for an amicable, agreeable, deferring, sweet, and passive woman, similar to *Naehun* (instructions for women) in the Korean classics. According to *Naehun*, a married woman has three roles: "to serve her parents-in-law, to be an obedient and dutiful wife, and to be a wise and caring mother."[17] Richard's concept of his future wife fits this description:

> What is more important, my wife should respect me. I am looking for an amicable woman, *wŏnmanhan yŏja*, who is not sharp but who is refined. These days it is hard to find a woman who knows how to respect others, who is not rude or self-centered. I admit that I am stubborn, *kojipchangyi*; however, I dream about a woman who is not stubborn. I like a *wŏnmanhan* ["amicable"], *yŏjadaun* ["feminine"], and *sangyanghan* ["sweet"] woman.

Richard further conforms to the stereotype of the conventional Korean male when he discusses double standards concerning sexuality and fidelity in a marital relationship:

> If possible we should prevent divorce by any means. In my opinion, divorces often occur due to problems with the couple's sex life. It is better for women to be tolerant of their husbands' "extramarital affair" *oedo*.[18] While men can keep their family life, despite their

oedo, women cannot. That's because once a woman has an affair, she is more easily liable to ruin her family physically and mentally.

Similar to Richard, all of the unmarried Korean American males that I interviewed preferred a parcel marriage with women from Korea. Gregory, who came to the United States at the age of six, explains this preference:

> Many Korean American men do "parcel marriage." That's because Korean American women lack such traditional Korean values as hard work and honesty. Again this is due to the fact that men have more responsibilities and therefore they retain far more traditional Korean values.

Richard, the first interviewee quoted, agrees:

> We, one-point-five generation, never turn to violence, which is again very different from first generation youth or the American youth. Therefore, the ideal marriage is the union between one-point-five generation Korean American men and women from Korea. These women not only are good at serving their husbands but also know how to appreciate such men, but not the same with one-point-five generation women.

On the other hand, unmarried Korean American women declared that it is not at all necessary to marry. They have constructed new concepts of marriage with emphasis on "political comradeship," "companionship," "partnership," "complementarity," "compatibility," "commitment," and "self-development." As a result, they do not often stress "respect" and "politeness" as their male counterparts do. Women are aware that these concepts are a convenient way to protect men's interests. Thus, these women see marriage as less of an "institution" and more of a "relationship."

Dr. Ha, a social worker who is in her forties, states:

> Marriage means that men and women who are in love with each other meet, and lead a shared life, through their sex life, hobbies, and communication. If not that, unless a man needs a cook, then why does he have to marry? Even so, these days people often eat out, so that cannot be a good reason to marry. Many Koreans marry just for the institution of marriage itself. Or, they say after a certain age, one has no choice but to marry. I swear that I am not going to marry for the sake of marriage. I do not want to marry by being forced by my family or relatives to see a guy *sŏnboda* (having an interview with a prospective [bridegroom]).

Accordingly, women in America, unlike their male counterpart, dislike the idea of parcel marriages, particularly between one-point-five generation Korean American men and women from Korea. Gloria, who came to the United States at the age of thirteen, says:

> I have a very pessimistic view of marriage. I have seen enough cases at my undergraduate institution here [where] many Korean couples were not happy with each other. In such cases, guys often go to Korea, and bring their brides back. They make such a big deal about their marriage, which I hate. Of course, they do not have a happy marriage, because of the problem with adjustment. It is very hard for me to understand those guys as the same one-point-five generation Korean American.

The Roots of Conflict

Increasingly, Korean women are participating in the labor market and they make as much money as men do. Or, men's contribution to the family economy seems to have declined. For some men, this development has produced new attitudes about gender relationships and marriage. But other men show little understanding of women's new role and changing consciousness. Mr. Song, a divorced painter, says:

> The starting point is the fact that women can obtain a job here. For example, often when the wife makes twenty-five hundred dollars, the husband makes two thousand dollars. [This discrepancy is due to the fact that Korean immigrant men are often restricted to marginal jobs.] Therefore, women, like my ex-wife, often think that they can survive without a husband. That's the new idea that they develop in their lives in America. At very least, they can survive by running a boarding house. Suppose that they charge four hundred dollars for each boarder, still they can save a lot. What else do they need money for except cosmetics?

Then, he continued:

> It is the way in Korea for women to follow men's decisions; here, however, it is not the same. Here Korean women become like foxes. Some even pretend to be widowed, despite having a husband. For example, those sewing factory women often announce that they are lonely widows. One woman I know crossed the Mexican border because she was asked to do so by her husband. Then within a month she left her husband. For a year she lived with another man and had a daughter. She even deserted that daughter. Now she lives with a third man. Still she insists that she's a widow. This is ridiculous!

Some men are determined not to divorce their wives, no matter what conflicts arise, as Mr. Song elaborates:

> I really did not want to divorce my wife. If one is going to end up a divorcé, why work so hard at dating and marrying her and finally producing children? I still do not understand how someone could bring . . . a new stepmother or father into the presence of their own children. However, these days, women, like my wife, start divorcing procedures without a husband's consent by hiring a lawyer themselves. How is it going to work? That's really bad.

In contrast, the men and women interviewees who are happily married arrived at a different concept of marriage and gender relationships. In the following case, Mr. Hong refers to premenstrual syndrome (PMS) to justify his wife's behavior and, thereby, her inferiority:

> I think that we argued over a small matter. For instance, she will say, "Other people make more money and are better off than us. When can we live like them? So-and-so travels to such wonderful places. When will we be able to do so?" This is certainly influenced by our social environment such as our neighbors and how they are doing compared with us. Besides, I admit I have little knowledge of women. For example, I did not know that they become very sensitive to trivial matters due to PMS and therefore they hurt a man's

pride. Now I will be more careful about making statements when she is about to have her period. I did not know that women are so delicate. God made them so. I hear they have more hormones, too.

With this view of women as materialistic, emotional, and biological beings, Mr. Hong sees marriage in terms of its sacredness and Korean classics:

For a harmonious family, I often preach a sermon referring to phrases in Korean and Oriental philosophy to my wife. The first important thing is *yŏpilchongbu:* Wives should follow their husbands. This means that women should obey the head of household. The second thing is *nampilchongch'ŏn:* Man should be conscientious. Then, finally, a harmonious family leads to world peace. As I repeat these phrases many times, she seems to listen to me.

Often men and some women suggest that this idea of following the husband is a parallel one to that of serving one leader, not two, in a nation. This attitude, I think, contributes to the perpetuation of dictatorships in Korea and in the family.

Mr. Kim works at a Korean silk-screening factory in south Los Angeles. He explains how he chose his wife and reveals the conventional view of Korean men toward women—Is this woman good at serving me and my parents?—in the following remarks:

When I first met my wife, I felt comfortable with her. I see a woman's attitude, manners, and other behaviors as more important criteria than her appearance. She should be able to serve others and to be generous. My wife seemed to know how to serve her parents and more importantly knew how to take care of my parents. As she is cooperative in managing family life, she is suitable.

Among women interviewees, only two stated that women needed to marry. In contrast to the men's attitude, they emphasized "companionship," "commitment," "political ideal," and "mutual beneficiality" in selection of marriage partners. Lisa came to America when she was eighteen years old. Once, when members of her Korean American Youth Group (a group devoted to unification on the Korean peninsula) saw her husband help her with the housework, they scolded her that it would harm his success in life. But he did not care, unlike other Korean men. Lisa says:

It has been five years since we were married. I would say, marriage is when each person complements the other's shortcomings and at the same time, as each person develops, is able to reach out to one's own ideal with mutual understanding. I want to emphasize that rather than being dependent, one grows to be a full person through marriage. Also, both spouses should be responsible for each other economically. It is the closest relation and requires honesty, including in sexual matters, with open communication.

The Emergence of Marital Incompatibility

An analysis of the marital experience among Korean American men and women reveals many problems arising from discrepancies in their concepts of marriage and gender. At the most extreme are cases of wife-beating. Except for one man, all male interviewees shared a positive attitude about marriage, despite marital conflicts. In other words, for them marriage remains a sacred institution that cannot be destroyed by women, even by divorce. In their opinion, it is imperative for a man and a woman to marry when they reach a certain age. They all believe that the success of a marriage depends on how well the wife serves her husband, how obedient the wife is towards her husband, *yŏpilchongbu*. To these men, marriage is predestined, and both husband and wife (although more so, the wife) should do their best to make it work through hard work and, more importantly, patience. It is evident that for these men, marriage is not simply a matter of finding the right person, or fulfilling a contract. Mr. Song reports:

> Well, if you live alone, you just go to a bar, *suljip*. There, you keep talking a lot and enjoy yourself, *nodakkŏrida*, with bar girls while spending money. I certainly married my wife not to fight with each other like now, but to be served a hot meal. *However, as my wife started to grumble, our marriage fell apart* [emphasis mine]. My wife never listens to me. There is a good reason to obey what the husband says, because a man seeks happiness and comfort for his family. My wife does everything her own way, acting perversely. As I see it, because she has lived in America for twenty years, she wants to live and treat me purely in the bad American way. She is horrible. In the evening, when I return home with an empty lunch box, she doesn't even bother to smile. It wouldn't kill her to smile. She does not care whether I come home or not, as if I were a dog. If she does not give me food, I go out and eat in a restaurant.

Mr. Kang, in his late thirties, works at an American company and has a similar complaint:

> If I ask my wife to do housework this or that way, she never listens to me. For example, when I see that the refrigerator is dirty, even though I have asked her many times to clean it, she will say, "You are narrowminded as a man." She even chose her own church, different from my church. How can we manage to have peace in our family? She chose a church full of widows and she is certainly contaminated by them. I would understand it if she went to church after doing the housework. But she does not and still comes home at midnight after church. How can I put up with that? I cannot take it any more. I cannot see such injustice as an honest man. She tries to harass this man. The stupid women tend to be battered; the wise women are never beaten. Please try and understand me.

He adds:

> Around me, I see two different kinds of women. The wife of a friend of mine gave her husband *hwadae*, funds for a female entertainer, *kisaeng*, because of her pregnancy. [Here he means that the wife of his friend provided her husband with money so that he could satisfy his sexual desire with prostitutes.] How nice she is! On the other hand, the wife of another friend expressed reluctance, *nunhŭlgida*, to have her husband's friend stay late, playing cards and drinking a lot. That's why Korean men would rather go to a bar. The women there do their best to serve their customers in order to earn their money. Otherwise, men are not that foolish to spend their money that way.

The behavior and attitudes of Korean American men raise questions about gender relations similar to those raised by Prell in the case of the Jewish American Princess: "Gender representations continue to express the tensions and conflicts surrounding assimilation, acculturation, and success which continue to be associated with one's family of origin and choice of marriage partner." Thereby, "Jewish women are associated with the desire for prestige, consumption, the continuity of the Jewish people, and the absence of erotic desire."[19] Similarly, many Korean immigrant and Korean American men like Mr. Kang blame materialism for the changes in Korean women's attitudes. I hold reservations about the contention that only Korean women are obsessed with the American dream of success.

> Unlike women, men are animals with carnal desire so it is natural that they can fall in love with other women mentally and physically. If you ask, more than 90 percent of Korean men have had a secret love affair, *parampiuda*. I am totally disgusted with Korean women, who are totally rotten. All they can think of is to try to catch a guy in a Mercedes-Benz. They think they can buy everything, including love, with money. They do not have any good values at all, I swear.

Christianity is also very important in influencing Korean immigrants' concept of gender. Mr. Pi, a wife-batterer and businessman in his early fifties, states:

> Everybody has to marry, except a priest or Buddhist monk. With marriage, one is "to wait with patience and tolerance," as written either in the Bible or a Korean classic. "Blessed are the people who keep patience." The degree of kinship between husband and wife is zero: so a husband and wife are very close to each other.[20] But they become distant when they are meant to leave each other. This tells us that a husband and wife cannot exist without love. However, as my wife admits, if we refer to what is written in the Bible, there were Adam and Eve. First, Eve was seduced by the snake to eat an apple, which was prohibited, and then she enticed Adam to do so. Ultimately, man committed a sin because of a woman.

In contrast to the above stories by men, the following story by a divorcée tells us about a new concept of marriage and gender. It was only by going through her divorce that Younghui developed her belief that marriage should mean companionship in her life. Her divorce transformed her from an upper-class Korean immigrant into a tough American woman. She had married a third-generation (*samse*) Korean American from Hawaii and joined her husband in the mainland United States. After three years, her marriage failed.[21]

> He and I are people of marked individuality. Secondly, our problems came from our completely different cultural backgrounds. Of course, our individual differences made matters worse. He was almost 200 percent American in that he was leading a very frugal life; he was very pragmatic. In contrast, I was coming from the Korean tradition in which people care about saving face, are formal, live in luxury, in particular if they are elite or upper class. In addition, as you know, we Koreans have to take off our shoes upon entering a room, but he not only did not remove his shoes, he put his feet, with his shoes still on, on the dinner table, which shocked me. Also, he used to make all of our furniture himself, as the frontiersmen did in the seventeenth century.

When her husband finally left for Hawaii by himself,

> I felt that the sky was going to collapse. At that time, I felt so hopeless. I didn't know what to do. As a last resort, I kept praying to God and was inspired by him, too. When I read the phrase "Serve your husband" in the Bible, I regretted rejecting my husband. I thought I had done so because of a character flaw in me. Then, I finally realized that God is with me all the time. I no longer had reason to fear. I saw God, Jesus Christ, in my dream.

She then found that she was not equipped with any kind of job skills, despite her master's degree in music.[22] At first, Younghui thought of becoming a secretary, which she felt would be the easiest and most realistic job that she could get in the United States. But, she did not know how to type. So she went to a secretarial training school:

> I had to borrow two thousand dollars for two or three months' training. I learned typing, shorthand, word processing, and bookkeeping. I made tremendous improvement. I was the worst at the beginning; by the end of the training, I became second in the class. Because of language barrier, I could not become the first. After a long struggle I was able to realize my economic independence. I was very excited. In Korea, I was defined by others: in terms of what to do and how to do it. In America, for the first time I realized my own independent identity. Luckily, I got a job at a women's organization, as predicted by God. First I was hired as a part-time typist, and soon a full-time position was created for me.

Younghui adds:

> Most Koreans marry, just following what others go through. After divorce, I learned a lesson: marriage is a process in which one adds maturity to one's life. If one finds a member of the opposite sex who can understand [her or his] themes, interests, needs, and hopes, with full understanding and respect, that person is the right person. In that case, one's life becomes richer than following the single life. Marriage is like heading in the same direction, but with another person. Marriage is only a means, not an end, particularly for a woman. Once one recognizes one's mistake, one has to divorce one's spouse, like me. After that, if you try to live together, it is not desirable for either of the spouses. A situation like this should be judged from one's own point of view rather than by social consideration.

In this case, although Younghui's husband left her first, it was she who refused him in the end. Her independent living made her realize the depth of her full potential. It is important to note that in the case of separated and divorced men, it was often their wives who left them first.[23]

Discussion and Analysis

For Korean American women, marriage mediates and structures inequality between men and women. They perceive gender as a sociocultural construction between men and women. Accordingly, they construct different interpretations of marriage than Korean American men. This disparity spans a generation after their settlement in America. Today's wage-earning Korean American women and, to a lesser extent, those in family businesses, seem to be reforming gender relations within the family as well as revolutionizing the entire marriage and family system.

Partly, this new awareness comes from the realization of their increased contribution to the family economy, in contrast to men's reduced role in America. In urban Korea, men's white-collar work is more or less sufficient to attain middle-class life, without women's paid work.[24] Korean American women relocate from capitalist Korea to a more advanced capitalist America. Their labor power is in demand in garment factories, grocery stores, beauty salons, and hospitals (mainly in nursing work). With immigration, the labor force participation rate of Korean women has doubled.[25] As a result, Korean women cannot keep their old ideals of marriage; they redefine their ideals.[26]

The American political climate concerning gender issues makes possible this "sudden and subtle change in Korean immigrant women's gender consciousness." Many women came to understand that they can be happy living by themselves. They know that they can take care of themselves. That is, they realize that they can lead a happy life without relying on husbands, children, or parents.

Three major material forces contribute to the changing gender relation/ideology of the Korean immigrant women: (1) the American legal system in relation to the family, (2) public expression of women's issues, and (3) Korean immigrant women's increased economic and social independence. While in Korea, many women expressed rather stoically their discontent or anger with gender relations; in America, they realize that there is an outlet, such as police, courts, and social service agencies. For instance, they do not have to put up with abuse or domestic violence; they can report it to police. Another major difference from their lives in Korea relates to public expression of gender inequality in America. Korean immigrant women find that women are vocal in the United States. They feel encouraged by other women and are inspired to speak out. Also, Korean immigrant women's sudden change in attitude can be attributed to recognition of their economic and social independence. Overall, they are going through speedy changes in a few years—often from mother and homemaker to business partner.

The above three factors have led Korean immigrant women to changes in consciousness of themselves, of "appropriate" gender roles, and of new ideas and practices regarding marriage and family. In addition, there are other facilitating factors, such as women-initiated immigration, that result in gender imbalance in the Korean American community; impact of American/Korean media;[27] and urbanization in Korea. At the same time, depending on generation/age and occupational category (e.g., wage work or work in a family business), the new gender consciousness differs among Korean American women.

The concept of marriage as understood by Korean American women involves a noticeable change from viewing it as an "institution" to perceiving it in terms of "companionship." Resulting from consciousness-raising, this new viewpoint represents a departure from traditional Korean culture. According to the Confucian ethic, gender relations in marriage are marked by "fatalism," "respect," and "*chŏng*" (familiarity and warm feelings). Innovative elements in the women's new concept stress "companion-ship," "compatibility," "commitment," and "self-development." My analysis suggests that these new ideals of self-development are primarily an outgrowth of a highly competitive economy and the associated beliefs in individualism and meritocracy. In addition, women tend to produce new meanings of marriage, because they know the old concept does not serve their interests.[28]

As mentioned above, Korean American women's notion of marriage differs from that of Korean American men. It is apparent that while men adhere to the traditional concept, women make different decisions about marriage, divorce, separation, and sexuality. While men still see marriage as a sacred institution, women question its sanctity. More important, some women develop new definitions of what men and women should be. This elevated gender consciousness is important in that it is "an awareness of one's self as having certain gender characteristics and an identification with others who occupy a similar position in the sex-gender structure."[29] The divorce rate for Korean American women in the United States has dramatically increased, which testifies to changing concepts of gender relations.[30]

One important question emerges: Why do men resist this new concept of marriage? Korean men are not socialized to deal with changing gender relations. Therefore, they feel threatened and betrayed by women's new gender consciousness. Currently, Korean American men perceive that "they may be losing some of their advantages and that more aspects of their social roles are subject to public challenge and renegotiation than in the past."[31]

Thus, in constructing marriage and gender relationships, Korean American men try to prove "male supremacy" by referring to various authorities such as biological and psychological explanations, the Bible, and Korean/Eastern classics. Korean American women are portrayed as biologically weak, narrowminded, picky, grumbling, inferior, sinful, and dependent on men. But, at the same time, Korean American men portray themselves as more emotional, instinctual, and babylike than women. Therefore, men's expectations of women are quite contradictory: women are weak, inferior beings, but at the same time are stronger and more rationally and morally superior than men. Meanwhile, men also apply a double standard towards women on the issue of sexuality, both within and outside the institution of marriage.

This conflict over gender roles occurs within the context of the dominant ideology in the Korean American community: the belief that establishing one's own small business is the route to realizing the American dream. However, increasing numbers of Korean American women find it difficult to define their lives according to this ideology. Thus, men often state that women are becoming "Americanized" and, therefore, difficult to control. They also blame the Korean American community's preoccupation with making money on women. In fact, it is mainly men's dream to become rich by opening up small businesses, and hence, to be accepted into mainstream American society.

Understanding this ideology is important because based on it, Korean American men see marriage as an institution to protect their interests at the expense of women. But the men's viewpoint is now being contested. Similar to the way that Western families have challenged prevailing assumptions about the family, Korean American women are asserting that they will not experience marriage and family in the same way that men do: "they have explored the differentiation of a family experience mystified by the glorification of motherhood, love, and images of the family as a domestic haven."[32]

Ultimately, the transformation of marriage that is now occurring in the Korean American community will hinge on how well Korean American women negotiate between their new gender consciousness and the dominant ideology in the community. Due to emphasis on families, Korean American women join their husbands' family businesses to help realize the dream of proprietorship in the United States. However, in their rejection of traditional gender roles, these women are now redefining marriage. For example, a small number of women have rejected the institution of marriage altogether, while others are delaying marriage and improvising paralegal unions. Those who cannot manage both work and housework may marry but refuse to fit into the traditional role of housewife.

Due to efforts by Korean American women, a new concept of marriage and gender is emerging in the Korean American community. However, this redefinition has so far produced only a limited transformation in relations between women and men; it has not yet deeply affected men's power and has left the patriarchal structure intact.[33] At best, the new concept highlighted women's struggle to negotiate a new gender role. At worst, it illustrates the breakdown of existing gender relationships, sometimes resulting in domestic violence. Nonetheless, change is occurring as Korean Americans redefine gender relationships.

Notes

1. Laura Nader related her critique to the positional superiority of Western women as symbolic of the positional superiority of the West. See her article, "Orientalism, Occidentalism and the Control of Women," *Cultural Dynamics* 7(3): 323–55, esp. 329.

2. In this essay, the term "Korean American" is used interchangeably with the term "Korean immigrant." Although the term "Korean Americans" normally refers specifically to those born in the United States, I follow my interviewees' usage.

3. Maria Grosz-Ngate, "Monetization of Bridewealth and the Abandonment of "Kin Roads' to Marriage in Sana, Mali," *American Ethnologist* 15(3) (1988): 501–14, esp. 502.

4. Joan W. Scott, "Gender: A Useful Category of Historical Analysis," *The American Historical Review* 91(5) (1986): 1053–75, esp. 1053.

5. Jane Fishburne Collier and Sylvia Junko Yanagisako, eds., *Gender and Kinship: Essays toward a Unified Analysis.* (Stanford, Calif.: Stanford University Press, 1987), esp. 10.

6. Since my research topic of marital history and love involves private and personal stories, my interviewees were recruited from my personal networks, such as Korean American feminist groups and Korean Family Counseling and Legal Service.

7. There were two men and women in their twenties, three men and women older than sixty, and the rest were in their thirties, forties, and fifties. In terms of marital status, nine women were

married and five were either unmarried or divorced. Four men were married; three were never married; nine were either separated or divorced. In terms of the women's occupations, eight were professionals, two were business proprietors, and four were homemakers and students. Among the men, three were professionals, six were business proprietors, five were workers, and two had other occupations. In terms of educational level, more women than men had postgraduate education. Seven women obtained graduate degrees, while only three men had pursued graduate studies.

8. G. Wong 1980, quoted in E. Chow, "The Development of Feminist Consciousness among Asian American Women," *Gender and Society* 1(3) (1987): 284–99, esp. 290.

9. Tai Hwan Kwon, Hai Young Lee, and Eun Sul Lee, "Ichon Survey: A Summary Report," *Bulletin of the Population and Development Studies Center* 6(27) (1977): esp. 28.

10. "In both the arranged and semi-arranged marriages, an intensive screening is conducted of a prospective marriage partner's virtue, family, 'integrity,' and socioeconomic status." Eui-hang Shin, "Interracially Married Korean Women in the United States: An Analysis Based on Hypergamy-Exchange Theory," in *Korean Women in Transition: At Home and Abroad,* edited by Eui- Young Yu and Earl H. Phillips (Los Angeles: Center for Korean-American and Korean Studies, California State University, 1987), 249–74, esp. 260.

11. Hyungsook Yoon, *Kinship, Gender and Personhood in a Korean Village.* (Ph.D. dissertation, Michigan State University, 1989), esp. 102.

12. Laurel Kendall, "Ritual Silks and Kowtow Money: The Bride as Daughter-in-Law in Korean Wedding Rituals," *Ethnology* (1985): 253–67, esp. 265.

13. For picture brides from Korea, see Alice Yun Chai, "Korean Women in Hawaii: 1903– 1945," in *Women in New Worlds,* edited by Hilah F. Thomas and Rosemary Skinner Keller (Nashville, Tenn.: Abingdon Press, 1981), 328–44. For picture brides from Japan, see Yuji Ichioka, "*Amerika Nadeshiko,*" *Pacific Historical Review* 48 (1980): 339–57 and idem, *The Issei,* pp. 164–75 (New York: The Free Press, 1988); Evelyn Nakano Glenn, *Issei, Nisei, Warbride: Three Generations of Japanese American Women in Domestic Service* (Philadelphia: Temple University Press, 1986); Yamamoto Ichihashi, *Japanese in the United States* (Stanford, Calif.: Stanford University Press, 1932).

14. This problem became more serious once the Immigration Marriage Fraud Amendment of 1986 was enacted. The residency provision may be challenged by INS if a marriage is dissolved. As a consequence, spousal abuse arising from bogus marriages has become more prevalent.

15. "The war and the subsequent continuing presence of U.S. military forces have created an economic and social environment conducive to intermarriage between Korean women and American soldiers." See Bok-Lim C. Kim, "Asian Wives of U.S. Servicemen: Women in Shadows," *Amerasia Journal* 4(1977):91–116. Sil Dong Kim, *Interracially Married Korean Women Immigrants: A Study in Marginality* (Ph.D. dissertation, University of Washington, 1979), esti-mated that about fifty thousand "internationally married" Korean women reside in the United States; and Tai Young Lee, "Comments on interracial marriages," *The Korean Central Daily News,* September 21, 1982, sec. 18, suggested the size of that population to be about eighty thousand in 1982. Considering the size of the Korean American population in the United States, "it is reasonable to assume that a great majority of Korean women who were admitted as immigrants under the category of 'wives of U.S. citizens' must have been Korean women married to U.S. servicemen formerly stationed in Korea" (Shin, "Interracially Married Korean Women in the United States," esp. 251).

16. This and subsequent extracts are taken from my field notes.

17. *Naehun* (instructions for women), the most important and influential textbook for women, was compiled in 1475 and taught girls the four basics of womanly behavior: moral conduct—women need not have great talents, but must be quiet and serene, chaste and disciplined; proper speech—women need not have great rhetorical talents, but must avoid bad and offensive language and speak with restraint; proper appearance—women need not be beautiful, but they must pay attention to such duties as weaving and entertaining guests. *Naehun* also elaborated on the roles a married woman had to fill: she had to serve her parents-in-law and be an obedient, dutiful wife and a wise, caring mother. See Martina Deuchler, "The Tradition: Women during the *Yi* Dynasty," in *Virtues in Conflict: Tradition and the Korean Woman Today,* edited by Sandra Mattielli (Seoul, Korea: The Royal Asiatic Society, Korean Branch, 1977), 1–48, esp. 6.

18. *Oedo* originally meant consorting with a whore.

19. Riv-Ellen Prell, "Rage and Representation: Jewish Gender Stereotypes in American Culture," in *Uncertain Terms: Negotiating Gender in American Culture,* edited by Faye Ginsburg and Anna L. Tsing (Boston: Beacon Press, 1990), 248–68, esp. 264–65.

20. In Korean kinship structure, the closer the kin relationship, the shorter the kinship distance.

21. Besides the problem of compatibility with Younghui's husband, the cancerous relationship with her mother-in-law was another cause for her divorce.

22. This is a common problem with many Korean immigrant women, who were highly educated but had never worked in Korea.

23. Many husbands or wives are reluctant to admit that they initiated divorce, because in their mind, divorce had much to do with ruining the family. Therefore, they attribute it to their spouse. Nevertheless, according to the Korean Consulate, it is more often women than men who initiate divorce in the Korean American community.

24. Personal communication with Eun Hee Kim, 1990.

25. Immigrant women, regardless of ethnicity, have always been more prevalent in the labor force than native white women. According to the 1980 Census, more than 54 percent of Korean immigrant females older than sixteen worked outside the household, as compared to 29 percent of women fourteen and older in Korea. Interestingly, 3 percent fewer white American worked outside the home. Moreover, only 19 percent of all married women are employed in Korea, whereas in the United States 56 percent of Korean immigrant married women are employed, which is 7 percent higher than married white American women.

26. Alice Kessler-Harris and Karen Sacks, "The Demise of Domesticity in America," in *Women, Households, and the Economy,* edited by Lourdes Beneria and Catharine R. Stimpson (New Brunswick and London: Rutgers University Press, 1988), 65–84, analyzed the impact of deindustrialization and the current structural transformations in the U.S. political economy on women's traditional roles. It is beyond the scope of this essay to discuss changes occurring among American women. Here, I restrict my discussion to the changes that Korean women undergo as they emigrate from Korea.

27. Media also portrays marriage in terms of companionship, influenced by Western thinking.

28. Judith Stacey, *Brave New Families: Stories of Domestic Upheaval in Late Twentieth Century America* (New York: Basic Books, 1990), 252.

29. E. Chow, "The Development of Feminist Consciousness among Asian American Women," esp. 285.

30. In Korea, 6.2 out of 1,000 women over fifteen years old are divorced, while in the United States the figure for Korean Americans is 36.8—almost a sixfold increase. The real figure might even be higher, as this rate is based on formally reported cases at the Korean Consulate. For men in Korea the rate is 3.6 out of 1,000, but increases to 15.0 after they immigrate to the United States. This number is still well below the figure of 93.7 out of 1,000 for all American men.

31. William Goode, "Why Men Resist," in *Rethinking the Family: Some Feminist Questions*, edited by Barrie Thorne and Marilyn Yalom (New York and London: Longman Inc., 1982), 131–50, esp. 147.

32. Thorne and Yalom, *Rethinking the Family*, esp. 2.

33. Nazli Kibria reported similar findings in "Power, Patriarchy, and Gender Conflict in the Vietnamese Immigrant Community," *Gender and Society* 4(1) (1990): 9–24.

Part III

Beyond Asian America
and Back

Karen Leonard

9   Identity in the Diaspora:
             Surprising Voices

To talk about ethnography and changing orientations in Asian American Studies, I explore here the two apparently dissimilar research projects that have involved me in Asian American Studies. The first project focused on the early Punjabi immigrants from India to California; the second focused on Indian immigrants from one particular place, the former princely state of Hyderabad, to the United States and several other nations. The two projects differ greatly with respect to the socioeconomic characteristics of the populations involved, the timing of the migrations, the conditions in India and the United States at the time of the migrations, and the stances taken by the immigrants to their old and new homelands. Both projects relied heavily upon ethnographic work, and although my research strategies and my location in the field were different, there are some surprising similarities. Comparisons and contrasts between the two projects illuminate and complicate the ways in which generation and gender can be seen to function among Asian immigrants (Lowe 1991) and help to reconcile the themes of "claiming America" and a "diasporic perspective" (Wong 1995).

Locating Self and Subjects

As a social historian of the princely state of Hyderabad, an outpost of the Mughal Empire in central India, I studied the interaction between members of a "caste" and the state administration in which they worked (Leonard 1978). Then I undertook a study of the Indian immigrants to California in the early twentieth century, thinking that it would not take me out of the India field for long. These men from farming backgrounds in the northwestern British Indian province of the Punjab came on their own to work in America, and almost four hundred of them stayed and married Mexican American women. These Punjabi Mexican biethnic families raised fascinating questions about ethnicity and identity, and the project took a decade to complete (Leonard 1992). Now

in an anthropology department (I began in an interdisciplinary program), I am looking
again at Hyderabadi history and culture, at Hyderabadis living and working outside
their homeland. Part of the project on diasporic[1] Hyderabadis deals again with South
Asian immigrants in the United States and Asian American history and culture.

The two immigrant groups have very different characteristics, and the timing of
their migrations, as well as the conditions in India and the United States at the times
they were leaving and entering them, are also very different. Men had been going
out of the Punjab province to work elsewhere in India and abroad for decades before
the West Coast of America became a destination; several thousand Punjabis migrated
to the United States between 1900 and 1924. They were from farming backgrounds,
mostly illiterate in English and perhaps even in Punjabi (or Urdu, the language of
education), and they took up agricultural work in the western United States. Constrained by the increasingly discriminatory immigration and citizenship laws of the
1910s and 1920s, those who elected to stay could not bring their wives or other relatives
from India[2] and settled down with women who were chiefly of Mexican American
ancestry. The "Mexican Hindu" or, more accurately, Punjabi Mexican children had
names like Yolanda Singh and Jose Akbar Khan, and they were bilingual in English
and Spanish. Most fathers were Sikhs, with some Muslims and a very few Hindus,
but the children were typically raised by their mothers as Catholics. Seemingly cut
off permanently from India, the Punjabi fathers deliberately deemphasized Punjabi
language and culture and set about becoming American—not able to take advantage
of the phone or the fax, or modern transportation for journeys back and forth, that
connect transnational migrants to their homelands and each other today. Despite a
fierce commitment to the Indian nationalist movement (mirrored in their fight for
political rights in the United States), on the whole their effort was to forget rather than
to remember their homeland, and their children had even more reasons to disengage
from the old homeland and claim the new one. In fact, the children think of themselves
as the first generation, firmly basing their identity in the new homeland.[3]

As a researcher investigating Punjabi Mexican ethnic identity in rural California,
my position seemed rather weak. I did not know Punjabi, and, thinking the project
would be a short one, I did not learn it or Spanish either. My knowledge of the Punjab
was relatively poor, although not so poor as my knowledge of rural California and
American history generally. There was much to learn, and I looked to the Punjabi
Mexicans for help.

It took me some time to understand how the Punjabi Mexicans saw me. I viewed
myself as an outsider to Punjabi history and culture, but the spouses and descendants
of the Punjabi pioneers knew themselves to be woefully ignorant about the Punjab
and India, while I had a doctorate in Indian history and culture. I knew little about
California and American history, but the Punjabi Mexicans' education, gained until
recent decades in segregated rural schools, was not good in those areas either, and
few had gone beyond high school. Furthermore, the knowledge differential was less
important than an assumed power differential. I was an Anglo and a faculty member
of the University of California system, a system to which few residents of California's

agricultural valleys send their children, and one known chiefly through its agricultural extension outposts that were sometimes at odds with local farmers. I also came from the city of Los Angeles, which looms as a threat not only to the Imperial Valley farmers' water supply but also to their relatively conservative social and political values. I spent ten years doing the research, however, continually underestimating the extent of the project and my own investment in it and neglecting to seek major grants. I made many short visits to check local records, talk to people, and participate in events like county fairs, family dinners, and funerals.

Demographic factors shaped the research, conducted in the 1980s when most of the Punjabi pioneers had died. But many of their widows were there, and so were their children (many in their fifties and sixties and themselves parents and even grandparents). The children of the immigrants spoke eloquently about family and community events and conflicts they had experienced and thought about over the years. My book features the kind of vivid details and personal perspectives simply unavailable except through ethnographic research (Schrager 1983; Yans-McLaughlin 1990; Chock 1987).

After completing the Punjabi Mexican research project, I returned to the history and culture of Hyderabad, to something that seemed completely different. Even though the new project involves the construction of identity by Hyderabadis in the United States, it is broadly comparative, both in terms of countries (the work involves Pakistan, Britain, Canada, the United States, Australia, and the Gulf countries of the Middle East) and in terms of generations (the first and second generations settling outside Hyderabad). In most cases this has been a recent emigration, dating from the late 1960s. The first generation immigrants are very much alive and dominate the interviews; the second generation is just coming of age, just beginning to leave home for careers and marriage.

Unlike the pioneer Punjabis, most Hyderabadis in the United States are highly educated professional people from India's fifth largest city (Hyderabad, former capital of the state). In America, they are part of the post-1965 South Asian immigrant population, which measured highest in terms of income and education in the 1990 Census.[4] Hyderabadis number in the tens of thousands and reside all over the United States, but since no nation, state, or locality keeps records by the designation "Hyderabadi," I cannot even attempt the closely contextualized examination that was possible for the localized Punjabi Mexican population of three to four hundred families. In this new study, I am comparing national legal and ideological frameworks with family and individual formulations of personal, ethnic, and national identity. This broader and necessarily more interpretive project rests on interviews, event narratives, and life histories obtained from willing participants in the many sites under investigation. I have spent time doing ethnography in each of the major sites, and again the work will take a decade.

While I am including in the population all emigrants who term themselves Hyderabadis, a contested term,[5] the population is dominated by those whose families were part of the former ruling class of Hyderabad State. It is they who, almost fifty years after the state's forced incorporation into India (1948) and forty years after India's linguistic states' reorganization broke the state into three (1956), still think of themselves as Hyderabadis. Hyderabad State had a majority Hindu population but was ruled by a Muslim dynasty, by the Nizam (governor, a Mughal title), and the majority of the ruling class was Muslim. So there are many Muslims among my interviewees, and fewer Hindus, Sikhs, Parsis, and Anglo Indians. The language shared from the days of the Nizam is Urdu, but other mother-tongues are represented, and English is well known to all. This highly literate group of immigrants has produced Urdu and English prose and poetry; therefore, in contrast to the earlier research on the Punjabis, much of the written material gathered for this research is produced by the immigrants themselves.

My location in the new project is both more immediately accepted and more problematic than in the earlier project. As an historian who has published on Hyderabadi history and culture since 1971, my work is known to many of my informants, who discuss and dispute it with me. However, much of the historical work on Hyderabad has been written by non-Hyderabadis, which is resented, and as a native-born U.S. citizen I represent a nation in which many first-generation Hyderabadi immigrants find themselves uncomfortable. Despite the opportunities that have drawn them to reside in the United States and the removal of most of the legal and social constraints Asians faced earlier, many Hyderabadis feel uneasy about their location in the United States. This, too, we discuss and dispute. I am no longer functioning as an historian and ethnographer, but as an informant myself whose views on both American and Hyderabadi contemporary culture can be solicited and challenged.

Unlike the Punjabis, for whom such choices clearly were not possible, many Hyderabadis want to "preserve and transmit" their cultural identity in their new setting. Yet many see contemporary America as a negative setting, lacking family and community values and even threatening the viability and safety of their families.[6] As members of transnational networks, they draw upon their considerable resources to stay in close touch with the homeland, import cultural products and performances, and build South Asian institutions and activities in the United States. Many not only do not want to become "fully American," they see South Asian practices and values as positive contributions they can make to the United States. This is a strong contrast to the stance of the Punjabis, who found positive political and social values in the United States. Inspired by the relative freedom they experienced outside the British colonial setting, the Punjabis founded the Ghadar party in California and gave money and manpower to its militant nationalist activities (Puri 1992; Jensen 1988; Vatuk and Vatuk 1969). Women brought up in the United States or Mexico became their wives, and despite some conflicts and divorces, most Punjabi men became convinced that love marriages were preferable to arranged marriages. They also supported women's education and equality for women in India (Leonard 1992). One can view the Punjabis as men of the world, cosmopolitan (perhaps even postmodern) in outlook, although they could not be transnational in behavior.[7] From a region accustomed to sending its men out for work, they were prepared to settle elsewhere. Travel was hard and political constraints were formidable, but once a journey was made there was an accommodation to the destination. Hyderabadis, on the other hand, were not travelers. Their ancestors may have migrated to Hyderabad at some earlier time from northern India, Iran, Arabia, or Madras, but once settled in the Nizam's kingdom, they did not leave. Conditions have changed dramatically, however. The initial catalysts for emigration were the political events of 1948 and 1956, but more recently both South Asian and global economies have propelled young people out of Hyderabad for education, work, and, increasingly, permanent settlement. The magnitude of the emigration was brought home to me when I attended, along with a thousand other people, the four hundredth birthday of Hyderabad city in Los Angeles, a celebration put on by the Hyderabad Association of Southern California in 1991.

Politics, Power, Generation, and Gender

So far, I have stressed the contrasts between these two immigrant groups, but there are also commonalities, and it is time for some theory to help address them. For theorizing, "one must stand in some experience of commonality or political alliance, looking beyond the local or experiential to wider, comparative phenomena" (Clifford 1989, 177). One experience of commonality that might serve here is the conflict between first- and second-generation immigrants, but Lowe cautions against interpreting Asian American culture in terms of master narratives of generational conflict and filial relations, thus displacing and privatizing class, gender, and national diversities into familial oppositions (1991, 26). I want to complicate a generational analysis by combining it with an emphasis on the formative political experiences, the political locations, of the first-generation immigrants. Not that these two populations had similar political experiences and locations, but both have been crucially shaped by their political experiences in ways that had consequences for the generational transmission of memories. The commonality, then, lies in the way these political markings are related to generational memory and to "claiming America" or taking "a diasporic perspective" in the American sociopolitical landscape today (Wong 1995). To start establishing this, I will emphasize two aspects of Clifford's characterization of migrants as people "changed by their travel but marked by places of origin, by peculiar allegiances and alienations" (Clifford 1989, 188).

First, the changes brought about by travel and resettlement deserve as much emphasis as the markings from the places of origin. This was quite clear for the Punjabi Mexicans, and it is increasingly clear for the Hyderabadis, even though few have married outside their communities. Second, we need to pay careful attention to the markings, the "peculiar allegiances and alienations" characteristic of the first generation migrants. Thus, the early Punjabi immigrants emphasized the language they shared rather than the religions they did not share, reflecting the situation in the Punjab at the turn of the century where relatively fluid pluralist paradigms had not yet been replaced by more uniform and exclusive Sikh, Muslim, and Hindu paradigms (Oberoi 1988; Oberoi 1994; van der Veer 1994, chap. 2). Then there is the Punjabi men's political positioning with respect to India, their passionate opposition to British colonialism and commitment to the nationalist construction of a greater India (Pandey 1990, 235). Paradoxically, India's achievement of independence seems to have freed the Punjabi pioneers to be proud of India and yet detached from subsequent struggles there. The descendants of Sikhs now distance themselves from the Khalistan movement (for an independent Sikh state), reflecting their fathers' or grandfathers' attachment to India rather than a regional or subregional unit.

The Hyderabadis are also marked by politics, by the traumatic loss of their state, a double loss—in 1948 it was taken over by India and in 1956 it was dismembered. Furthermore, the "fall of Hyderabad" was closely linked to the partition of British India into the secular state of India and the Islamic state of Pakistan and to the rise of communal (Hindu-Muslim) conflict in India and in Hyderabad itself (Copland 1988; Bawa 1992; Varshney 1997). Some Muslim Hyderabadis left for Pakistan after 1948, and some Hyderabadis continue to migrate because of increasing Hindu-Muslim tensions in India. In consequence, and because of the consolidation of the religious categories noted above, there has been an emphasis on religious identities for both those Hyderabadis staying at home and those going abroad.

While the overwhelming impression is that the new Hyderabadi immigrants throughout the United States are very dissimilar from the earlier, largely illiterate Punjabi agricultural workers, there are compelling similarities when one turns to issues of power, generation, and gender within the family. Since I have published much of the Punjabi Mexican ethnographic material, I want to concentrate here on the Hyderabadis. But a story told by a Punjabi Mexican man whose father was a Punjabi-speaking Muslim from India introduces the common issues well. This man grew up in the Imperial Valley, along the California-Mexico border east of San Diego; his mother was Mexican American, his religion was Catholic, his languages were Spanish and English. He went off and served in the U.S. Army in World War II, and when he came home his father took the whole family out to a Chinese restaurant to celebrate. The young man ordered sweet-and-sour pork, knowing that pork was prohibited by Islam, his father's religion, but wanting to demonstrate his maturity and independence. The father sent it back angrily, saying, "Not in front of me and not when I'm paying!"

The story points to generational tensions between immigrant parents and their children, and it directs our attention to issues of power, of parental authority and control. The Punjabis did not attempt much in the area of cultural or religious transmission, although they inculcated respect for difference, but they certainly were concerned with maintaining their authority over family members. In California's agricultural communities, where the early twentieth-century immigrant farmers from the Punjab expected their sons to work with them on the land the sons would inherit, tensions focused on the father-son relationship. Among the well-educated professional people now coming to the United States from urban South Asia, tensions seem more sharply focused on daughters, as well as on issues of cultural transmission.

First-generation Hyderabadi immigrants retain an allegiance to Hyderabadi culture from the Mughlai court era, characterized by elegant Urdu expressions and elaborate courtesies.[8] Older Hyderabadis carry this culture with them into (voluntary) exile, and the fact that there is no longer a homeland to which they can return only strengthens their nostalgia. Their horizons are both expanding and contracting, and the Hyderabadis seize upon a vanished world in which to ground their sense of self,[9] resisting redefinitions of self and community. The surprises promised by the title come largely from the children of the immigrants (as in the case of the Punjabi Mexicans), whose discourse shows the unpredictability, the unsettling and unsettled nature, of their identity abroad. Between the first- and second-generation Hyderabadis, there are slippages and ruptures that are changing the terms of parental recognition of their children and children's recognition of their parents,[10] changing the lines of control and authority, although perhaps "not in front of" the parents and not while they are still "paying."

The voices of the first generation show this firm grounding in that vanished world of old Hyderabad (and here I will draw upon immigrants in several locations). Most of these immigrants still have parents, other relatives, and property back in Hyderabad, and many have not made final decisions about their own citizenship or place of retirement. They may appear to be in a liminal state, going back and forth between two nations, yet their discourse is overwhelmingly one of loss and nostalgia. Some ten years ago, a story about Hyderabadis in London appeared in *Siyasat*, Hyderabad's leading Urdu newspaper. A longtime Hyderabadi resident in London, asked how far it was from Charing Cross to Hyderabad, placed his hand on his heart and told the inquirer, "Hyderabad is here, *janaab* [sir]." Not only do these older immigrants mourn their removal from Hyderabad and try to carry Hyderabadi culture with them, they mourn the loss of the homeland itself, which has "disappeared" in its original location ("disappeared" in the sense of "having been disappeared," "been obliterated" by those now in political power, the Andhras). Not only has the Hyderabadi "nation" been subsumed by the Indian nation and the state of Andhra Pradesh, even in Hyderabad city the engaging old Mughlai culture is being displaced. An Urdu poem ends: "Now the surviving remnants of the culture are few, *we* are the scattered history of the Deccan."[11] Doubly conscious, therefore, of their mission to "preserve" Hyderabadi culture, many of the first-generation Hyderabadi emigrants are forming Hyderabad associations abroad.

These Hyderabad associations talk loudly about the old Hyderabadi culture, the so-called "Deccani synthesis" presided over by a multiethnic/multireligious elite (Leonard 1973; Sirajuddin 1990; Butt 1990). Most often, however, the memberships of the Hyderabad associations abroad rather narrowly reproduce the old Muslim ruling class, and the Sunni Muslims at that.[12] Some of the associations have a direct connection to the Nizam's grandson, Prince Muffakham Jah, who was their instigator and patron. As Orvar Lofgren observes (1991, 161), loud voices indicate past arguments and the attempted silencing of other voices: to these members of families prominent in old Hyderabad, the Indian takeover came as a distinct shock, a challenge from the increasingly numerous and louder voices opting for an independent and united India. To reinforce the vanished vision of old Hyderabad, these associations typically celebrate the families of the Nizam and leading nobles of the former state; they hold annual dinners featuring Hyderabadi food, Hindustani music, Urdu poetry, and Urdu speeches about old Hyderabad.[13]

Not all Hyderabadis abroad base their identity on old Hyderabad. Some rarely attend the Hyderabad associations but join with others from India and Pakistan in linguistic or religious societies.[14] Marked by the traumatic and communally-tainted events bringing Hyderabad State's history to a close, many are emphasizing religion, and for these immigrants, reinterpretation of the old Hyderabadi culture proves necessary. Some of the religious reinterpretation is consciously done. Hyderabadi Muslims here often answer the phone with "Asalam aleikum," an Islamic greeting in Arabic, and answering machine messages may be in Urdu. This tells one that the person expects to be telephoned only by other Muslims and/or Urdu speakers; for some of these immigrants, the social world has narrowed upon moving to a country with at least as many ethnic and religious groups as in India. The familiar "Adab arz" or "respects" of Hyderabad was a secular and more inclusive greeting.

As Chambers writes, "Travel, migration and movement invariably bring us up against the limits of our inheritance" (1994, 115), and many first-generation Hyderabadi Muslim immigrants are deliberately redefining their Islam. One man in California talked to me about purifying Islam, cleansing it of practices developed in India that reflected other religions. He maintained that Islam in the Nizam's Hyderabad had been corrupted, and added, "Now, here in America, we have the opportunity to be real Muslims." He talked of rooting out the eclectic, non-Islamic customs, for example the joking rituals at weddings involving women, terming them "Hindu" and superstitious. His wife, who was also present, said, "Yes, we used to do that because we women got together so seldom; now we can see each other more, we all drive, we just get in the car and go." The husband looked at her with some surprise, not having thought about the gender implications of the changes in quite this way. The same couple, seeing that Hyderabadi children in the United States no longer learned Urdu, were prepared to give up the Urdu literary heritage. As the husband stated and the wife agreed, "We can follow Islam, teach Islam here, in English; our children need not learn Urdu. Urdu, and Muslim ways back in Hyderabad, reflected the Hindu influence too much." This question, of how much language and religion, or language and culture, are mutually implicated, is an important one, and immigrants take different positions on it.

Similar problems arise as the Hyderabad Association leaders try to teach their children their cultural heritage through associational activities. One Hyderabadi commented, "We older men are the leaders, and we don't want to sponsor the kinds of activities that we know the youngsters would like; we don't want to put on coeducational parties with music and dancing." These same first-generation leaders are also reluctant to give up use of the Urdu language—particularly poetry—at meetings, although they admit it is a barrier to the young people's understanding of programs. One exception to this preference occurred when a scholar, known for his excellent English as much as his knowledge of old Hyderabad, was asked to speak to the London Hyderabad Association in English so that the young people could follow his talk.[15] Thus, generational and gender considerations complicate the transmission of Hyderabadi culture.

Foregrounding Islam means alliances with Muslim immigrants from other countries and talk of a "Muslim way of life," "Muslim family values," and of fantasized universal norms (Nanji 1993) rather than the beliefs and practices experienced back in Hyderabad. This drive for a universal Islam falls afoul of the contextualizing influences that reconfigure other aspects of identity in the diaspora. Religion is taught to the second generation abroad through texts, not through everyday immersion in the South Asian context, and not surprisingly, its teaching often betrays the relocation and reorientation of the teachers. For example, a textbook for Islamic education produced in Orange County, California, for Muslim youngsters explains *zakat* (charity) thus: "Some have a lot and some have none. We live in America, the richest country in the world. We live in big houses, drive good cars, wear good clothes and play with the best toys. . . . We should also look at the other people here or in other countries who have nothing. . . ." (Ali 1991, 67). A striking example of this reorientation, simultaneously globalized and localized, is the recorded message on the machine of a Hyderabadi officer of a Los Angeles Pakistani association: it begins with "Asalam Aleikum," proceeds with a lengthy message in Urdu, and ends in English with "and have an awesome day."[16]

As Hall says, "all identity is constructed across difference" (1987, 45), and the national configurations of sameness and difference with which Hyderabadi emigrants work are very different (no one has failed to locate the "awesome day" quote in California). The kinds of national projects being undertaken by the states in which Hyderabadis are settling differ, from Pakistan's Punjabi-dominated and increasingly Islamic society to British, Canadian, Australian, and U.S. white-dominated versions of cultural pluralism. In Britain, a "black" politics may engage some Hyderabadis,[17] while in the United States most such emigrants perceive themselves as "white." Local, regional, and national demographic patterns also play important roles here, and there can be considerable variation within each country. In the United States, there is the possibility of working with others of Asian immigrant descent under the Asian American banner; at least so far, the "Muslim American" identity must be seen as a competing one (Williams 1991).

How to connect to the new national culture, how to work with others in the new national context, is a major question for community leaders. The Punjabis wanted to become citizens and join the mainstream. But many first-generation Hyderabadis see themselves as inhabiting a space "both inside and outside the West" (Keith and Pile 1993, 18), and this poses a dilemma. Critical of the culture in which they find themselves yet also being at a power disadvantage, they hopefully offer better family values, better community values, greater respect for elders and women to their host societies, seeking that "common ground" so eloquently written about by Radhakrishnan (1987).

Are these hopeful offerings Islamic values, Hindu values, South Asian values, or universal values, and what are the differences? It sometimes seems that Hyderabadi Muslims have more difficulty disentangling these because they assume that they share more values with the majority Christian community than do Hindus. This question of a special relationship has persisted from long before the time of Sir Walter Scott's *The Talisman* ([1825] 1958) to the present. That tale, set in Crusader times, delineates the similarities and the growing friendship between the knight Sir Kenneth and the Saracen *emir* (ruler) Saladin, but as this male bonding proceeds (although different notions about gender are a significant source of difference between them), the reader notices that the real tensions, the sharpest animosities, are between the English and the Scots within King Richard's coalition.

One is reminded by Scott's tale of the discourse of Muslim American writers and speakers who stress that Christianity and Islam are monotheistic, share some prophets, and are "religions of the book" and therefore share basic values. A Muslim American leader writes that "Muslims believe in the same values for which this country [the United States] was founded. . . . They feel closer to the founding fathers than what America has become. . . . Those Muslims who have the strength of character to withstand the agonies [will] remain in America to re-instill the American values of [*sic*] which the American themselves have lost" (Athar 1994, 7). He also writes about major divisions within Islam, such as Shia and Sunni, that hinder united actions by Muslim Americans. Other leaders downplay such divisions, but they are in fact sharp ones, like the English/Scots divisions above. Even more significantly, Muslim American leaders overlook the fundamental differences between Muslim American and mainstream American family and community values having to do with gender.

These same Muslim leaders who celebrate shared societal values speak strongly for separation of the sexes in social settings and equate dating with engaging in premarital sex. They advocate modest dress, perhaps the *hijaab* (head scarf), for Muslim women and complementary sex roles within the family and society. Most also oppose abortion and the feminist movement. One man talked to me about how "Western women's liberation" invited criminal acts against women, earnestly informing me that "walking about, dating, going in the dark, this leads to rape and worse." On the subject of feminism, he said, "Don't you believe that a woman is by nature delicate, a flower, not to be opened to the public?" "No, I don't," I answered, moving the interview into a new and interesting phase that included an exploration of our differing views of the origins and permissibility of homosexuality, another major concern of Muslim Americans.

Perhaps "family values" can be used to reinterpret the currently dominant South Asian and/or Muslim ideologies concerning gender. I am thinking, from the earlier research project, of the two Punjabi Mexican daughters of a Punjabi Muslim who objected strongly to the way new Muslim immigrants conducted their father's funeral: "they didn't have any family values; they made the men and the women sit separately." From my current research project, there have been two similar incidents. At an Id commemoration (the annual month-long feast) in a Virginia community center in 1992 with Muslims from many countries, men from Pakistan fruitlessly tried to force family members to reseat themselves at sex-segregated tables; people simply stayed where they were, in family groups. Then there was a memorable Hyderabadi Muslim wedding banquet following the *nikah* ceremony in a Buena Park hotel in southern California. A family that included an American-born daughter-in-law led the way into the dining room, and the Mexican waiters attempted to direct men and women to tables on opposite sides of the room. But the young daughter-in-law went to a middle table, saying, "We will sit family style, as a family, thank you." Amused, the waiters gave up trying to regulate the seating, and the other wedding guests sat as they wished.

Surprising (But Still Muted) Voices

This brings us to the second generation and its new conceptions of personal, ethnic, and national identity. The Hyderabadi children being raised abroad cannot share that vanished world still inhabited by so many first-generation immigrants. The parents may think of their children as South Asian and Hyderabadi, heirs to an identity that is an extension in space and time of "a prior natural identity rooted in locality and community" (Ferguson and Gupta 1992, 7), but "culture" proves not to be a bounded and portable thing. It is true that the last Nizam's grandson came from London to report to Los Angeles Hyderabadis at a festive dinner in 1992 that Hyderabadi culture was a "backpack culture" that could be transported to new countries, and furthermore it could be transmitted in English. Luckily so, since the younger generation is proving not very competent in Urdu.[18]

The children locate themselves in the American social landscape, positioning themselves in the history, culture, and language of the new homeland. They did not undergo the traumatic years of the "fall of Hyderabad" or experience the physical space or the cultural landscape romanticized by their parents. Few can read and write Urdu, and even those who speak it find the poetry elusive. They may be linked to their peers at school—their classmates—as strongly as their parents were to their classmates back in Hyderabad (and this is the strongest tie I found among members of the older generation), but they and their classmates are co-learners of American, not Hyderabadi, culture.

As Gilroy's title succinctly puts it, "It ain't where you're from, it's where you're at" (1993), and Hyderabadi parents and youngsters made this point repeatedly. When I asked one Hindu grandmother if her grandchildren, who are being brought up in Texas, are in any way Hyderabadi, she replied despairingly, "Hyderabadi? They're not even Indian," and then cried as she told me that her granddaughter asked her to wear some other clothing, not a sari, when accompanying her to school. In another interview, an adult son who settled near San Diego, California, made his identity clear by insisting on watching the Super Bowl in the main living room while I interviewed his aging parents, visiting from Karachi, in a smaller room. His rudeness was atypical; sent to the United States at an early age for schooling, his were not Hyderabadi manners.

Because the members of the second generation are just coming of age, it is difficult to talk to them apart from their parents. Young people are almost always part of the small Hyderabadi groups I am interviewing in homes in America and elsewhere, but they are quiet and very respectful of their parents and other elders who are present. These same youngsters, however, when delegated to drive me back to my place, speak openly about their differences with their elders. Their voices are muted but inventive and diverse. Even in Pakistan, where the first-generation migrants went to be with fellow Muslims and become Pakistani, and where they certainly wanted their children to become Pakistani (those coming to the United States are ambivalent about their children becoming American), Hyderabadi parents still maintained a distinction between themselves and other Pakistanis. In fact, Hyderabadis in Pakistan are still viewed by the members of other "ethnicities," the territorially-based vernacular cultures, as *muhajirs* (exiles or refugees). Yet their children reject this separate identity and are speaking out, terming themselves "Sindhi," "Karachiite," "Punjabi," "certainly not Hyderabadi."

One son in Pakistan expressed himself especially forcefully as he drove me back to my Lahore residence, relating the reason for his marriage to a Punjabi rather than Hyderabadi girl there; his own very young son was in the back seat, "a very smart kid, a cross-breed," he said. His father had always advised his several sons to "keep away from those Punjabis, avoid problems," and one by one the older boys were married to girls from Hyderabadi families. Then their mother died, and who came to her funeral? "Our father's brother and sister from Hyderabad, I never did see them; my friends and my brothers' friends, they all came, they stood with us, crying, saying 'Our mother has died.' No relatives came from Hyderabad, and I said, to hell with them, they are in India, they'll always be there, but we live here. Why not have relations with these people, who are here when we need them? We need relations who can stand with us, be here for us." He went on to ridicule his father's allegiance to Hyderabad by invoking Islam: "We are Muslims. Muslims have no particular land. What is this village, what is that city Hyderabad, what is that Char Minar [a famous landmark in the old city], to us. . . ."

I think also of the young woman in Melbourne, Australia, who drove me back after a meeting designed to organize a Melbourne Hyderabad Association. A staunch Muslim who criticized Saudi Arabia as un-Islamic because it did not value women, she was fighting for the right to wear a tank-top, telling her mother, an occasional sari-wearer, that the sari blouse bared the midriff just as much as a tank-top and was un-Islamic besides. The same girl said that she and other young people from Hyderabadi families were not at all interested in the proposed Hyderabad Association, and that they find it ridiculous that they can't invite friends from Mumbai and other parts of India to the existing "one dish" potluck group of some ten Hyderabadi families. Ironically, many in this particular set of parents had joined the Melbourne Pakistan association, not the India association, suggesting that both first- and second-generation Hyderabadis are redefining where they're "from" as well as reacting differently to where they're "at." The parents above are emphasizing Islam and moving to claim Pakistan rather than India, while the children are claiming India rather than Hyderabad as their ancestral homeland. Perhaps even more remarkable is the turnabout of many of the younger Hyderabadi Anglo Indians who have ended up in Australia with their parents, often after unsuccessful "returns" to England. They are rejecting the British identity and electing to call themselves Indian, affirming a racial identity strenuously resisted by their parents in earlier days in both India and Britain.

Frustrated by the almost clandestine and somewhat random nature of my encounters with members of the second generation, I tried a systematic method of getting their views through questionnaires. The process of developing the questionnaire was itself an exercise in negotiating the issues of power, gender, and generation. A senior social scientist from Hyderabad, a retired eminent Muslim educator, urged me to expand the simple one-page questionnaire I was using to keep track of people. Stuck for long periods of time visiting his sons in their southern California suburban homes, he offered to work with me on a more ambitious effort to garner facts and opinions through survey questionnaires.[19] He assumed that the (male) head of the family would fill out a questionnaire for each family. However, I wanted the same questionnaires to be filled out by women and young adults, so that we could look for gender and generational patterns. But the head of the family could fill out the questionnaires for the others in the family, my colleague said, if I really wanted them for the women and children. We compromised: the women and children would fill out their own questionnaires, but they would be questionnaires designed to capture the issues and perspectives unique to women and children. We then designed three different questionnaires: a five-page one for male heads of household with questions about work, Hyderabadi culture, and political participation in the old and new countries; a four-page one for women omitting some of the questions related to work, culture, and politics, and adding questions about domestic practices and childcare; and a three-page one for members of the second generation. Unlike their elders, the youth were not asked, "Do you approve of extreme Western individualism? Yes or No?"

It was hard to get Hyderabadis to fill out these questionnaires (and some filled out the wrong ones). Just as I was generally unable to interview young people alone, I could not send questionnaires independently to family members. Questionnaires for each family were sent in one packet to the family head, or they were handed out at family and community events. The fathers, charged with collecting the filled-in questionnaires and sending them back, could be expected to read them as they did so. One young man sent his questionnaire back a full year after he had gotten it, explaining: "My father wanted to get it from me and send it back, so I couldn't fill it out. I took it myself, away to law school, where I could fill it out and send it back myself." He wrote that he thought the first-generation immigrants were close-minded people who had a hard time adjusting to life in the United States, and he asked me to call him long distance for additional comments. I did that, and he told me that while his father thought assimilation would be slow and take several generations, he himself expected that it would be rapid and that changes would be striking. Explicitly rejecting the "Hyderabadi identity" that they so much wanted him to take up, he did agree with his parents' strong emphasis on education and family values, but he didn't like the methods with which these two were furthered. For example, he said, on his mother's side, he is one of sixteen cousins, thirteen of whom are going into medicine; he is going into law and the other two, both girls, are married to doctors. He called the preference for the medical profession "insane" and was dubious about arranged marriages, too, thinking they would not be easy, and stating that he would prefer to know his future spouse beforehand.

The management of sexuality and marriage is an area of crucial negotiation for second-generation Asian Indians, undoubtedly the most significant area in which they resist and reformulate the identities imposed by their elders.[20] Hyderabadi and other South Asian youngsters are learning, as members of American culture, that parental love is legitimate and to be honored, but that parental power can be resisted as one empowers oneself, becoming an autonomous individual. Almost all South Asian immigrant parents oppose dating and "love marriages," and this puts the children of South Asian immigrants in a difficult situation. They do not want to break with their parents, so they control and limit what their parents learn of their feelings and activities. The focus is on daughters more than sons, and both sons and daughters are dating secretly, a very few even marrying secretly (Leonard 1997, 1999b). "Not in front of me" nondisclosure seems the least risky path to take.[21] To make public the betrayal of their parents' trust, to show that they have made their own decisions in matters so crucial to each generation's sense of self, would be a major rupture.

Most Hyderabadi young people are generally going along with arranged marriages, even transnational marriages arranged by their parents with other Hyderabadis. The evidence is mounting, however, that such marriages entail risks. Children who have been brought up in different countries, even if they are cousins (cousin-marriages are common among Muslims), turn out to have very different expectations about marriage, sex roles, and many other things. Everywhere, members of the second generation abroad are as comfortable with Apache Indian's casual British cynicism about Indian arranged marriages and Indian culture and Madonna's breathy lyrics about sex and love as with the coy "Choli ke Pichee" (What's behind the sari blouse?) and similar popular Hindi film songs in India and Pakistan. Divorce has become not only a distinct possibility but an option increasingly exercised. Despite this, most members of the second generation are moving cautiously with respect to making their own choices of spouse. The preference may even be to let the parents make a mistake, then arrange for a quick divorce and another try at marriage.[22]

"Not in front of me and not when I'm paying," as the old Punjabi said, and the second part of his statement also applies to marriages. One gets married in front of one's parents and at their expense, in fact in front of large numbers of relatives and friends of one's parents and at a very big expense. At these major events in family and community life, parents proudly display their ability to start a young couple on its way. Dowries can include not only clothing and jewelry but home furnishings, the house itself, a car, and perhaps the bridegroom's continuing educational expenses. Guests typically number from three hundred to thirteen hundred, and some of them may be flown from India or Pakistan and put up in local hotels. If one marries against parental wishes, there will be no big wedding, no beautiful photo album, no two- to six-hour video. And there will be no parental approval of or investment in the marriage.

Family arrangement of and investment in marriages also means some control after the event. One young couple who had made a love marriage explained that the husband had enrolled in higher education in the United States in business school only to find that he really wanted to do a Ph.D. in political science. Had he accepted an arranged marriage, in which his wife and her parents would have considered their contribution to his educational expenses their investment as much as his, he would have felt obligated to carry out the original plan. But with the strong backing of his wife, he felt he could risk making a change to a Ph.D. program.

Almost all aspects of the weddings, down to the details of the festivities, are still planned by the parents without much consultation with members of the second generation. Sitting at a kitchen table in London with a father and son, I asked about the guest list for the son's future wedding. Consternation dawned as the father realized I was thinking some of his son's school friends might be invited. Carefully he explained to me that he could not afford more than three or four hundred guests, and already there were more Hyderabadi relatives and friends than that who would expect to be invited. Issues like the composition of the guest list, whether or not to let Pakistani and/or Punjabi friends dance the *bhangra* (a lusty Punjabi folk dance, not congenial to old Hyderabadi wedding tastes), and whether to enforce gendered seating at the wedding or the wedding dinners are still determined by the first generation.

Diasporic and American Perspectives

Stepping back and comparing the two experiences of South Asians relocated in the United States, the Punjabis in the early twentieth century and the Hyderabadis in the late twentieth century, many issues of generation, gender, and power within the families appear similar. Yet their sociopolitical locations with respect to both the old and new homelands show sharp differences. The identities being constructed in the diaspora are highly contextualized ones, with the first generation in the Punjabi case consciously participating in the redefinition and in the Hyderabadi case consciously resisting it. The Punjabis came as colonial subjects, unified against the British, and they became active agents of sociopolitical change in both India and the United States. The Punjabis proudly gained two nations, the United States (by becoming eligible to citizenship after 1946) and India or Pakistan (at their independence in 1947). Many of the Hyderabadis came with the feeling that they had lost a country, yet they hesitated to embrace America as their new country. They tried to retain memories of a princely Urdu-speaking state now reconfigured as Indian and Telugu-speaking. Their nostalgia for Hyderabadi culture to some degree represents opposition to India and also to what is seen as a decadent dominant culture in the United States.

The Punjabis applied their fighting political spirit to both Indian and U.S. politics, and when the nationalist movement came to power in India they felt enormous pride but had become distanced from the details of the struggle. They and their children identified with India or Pakistan, with the new nation states, rather than with subsequent conflicts.[23] The Hyderabadis lost their kingdom in 1948, and many members of the first generation are somewhat ambivalent about identifying with India; the second generation has less hesitation about doing so. Hyderabadis have little chance to "forget" Indian politics, since the ease of transnational travel and communications keeps them all too aware of the communal conflicts of contemporary India. Religion plays a powerful, divisive role as diasporic communities finance and support Hindu and Muslim institutions and activities in both homelands.

With respect to cultural transmission, the orientations again are very different. Migrating in the early twentieth century, the Punjabis faced legal, technological, and familial constraints; they gave up their early expectations of keeping in touch or returning to India. They had limited resources and little specialized knowledge. The Punjabi men's choices when it came to selecting partners in marriage were restricted, and they could not select partners for their children either, so their parental authority centered on property and therefore on sons. Punjabi values about hard work and a strong martial tradition reinforced this focus on the male line.

The Hyderabadis are very concerned with cultural transmission and feel they have the knowledge and resources to ensure it, deciding what institutions to build, what teaching materials to develop, and what language to use. With respect to their children's marriages, again the Hyderabadis feel they have many choices. They can build transnational marriage networks, so parental authority centers on marriages and especially on daughters. The "traditional" complementary sex roles for men and women in society remain an ideal in the diaspora (even as within India the gender system is changing in the middle classes).

In both cases the second generation locates itself generally on the side of the new nation states—India and Pakistan. It also roots itself in the U.S. sociopolitical landscape, the Punjabi Mexicans openly so from their births and the Hyderabadis muting their voices, avoiding confrontations by compartmentalized and acquiescent behavior. The second Hyderabadi generation is still relatively young in age, and what its members will say when they reach the age at which I interviewed the Punjabi Mexicans is hard to predict. But the young Punjabi Mexicans started a club for themselves in their late teens, barring people over forty years of age from membership in a transparent attempt to stave off paternal participation. The young Hyderabadis are not taking this approach. Instead, many are resorting to nondisclosure.

The roles played by religion and by "family values" in the diasporic communities are also different, with the first-generation Punjabis deemphasizing religious differences between themselves and the majority Christian community in the United States, and bringing up their children as Christians. The Hyderabadis are very conscious of their religious differences, among themselves and with the majority community in the United States, and many spend time reconceptualizing their religious identities. Part of this effort involves an emphasis on the positive contribution Asian or Muslim family values can make to American life.

In the context of the tension within Asian American Studies between "a diasporic perspective" and "claiming America," the consideration of immigrants' political positioning with respect to old and new homelands adds explanatory power. A generational analysis, rather predictable within the family with respect to issues of gender and power, is deepened by this additional dimension. First generational stances towards old and new homelands may differ from one another, as we have seen, but subsequent Asian American generations ground themselves in American history and politics.

I have argued (1992, chap. 11) that the Punjabis and their descendants exemplify what some call postmodern identities: hybridity, mongrelization, "how newness enters the world" (Rushdie 1990, 3–4). Such features are linked, I think wrongly, to recent globalization or transnationalism. But other features of immigrant life are very strongly linked to the recent phenomenon of transnationalism, such as one's sense of connection to more than one location. Hall writes that one is "located in relation to a whole set of notions about territory, about where is home and where is overseas, what is close to us and what is far away" (1992, 22). Henderson and Castells (1987, 7) write memorably that the internationalization of postwar capitalism is producing lived experience in which "the space of flows . . . supersede[s] the space of places." Some words for this—"deterritorialization," or Wong's term, "denationalization" (1995)—have negative connotations. Other writers emphasize the positive aspects of experiencing various horizontal planes of experience all at once, as it were, instead of in an historical, linear fashion.

This postmodern geography resonates with the political experiences of the Punjabi and Hyderabadi immigrants. Both sets of first-generation immigrants were marked by dramatic political events in India, but for the Punjabis the effects were linear. They really had no alternative to "claiming America." Despite the legal constraints that they faced in the United States, barriers against meaningful continuing connections with India were stronger. The Punjabis themselves erased memories and sharply changed direction, repositioning themselves in the American landscape, and their children confidently claimed the new homeland. First generation Hyderabadi immigrants to the United States stretch across nations. They live in a transnational setting where technology allows them to maintain multiple connections; many legal constraints have been removed and others, given their resources, can be negotiated. Some reject the reconfigured, now Indian, homeland but claim an imagined past; others reinvent their religion and project it onto the new homeland; and many reject some realities of the new homeland. The members of the second generation in the Punjabi Mexican and Hyderabadi populations are more similar than those of the first, both politically positioned to claim the new homeland and a larger version of the old (India rather than the Punjab, or India or Pakistan rather than Hyderabad). The children of the Hyderabadis may not keep up their parents' transnational networks, and they are part of the new homeland in important ways. They may claim it more confidently when the parents are no longer paying their way.

Notes

1. For the changing use of the term "diaspora," see Safran (1991, 83–84 and 88–89). I discuss the extent to which the Hyderabadis and other South Asians fit this in "Construction of Identity in Disapora" (Leonard 1999a).

2. For the U.S. immigration laws of 1917 and 1924, California's Alien Land Laws of 1913 and 1920, and the Supreme Court Thind decision of 1923 denying South Asians naturalized citizenship on the basis of race, see Leonard (1992, 21, 31–32, 55–57).

3. I argue this in "California's Punjabi Pioneers: Remembering/Claiming Homelands" (Leonard, forthcoming). The "first generation" usage has been reported by other ethnographers, particularly Dorothy Angell Rutherford, personal communication, 1995.

4. Those born in India had the highest median household income, family income, and per capita income of any foreign-born group in the 1990 Census. The immigrants born in India also had the highest percentage with a bachelor's degree or higher and the highest percentage in managerial and professional fields (India- West, October 1, 1993). Leon Bouvier and David Simcox's study on foreign-born professionals for the Center for Immigration Studies, 1994, showed foreign-born Indians to be the highest paid among foreign-born professionals (with an annual median income of $40,625) (India-West, April 22, 1994).

5. Mulki, or countryman, was an important administrative category: membership in it could be restricted to those resident in the Deccan since the mid-eighteenth century (the Mughal conquest), or it could include immigrants to Hyderabad up to the late nineteenth century but bar those coming in after that (Leonard 1978).

6. People have expressed fears about inability to physically discipline their children because they may be reported to the police, and they have also expressed more general fears of violent crime.

7. Hall (1992, 275–77) remarks on the sociological subject and the postmodern subject, the former constituted by an interaction between the self and society, the latter far more fragmented, shifting, contextually and constantly reformulated.

8. A good analogy for the fall of Hyderabad is that of the old South in Gone with the Wind. The two societies had much in common: an hereditary aristocracy; a society divided by race, class, national origin, and gender; men concerned with horses, hunting, drinking, and the manners appropriate to their status; sheltered and protected women concerned with apparel, jewelry, food, and other domestic arrangements; heavy dependence on servants or slaves; and even arranged marriages, including cousin marriages. Both cultures were said to be soft, indolent, and gallant, with family background valued more than education and a contempt for commercial activities; however, Hyderabadi men were better educated, on the whole, and very fond of wordplay, Urdu lending itself so beautifully to poetry and jokes. Even more than Antebellum southerners, Hyderabadi men were said to be too courteous and polite, and to compete aggressively in their new worlds after "the fall."

9. I recognize that the designation "Hyderabadi" inaccurately projects "a group of people

as a unified actor," as Richard Handler puts it (1985, 178–79). Still, I am trying to follow self-identified "Hyderabadis" as they become part of other societies in different ways.

10. The discussion here draws on Gilroy (1993), Hall (1992, esp. 279 citing Laclau), and Bhabha (1987, 5–11).

11. Aziz Ahmed, London, 1991, telling of the story he sent to *Siyasat* some years ago about the London Hyderabad organizations; for the poem (my translation), "Baqi hai tamuddun ke namunee ab chand; bikree huii tarikh i Deccan hai, ham loog," Nawab Mohsin Ali Khan, London, 1991.

12. This is not surprising, given that many of the associations were formed by early emigrants to observe the Muslim Ids.

13. Program attendance and newsletters from Chicago, Los Angeles, Toronto, and London Hyderabad associations.

14. There are big Telugu, Marathi, and Kannada language societies, and Urdu societies include both Indian and Pakistani Hyderabadis, along with Punjabis and other Urdu enthusiasts. There are diverse Muslim, Hindu, Parsi, and Christian societies, and the societies based on schools, with their old-boy and old-girl networks.

15. This was Professor Syed Sirajuddin, retired from Osmania University's English department.

16. From an officer of the Pakistani American Association, Inc., 1992.

17. See Chambers (1994), who states: "Here to be 'black' can be a political and cultural term of identification among diverse groups of Caribbean, African and Asian inheritance held in a shared field of representations, rather than employed as a self-referring biological category or racial bloc" (p. 86); and Gilroy (1987). (I have not found a Hyderabadi yet engaged in this "black" politics.)

18. Prince Muffakham Jah of Hyderabad and London attended the Los Angeles Hyderabad Association annual dinner as chief guest on October 11, 1992; he was quoting a young Hyderabadi, and he repeated the view to me in London on December 20, 1992. The younger of two grandsons of the seventh and last Nizam, Muffakham Jah is widely respected by Hyderabadis.

19. Despite the humorous tone taken here, I learned a great deal by working on the questionnaires with Professor M. A. Muttalib, of Hyderabad, where he heads MUAVIN (Mutual Assistance for Voluntary Organizations in India), and Los Angeles, California.

20. James Ferguson and Akhil Gupta (1997) discuss resistance "as an experience that transforms the identity of subjects," quoting Foucault (1991, 27). They talk about how resistance "transforms the way in which they are subject to someone else" and "serves to reshape subjects by untying or untidying that relationship"; the remarks apply to the youngsters and their parents.

21. Recent films about and by South Asian young people show the nondisclosure of actions. In Elise Fried's *Do You Take This Man: Pakistani Arranged Marriages,* a mother says that love for one's parents means trusting their choice of one's spouse—a daughter who insists on choosing her own spouse is rejecting parental love. The British Asian filmmaker Gurinder Chadha's *Bhaji on the Beach* features a love relationship kept secret from the girl's parents.

22. The continuance of marriages with close relatives, among Muslims or South Indian Hindus, is one way of avoiding risks. Young women raised in the United States and Canada are said to have no patience, to be unwilling to spend years trying to make a marriage work.

23. The Punjab was divided into two parts at partition, and the Punjabi descendants of Muslims from Pakistan felt enough emotional attachment to reclassify themselves as Spanish

Punjabis, though there is little effort to follow Pakistani politics. The Hyderabadis also divided into Indian and Pakistani Hyderabadis, since many Muslims migrated to Pakistan at that time. Space does not permit a discussion in this essay of the Pakistani Hyderabadis, now quite different from those in India.

References

Abelmann, Nancy, and John Lie. 1995. *Blue Dreams: Korean Americans and the Los Angeles Riots.* Cambridge, Mass.: Harvard University Press.

Ali, Faiz-u-Nisa A. 1991. *The Path of Islam, Book 3* (3d ed.). Tustin, Calif.: International Islamic Educational Institute.

Athar, Shahid. 1994. *Reflections of an American Muslim.* Chicago: KAZI Publications, Inc.

Bawa, V. K. 1992. *The Last Nizam: The Life and Times of Mir Osman Ali Khan.* New Delhi: Penguin.

Bhabha, Homi. 1987. Interrogating Identity. In *Identity.* Edited by Homi Bhabha. London: Institute of Contemporary Arts, 5–11.

Butt, Helen B., ed. 1990. *The Composite Nature of Hyderabadi Culture.* Hyderabad: Intercultural Cooperation Hyderabad Chapter and Osmania University.

Chambers, Iain. 1994. *Migrancy, Culture, Identity.* London: Routledge.

Chock, Phyllis Pease. 1987. The irony of stereotypes: Toward an anthropology of ethnicity. *Cultural Anthropology* 2:3, 347–68.

Clifford, James. 1989. Notes on Theory and Travel. In *Traveling Theory Traveling Theorists.* Edited by James Clifford and Vivek Dhareshwar. Santa Cruz: Center for Cultural Studies, 177–88.

Copland, Ian. 1988. Communalism in princely India: The case of Hyderabad, 1930–40. *Modern Asian Studies* 22:4, 783–814.

Ferguson, James, and Akhil Gupta. 1992. Beyond "culture": Space, identity, and the politics of difference. *Cultural Anthropology* 7:1, 6–23.

———. 1997. *Culture, Power, Place: Explorations in Critical Anthropology.* Durham, N.C.: Duke University Press.

Foucault, Michel. 1991. *Remarks on Marx: Conversations with Duccio Trombadori.* Translated by James Goldstein and James Casciato. New York: Semiotext(e).

Gilroy, Paul. 1987. *There Ain't No Black in the Union Jack: The Cultural Politics of Race and Nation.* London: Hutchinson.

———. 1993. " 'It Ain't Where You're From, It's Where You're At': The Dialects of Diaspora Identification." In *Small Acts: Thoughts on the Politics of Black Cultures,* edited by Paul Gilroy. Pp. 120–43. London: Serpent's Tail.

Hall, Stuart. 1987. Minimal Selves. In *Identity.* Edited by Homi Bhabha. London: Institute of Contemporary Arts.

———. 1992. The Question of Cultural Identity. In *Modernity and Its Futures.* Edited by Stuart Hall, David Held, and Tony McGrew. London: Polity Press, Open University, pp. 273–316.

Handler, Richard. 1985. On dialogue and destructive analysis: Problems in narrating nationalism and ethnicity. *Journal of Anthropological Research* 41:2, 171–82.

Henderson, Jeffrey, and Manuel Castells. 1987. *Global Restructuring and Territorial Development.* Newbury Park, Calif.: Sage.

Jensen, Joan M. 1988. *Passage from India: Asian Indian Immigrants in North America.* New Haven: Yale University Press.

Keith, Michael, and Steve Pile, eds. 1993. *Place and the Politics of Identity.* London: Routledge.

Leonard, Karen Isaksen. 1973. The Deccani synthesis in old Hyderabad: An historiographic essay. *Journal of the Pakistan Historical Society,* 24(4), 205–18.

————. 1978. Mulki—non-Mulki Conflict in Hyderabad State. In *People, Princes and Paramount Power: Society and Politics in the Indian Princely States.* Edited by Robin Jeffrey. Oxford: Oxford University Press, 65–108.

————. 1992. *Making Ethnic Choices: California's Punjabi Mexican Americans.* Philadelphia: Temple University Press.

————. 1997. *The South Asian Americans.* Westport, Conn.: Greenwood Press.

————. 1999a. Construction of Identity in Diaspora: Emigrants from Hyderabad, India. In *The Expanding Landscape: South Asians in Diaspora.* Edited by Carla Petievich. Delhi: Manohar.

————. 1999b. The Management of Desire: Sexuality and Marriage for Young South Asian Women in America. In *Emerging Voices: South Asian American Women Redefine Self, Family and Community.* Edited by Sangeeta Gupta. Newbury Park: Sage.

————. Forthcoming. California's Punjabi Pioneers: Remembering/Claiming Homelands. In *Movement and Memory: Pre- Partition India.* Edited by Paul Greenough.

Lofgren, Orvar. 1991. Learning to Remember and Learning to Forget: Class and Memory in Modern Sweden. In *Erinnern und Vergesse.* Edited by Brigitte Bonisch-Brednich, Rolf W. Brednich, and Helge Gerndt. Gottingen: V. Schmerse, 145–61.

Lowe, Lisa. 1991. Heterogeneity, hybridity, multiplicity: Marking Asian American differences. *Diaspora* 1:1, 24–44.

Nanji, Azim A. 1993. The Muslim Family in North America: Continuity and Change. In *Family Ethnicity: Strength in Diversity.* Edited by Harriette Pipes McAdoo. Newbury Park: Sage.

Oberoi, Harjot S. 1988. From Ritual to Counter-Ritual: Rethinking the Hindu-Sikh Question, 1884–1915. In *Sikh History and Religion in the Twentieth Century.* Edited by Joseph T. O'Connell et al. Toronto: Centre for South Asian Studies, University of Toronto, 136–58.

————. 1994. *The Construction of Religious Boundaries: Culture, Identity and Diversity in the Sikh Tradition.* New York: Oxford University Press.

Pandey, Gyanendra. 1990. *Construction of Communalism in Colonial India.* Delhi: Oxford University Press.

Puri, Harish K. 1992. *Ghadar Movement* (2d ed.). Amritsar: Guru Nanak Dev University Press.

Radhakrishnan, R. 1987. Culture as common ground: Ethnicity and beyond. *MELUS* 14:2, 5–19.

Rushdie, Salman. 1990. *In Good Faith.* London: Granta.

Safran, William. 1991. Diasporas in modern societies: Myths of homeland and return. *Diaspora* 1:1, 83–99.

Schrager, Samuel. 1983. What is social in oral history? *International Journal of Oral History* 4:2, 76–98.

Scott, Sir Walter. [1825] 1958. *The Talisman.* London: Collins.

Sirajuddin, Syed. 1990. Deccan-Hyderabadi Culture. Unpublished ms., Hyderabad.

van der Veer, Peter. 1994. *Religious Nationalism: Hindus and Muslims in India.* Berkeley: University of California Press.

Varshney, Ashutosh. 1997. Postmodernism, civic engagement and ethnic conflict: A passage to India. *Comparative Politics* (October): 1–20.

Vatuk, Sylvia, and Ved P. Vatuk. 1969. Protest Songs of Indians on the West Coast, U.S.A. In *Thieves in My House: Four Studies in Indian Folklore of Protest and Change.* Edited by Ved Vatuk. Varanasi: Vishwavidyalaya Prakashan, 63–80.

Williams, Raymond. 1991. Asian Indian Muslims in the United States. In *Indian Muslims in North America*. Edited by Omar Khalidi. Watertown, Mass.: South Asia Press, pp. 17–25.

Wong, Sau Ling. 1995. Denationalization reconsidered: Asian American cultural criticism at a theoretical crossroads. *Amerasia Journal* 21:(1&2), 1–27.

Yans-McLaughlin, Virginia. 1990. Metaphors of Self in History: Subjectivity, Oral Narrative, and Immigration Studies. In *Immigration Reconsidered: History, Sociology, and Politics*. Edited by Virginia Yans-McLaughlin. New York: Oxford University Press, 254–90.

Louisa Schein

10   Forged Transnationality and Oppositional Cosmopolitanism

A couple years ago I found myself in an unexpected position. As an anthropologist working with the Miao in China and with Hmong refugees from Laos, I had suddenly landed in the role of transnational marriage broker. Certain Hmong men, troubled by the unnerving Americanization of "their" women, had begun to seek more "traditional" marriage partners among their putative co-ethnics in the romantic Chinese homeland. These men—who were steeped in dreamlike memories of a Laos they felt they had lost due to U.S. withdrawal from the anti-Communist effort they had fought passionately as their own—were turning now to an imagined China their ancestors had left many generations before. It was a China that, on the one hand, they abhorred, as the once-Imperial now-Communist oppressor of their people. But it was nevertheless this same China that purportedly housed the most archaic pockets of their tradition left on earth. This tradition could be had through an importing technique akin to the mail-ordering of brides from Asia by nostalgic "first world" men that has been interrogated elsewhere (Tolentino 1996; Villepando 1989; Wilson 1988). Wielding their Americanness, Hmong men could get culture back by playing on the desires of Miao women within China, desires for a liberation that their future husbands would both proffer and deny.

But it was not Hmong men who were asking me to be their agent. Rather, Miao women, during and after a trip I made to China in 1993, hoped that I would make introductions and convey photographs.[1] Moreover, once communication was initiated, language issues might arise. Some of the Miao dialects were so unintelligible with Hmong dialect as to make telephone conversation nearly impossible. Beyond that, Miao knew Chinese, and Hmong knew English, but that meant that courtship letters had to be painstakingly composed through interpreters. A final recourse was the American anthropologist, who could translate faxes and phone calls, paving the way for more intimate communications and expediting the crafting of an ethnic bond into a transnational marital union.

I want to begin my reflections on this and related stories yet to be told by exploring the potential space opened by Bruce Robbins in an essay on "Comparative Cosmopolitanisms" (1993). Robbins travels through critiques of multiculturalism, the problematic of situatedness, the commentary on global culture, through Mohanty, Spivak, Said, and especially Clifford (and this is not a complete list), to arrive at a revision to our recoil from the notion of cosmopolitanism as nothing but a circumscribed site of privilege from which "free-floating intellectuals" reproduce their elitism through assertions of universality. The antidote for the queasiness of totalizing privilege, Robbins argues, cannot be as simple as valorizing the particularity of the local. Instead, Robbins builds on Clifford's notion of traveling cultures, on the latter's assertion that "the representational challenge is . . . the portrayal and understanding of local/global historical encounters, co-productions, dominations and resistances" (Clifford 1992, 101). The space Robbins makes is for cosmopolitanism to be more widely distributed, to be non-elite, situated and yet somehow worldly. "Instead of renouncing cosmopolitanism as a false universal, one can embrace it as an impulse to knowledge that is shared with others, a striving to transcend partiality that is itself partial, but no more so than the similar cognitive strivings of many diverse peoples" (Robbins 1993, 194). Variant cosmopolitanisms could be located, then, among those who have long constituted elite cosmopolitanism's "others": among migrant workers, for instance, or among indigenous intermediaries that intervene in the construction of ethnographies, or among diasporic groups imaginatively traveling toward "home." "The world's particulars," Robbins proposes, "can now be recoded, in part at least, as the world's 'discrepant cosmopolitanisms'" (1993, 194).

From this point of departure I want to wander further, to consider the *discrepancies* between cosmopolitanisms as vital interstices from which oppositionality could be enunciated. I want to push beyond the recognition that cosmopolitanisms will vary predictably according to the degree to which they emerge, on the one hand, from power and privilege—as in the case of, say, tourists or mobile capitalisms—or, on the other hand, from constraint or economic disadvantage—as in the case of, say, refugees or guest workers. Cosmopolitanisms, in their multiple incarnations, ought instead to be thought of as processual and as *potentially* renegotiating precisely that nexus of privilege and constraint that conditions them. This is, obviously, an optimistic scenario, but one that, given what I will present below, may deserve to be examined.

In a recent essay, community studies specialist Michael Peter Smith affirmed the importance of looking at the kind of multilocal grass roots political activism that takes place in transnational contexts. This is a kind of activism that reflects what he calls the "polyfocality" (1994, 28) of human agents who reveal themselves to be capable of "thinking and acting simultaneously at multiple scales" (p. 25)—particularly those of the subnational and the supranational. Translocal activism, Smith holds, not only evades state structures, but may in fact erode their sovereignty (p. 31). Critical to this destabilization is the work of fashioning identities that accompanies or propels social movements:

> The reprocessing of identity by those who once saw their lives as more or less predictably constrained by the givenness of established orders may produce new emancipatory social movements with a high degree of political efficacy. (Smith 1994, 31)

Smith's comments are provocative, especially for formulating transnational research agendas, but I would suggest that as anthropologists we may want to cast our nets considerably wider than the focus on social movements and overt activism would entail. I suspect that ethnographies attentive to multilocal linkages will turn up a great deal of subterranean activity that may not name itself as activism, may not focus around oppositionality, but may in fact have the *effect* of subverting the constraints of the territorially-based state. As ethnographers, then, and interpreters of ethnographic data, let us attend not only to resistance *per se* but to oppositionality as an effect of translocal practices—especially those practices concerned with identity production.

Attending to cosmopolitanisms' effects, then, raises a number of questions at different levels. Specifically, how might the active forging of transnationality to which diasporas have lately given rise unsettle the logic of the nation-state and of superpower politics? Must the identity politics of such transnational moves inevitably devolve into reinvented particularisms, no matter how globalized? Is it conceivable that they could be anything other than complicit with and structured by global capitalism? When translocal identities defy particular states, how likely are they to instead be complicit with global capitalism?[2] And, finally, should the voluntary unions of Miao women from China and Hmong refugee men in the United States (through the less than voluntary brokerage of an American feminist anthropologist) be read as some form of critique or only as the latest incarnation of a nostalgia-driven practice of raiding the "third world"?[3]

This essay will entertain these and other questions through looking ethnographically at what I call "identity exchanges" between Hmong and Miao across the Pacific. I intend my use of "ethnographic" to be provocative, since the character of this kind of research is necessarily divergent from a conventional sense of ethnography. Because it is siteless and lacks any fixed duration, I have cast it as "itinerant." I will expand upon this issue of itinerant ethnography further after a brief introduction to Hmong-Miao transnationality. . . . Throughout this essay, I will enact my own polyfocality, shifting rapidly between the perspectives of the minority and the state, and those of China and the United States, in order to demonstrate how densely articulated these positionings are.

Cultural Production and the Forging of Transnationality

The ethnic bond that Hmong and Miao agents have been avidly kindling in recent years is being forged virtually "from scratch." The cumbersome umbrella term
"Miao," which became naturalized as an official category of ethnic agency in China's
Maoist decades, refers to a number of disparate groups totaling 7.5 million people,
speaking three mutually unintelligible dialects and scattered over seven provinces
in southwest China. One to two centuries ago, several hundred thousand of these
people migrated out of China into Vietnam, Laos, and Thailand after conflicts with
the Qing state. These are the people who, by Southeast Asian and Western convention,
are referred to as the Hmong. This migration took place enough generations ago that
direct kinship ties and living memories of the Miao in China have been forgotten.
What has not been forgotten is that China represents the homeland.

Several generations of Hmong migrants to Southeast Asia have assiduously kept
the memories of China alive through folklore and oral history. In funerals, for instance,
when a Hmong ritualist anywhere in the world guides the soul of a deceased person
back to a place where it can be at rest, the ultimate destination is a mythologized
China, shrouded in authenticity and the aura of origins. Those Hmong who left their
subsistence agrarian lives in Laos to resettle in American cities long not only for the
land they inhabited most recently. Like other refugees, their longing for the land of
earliest origins has become hyper-acute as a consequence of what they remember as
an involuntary ejection from the peaceful, independent, pastoral lives they once led.
The obsession with loss has inspired a tremendously productive array of cultural
practices, many of which are directly concerned with recovering China. Hmong
cultural producers have thrown themselves into reinventing both their homeland and
their ancestors, unflinchingly creating ties of putative kinship out of the vacuum that
was centuries of isolation. At the same time, the political and economic ramifications
of this recuperative project are not lost upon them. Their practices constitute what
Stuart Hall has so aptly called "identity as a 'production'" (1989, 68). The artifact that
emerges from this identity production is a multivalent and potent transnationality.

What are the strategies through which Hmong refugees are crafting this transnationality? The players in this project are not the "transmigrants" that Basch, Glick-
Schiller, and Szanton Blanc (1994) have described, nor exemplars of the "flexible
citizenship" identified by Ong (1994). Firmly based in territorial sites, Hmong-Miao
identity production is heavily conditioned by the U.S.-China disparity. Periodic travel,
as well as the movement of objects, images, and most recently brides, comprises the
ground on which identity elaborations are being constructed. A general notion of
fraternity as well as more particularized bonds of fictive kinship and marriage alliance
are the idioms out of which a sense of mutual obligation is produced—as discussed
further below. What does it mean to do research on a vagrant identity-in-production?
Because of the mobility of the cultural producers and their products, my research on
this process has of necessity been multisited and episodic. Indeed, to talk about "sites"
seems not the point since there is no *place* one can go to watch this process unfold.

Often, too, as in the case of the marriage negotiations above, the encounter with "data" has been unplanned or incidental. This itinerant ethnography compels me to chase cultural products and events around the globe, and often to settle for their discursive traces in anecdote or written account. The story is assembled piecemeal, then, and on its own schedule. I must be consigned to stay home and answer the phone, or to collect representational objects and second-hand accounts of events. Sometimes, I travel great distances to do participant observation at international gatherings as far-flung as California, Minnesota, or Hunan. I want to make a case for these nomadlike methods, not as second order or secondary, but as the legitimate primary sources for a research that works out of whichever margins its subjects are working within. These margins are akin to those that Anna Tsing (1994) has theorized as significant sites for new forms of cultural analysis, but unlike Tsing's, these margins are not situated only in what she calls "out-of-the-way places" (p. 284).

What have been the consequences, then, for the once-idealized detachment of the researcher when she works in these shifting venues? In addition to itinerancy, my privilege has been called upon as my resources and mobility have been targeted as vehicles for transpacific identity exchanges. Over fourteen years of research, I have been a porter, a translator, a keynote speaker, a networker, a broker. I have been a transmitter of messages, of precious objects, of texts. I have been the link through which many a transnational relationship has been inaugurated. Throughout, my partisanship to Hmong-Miao unification has gone unquestioned. How else could I better deconstruct my ethnographic authoriality than to let myself be thus employed as a conduit for the agency of the other? How contradictory, then, that I should embark on writing about it, as I am doing here.

Video Hegemony

One of the chief means by which the Miao of the Chinese homeland are being recovered by Hmong in the West is the video image.[4] Some Hmong businessmen who have saved money in other enterprises have invested in video cameras and, upon attainment of a U.S. passport, have jetted off to China as tourists in search of roots. Touching down on homeland soil, their cameras play lovingly over every detail: the curve of the mountains, the costume of the young women, a toast of liquor from their hosts, a villager's song. Shepherd children head up the mountainsides straddling water buffaloes . . . women beat the filth out of clothing at sparkling streams . . . families squat around a communal hot pot of bubbling pork, bak choy, and chilies. Thick with nostalgia, this type of video image is most marketable to the Hmong American elderly, who have lost the strength to travel themselves, but retain an inviolable sanctuary in their memories for the pastoral lives they lost.[5]

Pristine visions of their Miao co-ethnics are not the only images they bring back, however. Some would-be documentarians never make it to Miao villages since they travel under official tourist statuses. Instead, they turn their cameras onto China itself—the figure, simultaneously, of the historically oppressive other, but at the same time of an ancient, originary power with which to affiliate. Scenes of the Great Wall, of city streets, of staged ethnic performances, of the tour buses themselves, fill these taped narratives of the travel experience. Such visual musings seem to intimate a subtextual wondering: "What would it have been like if we had never left?" Here the "we" is distilled into an historical agent, the one who took the giant step out of China that eventuated in their exile to the West. The videos, then, simulate a traveling backward in time, a retracing of migratory paths—hence the interest in travel narratives themselves as subject matter.

Faye Ginsburg has proposed looking at indigenous, or more generally fourth-world, media production practices such as these as positive trends in the context of a global economy of representation that still leaves fourth-world peoples relatively mute:

> Indigenous media offers a possible means—social, cultural, and political—for reproducing and transforming cultural identity among people who have experienced massive political, geographic, and economic disruption. The capabilities of media to transcend boundaries of time, space, and even language are being used effectively to mediate, literally, historically produced social ruptures and to help construct identities that link past and present in ways appropriate to contemporary conditions. (Ginsburg 1991, 94)

From this perspective, the video cassette and its tremendous portability is a formidable medium for ethnic learning across great spatial divides. Produced in Hmong language, exclusively targeted for intra-ethnic consumption, the China tapes constitute means for the simulated reduction of the cultural distance engendered by history. The tapes circulate widely in the West and, for Hmong that lack the resources to travel themselves, they function as a salve to the wounds of their own war-induced dislocation. Voraciously consumed, they offer the next best thing to being in the homeland.

But there is more to be read in the manufacture of these cultural products. In most cases, their producers are not merely disinterested disseminators of cultural messages. They are entrepreneurs who have hit upon a means to derive profit from the relative disadvantage of their co-ethnics. They often have their own video companies—I know of at least twenty in the United States—with names such as Mong Enterprises Home Video (Minneapolis), S. T. Universal Video (Fresno), Southeast Asia Video Production (Chicago), and Hmong Traditional Video Cassette of China and U.S.A. (Minneapolis). In addition to China documentaries these companies also produce a range of genres— love dramas, war and martial arts stories, music videos of Hmong bands—all intended for Hmong consumption. Their products, including the China tapes, are packaged slickly in illustrated, shrink-wrapped boxes with copyright warnings printed on the outside and repeated along with the credits on the leaders to the videos. The cultural material therein is transformed into the intellectual property of the video producers. Not for random copying, they are for sale only. They are distributed by mail order and at large-scale ethnic events such as the Hmong New Year fair in Fresno, California, where stall after stall of small vendors offer official copies of these tapes for twenty to thirty dollars apiece. For the majority of less affluent Hmong refugees whose dreams may be limited to earning minimum wage, the homeland can be vicariously had, but only for a dear price.

This marketing of origins is also significant in terms of the relation it establishes between elite Hmong travelers and their landlocked objects of ethnic recuperation in China whose own prospects for travel are virtually nonexistent. It is the Miao peasants in the southwest China highlands who are the source of the greatest fascination for the nostalgic eyes of Hmong refugees in the West. For centuries, exoticizing dominant Han representations derogated the Miao as figures of wildness at the fringes of the Chinese empire. Then, in the Maoist and post-Mao decades their cultures were promoted and celebrated, but according to a pernicious logic that blithely conflated their essentialized "tradition" with the stigma of backwardness. From the perspective of Miao peasants, then, while the fascinated gaze of their own co-ethnics is undoubtedly far more welcome than that of a contemptuous majority other, it nonetheless preserves the asymmetry of the gaze—an asymmetry rooted in differential economic conditions. For Hmong Americans, Miao co-ethnics are largely a leisure activity, spicing up their idle hours with spectoral entertainment while Miao peasants, on the other hand, don't have VCRs in *their* living rooms on which to watch reciprocal images of their migrant "cousins" going about their first-world lives.[6]

Elite Hmong cultural producers, then, cannot be immune from the kind of cautions that Rey Chow has posed for the category of "third world intellectuals" in the West. For Chow, these discourse-producers, among whom she classes herself, "need to unmask [themselves] through a scrupulous declaration of self-interest" (1993, 117), in which their championing of minority discourse is no less implicated in what Spivak called "empire-nation exchanges" (1990, 90) than that of Euro-American intellectuals who would presume to speak for the voiceless other. For Chow, the identification with the "third world" implicit in diasporic claims harbors special dangers:

> Physical alienation . . . can mean precisely the intensification and aestheticization of the values of "minority" positions that had developed in the earlier struggles and that have now, in "third world" intellectuals' actual circumstances in the West, become defunct. The unself-reflexive sponsorship of "third world" culture . . . becomes a mask that conceals the hegemony of these intellectuals over those who are stuck at home.
>
> For "third world" intellectuals, the lures of diaspora consist in this masked hegemony. . . . Their resort to "minority discourse," . . . veils their own fatherhood over the "ethnics" at home even while it continues to legitimize them as "ethnics" and "minorities" in the West. (1993, 118)

The production of Hmong video, then, is a powered practice that cannot circumvent some form of first world—third world asymmetry. The fact that its circulation is intentionally and almost entirely intra-ethnic, however, also positions it to be deployed otherwise in ways that potentially foil dominant appropriation. When contextualized in light of the practices of Miao cultural producers *within* China, its power appears more multivectoral. The unilateral character of Hmong production of the romanticized Miao other is tempered by the ways in which Miao are deploying *self-representation*. . . .

Identity Exchanges

Hmong refugees come to the encounter with homeland Miao with multiple intentionalities, the most salient of which are the quest for roots and the quest for profits. In addition to video and travel, however, there are additional ways that Hmong in the West have been consuming the Miao of China. Hmong ethnic style, for instance, has begun to bear the mark of the recent encounter with Chinese origins: at festivals and on special occasions on which Hmong refugees dress in ethnic garb, imported clothing from the Miao in China has become quite fashionable. Although the variation from their original Southeast Asian style of festival dress may be minimal, these imported styles are instantly recognizable to Western Hmong as prestige emblems because of their association with the homeland. The adoption of an obviously differing style of dress than that of one's own subgroup is a decisive announcement of pan-ethnic identity and of a disregard for intragroup distinctions. In the context of the Hmong becoming an American minority, this dress practice could also be seen as symbolizing what Kobena Mercer called a "reconstitutive link" (1990, 253) with the homeland— one that asserted a pristine unity prior to segmentation by the political borders of modern states.

Beyond adopting imported dress, Hmong refugees are also importing actual Miao from China, especially as objects of entertainment at festivals. The craving to gaze upon a homeland native and putative bearer of one's most ancient traditions has inspired Hmong refugees to collectively put up funds for all-expenses-paid visits to the United States for Miao who have particular cultural resources to offer. At the 1993 Fresno Hmong New Year fair, for instance, three young women from China's Yunnan province were brought over. Bedecked in multilayered embroidery and silver, weighted down with cumbersome headdresses, they were asked to appear on stage over and over again to sing the songs of courtship, hospitality, and folk history that U.S. Hmong longed to hear. As emblems of authenticity, they were paraded about in costume, drawing stares and whispers from Hmong fair-goers who imagined themselves to be witnessing their very past incarnate.

So far, the sketch I have drawn of U.S. Hmong consumption of their homeland co-ethnics is one that smacks of unilateral objectification. Celebratory as it is, it amounts to a production of the other as both other and constitutive of the self, but not as autonomous agent. The Miao in China who encounter this appropriation, however, do not resent it but, on the contrary, welcome it as a fraternal embrace. Their own cultural practices are highly complicit with Hmong representation of them as less "modern" and as bearers of tradition. In fact, they offer themselves and their purported cultural expertise almost as prestations in an ongoing exchange that they hope will have other consequences. What strategies are Miao pursuing in their nurturing of identifying bonds with diaspora communities?

The recent years of the post-Mao reform experiment have seen significant political and regional realignments for the people who inhabit China's remote interior. Reform policy in the 1980s was one of what I have called "scripted difference" (Schein 1996) in which relative economic stasis was what was prescribed for the subsistence producers of the hinterland while capital was relentlessly extracted for joint venture investment in Special Economic Zones along the coast. Minority peasants were particularly set up for exclusion from the putative economic miracle that transformed the coast and many urban sites; their economic marginalization was rationalized precisely by their imposed and valorized role as cultural conservators.[7] With few resources for household enterprises, many families have resorted to sending their teenaged children to labor for wages on farms and in factories in more rapidly developing regions. In addition to their omission from China's grand prosperity schemes based on enforced uneven development, minorities and others in the interior saw decentralization, structural reform, the responsibility system, and other reforms smash the iron rice bowls on which many had come to depend. Concomitantly, reduced state intervention in affirmation action-type policies that had ensured minority places in education, jobs, and government likewise resulted in their progressive exclusion and impoverishment.

Miao elites—intellectuals and party cadres—alarmed and angered at the acute consequences of post-Mao reforms for their people, turned to the embrace of identity politics as a vehicle for voicing their concerns.[8] Many of these elites who, during the Maoist and early post-Mao days were well on the way to a kind of intra-ethnic class formation in which they would have constituted the upper stratum, have done an about face and become passionate advocates for less advantaged members of their ethnic group. Ironically (since many of them are still speaking from within the state), it was precisely the withdrawal of state presence from their lives—the decline in state planning, protection, and redistribution—that they were protesting. The overarching objection was to the velocity with which their region and their people were being pushed to the ever more distant margins of Chinese economic life. Their requests, then, were addressed to the state and comprised of demands for greater inclusion in the national economy and in what are perceived as its newfound riches, for representation in advocacy positions in the government, and for protected opportunities in education and employment. But these requests, in the assessment of Miao proponents, go largely unheeded.

The arrival of what appear to them as tremendously prosperous overseas Hmong has coincided with the formation of this increasingly organized and oppositional Miao elite. Hyper-aware of the way in which Chinese state policy circumscribed their futures, Miao see an opening up of alternative possibilities embodied in these roots-seeking co-ethnics who hail from the first world. If Miao peasants represented an object of nostalgic longing for urban American Hmong, the latter likewise have come to represent a focal point for the desires of Chinese Miao who seek to circumvent the limits imposed upon them by a Chinese national plan that allocates to them only sacrifice and patient labor.

These Miao elites, then, have elaborated myriad ways of enmeshing the U.S. Hmong with them culturally and economically. Some are purchasing or manufacturing ethnic costumes to be shipped or carried overseas for sale through Hmong brokers for what constitute high returns by Chinese standards. Some organize international Miao studies conferences to which overseas Hmong are graciously invited as the most special of guests. Some record and send audio tapes or develop pen pals in order to foster long-term communication. Some have designed language or culture classes that they hope to market to Hmong travelers-turned-pupils who will stay in China long enough to embark on a course of study to learn where they came from culturally. In 1996, the Institute of Cultural Research of the Miao Nationality in Hunan offered an eight-week course promoted through contact persons in the United States. The preamble to the course description went as follows (note the language of "compatriots" and that the Miao authors do not use "Hmong"—the preferred ethnonym in the United States):

> Through two international seminars on the Miao nationality, we understand many scholars mentioned that they didn't know much about the history and culture of the Chinese Miao nationality, and hope to have an opportunity to come to China for studying the history and culture of the Miao nationality. In order to meet the demands of our compatriots of the Miaos in foreign countries, we decided to run a class for advanced studies of the Miao's history and culture. Our compatriots of the Miaos in America are welcome to take an active part in the class.

With a tuition of four hundred dollars, the course offered not only classroom instruction in history and culture, but also training in Chinese language for those interested in widening their ventures in China, and "on the spot" investigation for those interested in first-hand visits to their rural origins. In this way, through a structured and academicized medium, culture was delivered and the homeland saw returns.

These ventures are not reducible, however, to the instrumentality of economic transactions. Central to this project is the cultivating of Hmong obligation based on appeals to common cultural idioms of indebtedness. Miao elites hasten to host Hmong visitors to China offering conveniences such as arranging their touring and accompanying them at every moment. Most common is the banquet thrown to enact Miao hospitality rituals, bestowing the glow of cultural intactness on the nostalgic travelers. No matter how limited their means, Miao hosts struggle to put on lavish spreads of high-prestige food and to assemble an entourage to dine along with the guests. The proffering of liquor to the guests' lips, accompanied by ceremonial welcoming songs, constitutes the most significant offering. In the course of these meals an aura of kin-bonding is created; brothers are constituted out of strangers through partaking in the ritual feast. Kin obligation comes to function very powerfully in these forged familial ties. To the dislocated Hmong, Miao offer identity; in exchange they hope for concrete returns in the form of sponsorship for overseas study or travel, joint venture investment in Miao-run enterprises, charitable donations for the Miao poor, subsidies for education, and academic publishing.

But immediate concrete returns are not the only aim of these offerings. On the contrary, as I've said, they are better seen as prestations that, according to the age-old logic of reciprocity, put the Miao in long-term positions to make claims on their privileged co-ethnics overseas. The Miao elites who enter into these identity exchanges envision a growing thicket of linkages that will consolidate the Miao in China with the Hmong in the West in a potent alliance of mutual aid, an ethic of reciprocal commitment born of their shared lot as minorities wherever they are located. I turn now to examining the process by which such cultural and economic exchanges come to assume political valences.

Oppositional Cosmopolitanism

There is a noteworthy dissonance in the intentionalities that Hmong in the West and Miao in China bring to their enthusiastic reunion. While the former seek a territorial centering—a return home, a recovery of the land of origins—the latter envision themselves detached from the land, despite their boundedness to it in terms of livelihood and legal citizenship. Dislocated Hmong in diaspora feel flung to the farthest reaches from what they consider home. The direction of their movement, both psychic and spatial, is centripetal—toward an imagined locus both of the steadfastness of culture and of a potential wellspring of political vitality. When anomic youth gangs began to form in refugee Hmong communities, some Hmong elders invited a visiting Miao intellectual from China to meet with the young gang members to instruct them in how to be upstanding members of their ethnic community. In addition, some U.S. Hmong leaders have strategized for the loyalties of Hmong refugee followers by invoking whatever ties they have forged with Chinese Miao as a basis for their claim to power. That inalienable territory of the homeland, then, constant and stalwart, has become a leitmotif in the social imaginary of Hmong "out of place."

Meanwhile, Miao desires for transnational identification aim to defy space. Their strategy is to fan out over the globe through diasporic ties, to derive political strength precisely from their irreverence for national borders. This represents a significant realignment in their conceptualization of belonging. I hold that, for the post-1949 era at least, it was not until the last few years of the reform period (i.e., the 1990s) that Miao developed a sense of oppositionality toward China. In the Maoist (1949–1979) and early reform (1979–1989) periods, they were caught up in nationalist projects, building a strong sense of Chineseness vis-à-vis the West, throwing their cultural essence into the amalgam that was to constitute the multi-ethnic Chinese people. The Chinese state, for the most part, was seen as their patron, their benefactor, their protector from the vagaries of economic caprice to which both nature and the market had subjected them in centuries past. Deeply disaffected with the trajectory that post-Mao reform took, however, they then turned away from a Chinese national project that had devolved into the proliferation of invidious difference. They have turned more recently toward a transnational source of identity that could yield the possibilities for development that the reform process had denied them.

The coalescence of interests that impels the Miao-Hmong forging of transnationality has permitted the elaboration of common identity despite communication barriers and cultural disjunctions. An article in a newsletter of the Hmong American Partnership (HAP) aptly exemplifies the coevalness of concrete exchanges and identity production. I quote at length to reveal the interweavings in the text:

> The gap between Hmong Americans and Hmong Chinese became a little narrower last spring, when HAP had the honor of briefly hosting Mr. Wu Zi Ming (Nom Kav Vwj), a Chinese-Hmong government official . . . to explore the possibility of developing formal relationships with organizations . . . to promote educational, economic and cultural exchange between Hmong communities of our two nations. . . . The brief meeting was a momentous occasion for all who were there. . . . Everyone who was there walked away enriched by the experience and the opportunity to reach back in time and connect with Hmong history and Hmong heritage. It is hoped that there will be more contact with our fellow Hmong in China and elsewhere as Hmong Americans continue to strive for prosperity and the world becomes an increasingly smaller place. (Hmong American Partnership 1996, 3)

Similarly, idioms of kinship are elaborated not on the basis of spatial proximity, but precisely on the basis of their ability to bridge the vastness of space and the gulfs between cultures. When a Miao intellectual from China visited a Hmong family in Washington, D.C., they had no one to translate their mutually unintelligible dialects. They called me in New Jersey to act as interpreter and passed the phone back and forth for a brief interchange. The Hmong American host asked whether the food they cooked was palatable. Yes, if I stick to Hmong food and stay away from Western food and raw vegetables, he offered back, stressing ethnic solidarity. Would he like them to place an international call so he could talk to his family in China? That would be nice, but not necessary, he demurred, highlighting his hosts' role as surrogate kin: he was happy just to be visiting with them. The host then made a short speech, proclaiming his joy at being able to receive a cousin from such a distant land right there in Washington, D.C. The invention of this type of extended kin network, I propose, has its lure precisely in its deterritorialized character, in its cosmopolitanism. While the space of the homeland comprises an alluring trope to be deployed in the crafting of common essence, it is, on the contrary, the *multisite* feature of this newfound identity that makes it so compelling.

Hmong in the West and Miao in China have encountered, both historically and in the present, a relentless marginalization at the hands of large states that would incorporate them as others even as they maintain their difference. And both groups have been the targets of venomous national discourses—discourses that may exemplify the nationalist "pedagogy" that Bhabha (1990, 297) identified—that construct them as part of the nation-people either by exacting their selfless contribution or by chastising them for withholding it. In the current period, Miao have been expected to enact their loyalty to China by laboring patiently at eking subsistence rice out of scrappy mountain terraces while entrepreneurs on the coast prosper unimaginably. Hmong in the United States have been challenged to prove themselves worthy of the American citizenship they were promised by exchanging the everyday autonomy they retained on federal cash assistance for subjection to the wage work process.[9] And those who have "failed" to do so have in turn contributed inadvertently to their groups' imaging by journalists and social scientists as culturally "unfit" for U.S. society. One American anthropologist, for instance, pronounced with authority: "Taking into account their traditional existence . . . of the various Southeast Asian refugee groups the Hmong are culturally the most disparate from the receiving society" (Scott 1982, 146). *Newsweek*, resorting to racializing discourse, sneered, in a classic social-evolutionist slur: "The gene for adaptability is an elusive one; those who have it survive, those who lack it may not. . . . [The Hmong embroidered squares] don't quite fit in, like Hmong themselves" (*Newsweek*, July 7, 1980, p. 34).

Remaining as they do on the cultural and economic margins of the states in which they reside, the choice to travel the postnational, translocal trajectory that Appadurai (1993) has described seems almost ineluctable. An alternative identification forged out of cultural production and what I have called identity exchanges appears to Hmong and Miao as a potent antidote to a state loyalty gone sour. This identification defines itself, as Clifford noted, against both the "norms of nation-states" *and* those of "indigenous, and especially autochthonous, claims by 'tribal' peoples" (1994, 307). It can be viewed as oppositional precisely because of the way it mocks the constraints and exclusions that the state would impose, instead envisioning a plethora of linkages across the globe.[10]

Several qualifications must be raised, however, in entertaining this notion of op-positionality. First, it should not be conflated with secessionist impulses and with a diversion of interests entirely away from the state and from the national base in which each group is operating. Indeed, both Hmong in the U.S. and Miao in China juggle their transnational strategies and their local ones, striving, despite exclusions, for greater integration at home.[11] Second, as I have argued elsewhere (Schein 1998), the forging of transnationality may be not simply a set of autonomous moves, but may in fact be or appear consequential for the respective states. Certainly, China has been proactive in promoting the soliciting of donations, investments, and remittances from overseas Chinese (cf. Ong 1997, 174–75). Hmong of Lao origin, because of their homeland attachment to China, could conceivably come to occupy this position as well. Hence, oppositionality needs to be conceived in part as a product of involvements with the state, both consistent with and resistant to state aims. Third, this is an oppositionality the effects of which remain to be seen. Christoffersen holds that for the region of Xinjiang, "transnational forces contributed to Xinjiang's closer integration into the Chinese polity" (1993, 132) through a "bargaining" process in which strength gained through economic ties abroad enabled this peripheral region to achieve more of its economic aims within the domain of Chinese policy. It is early to assess whether Hmong-Miao transnationality will be so consequential—either in China or the in

United States—and certainly it is by no means comparable with global pan-Islamism or, for that matter, the economic might of the "Greater China" alliance (Ong 1997). But it is conceivable that bonds could strengthen to the extent that they gain significant state notice.[12]

What emerges out of a close reading of the Hmong-Miao forging of transnationality is a sense of a solidarity complexly fraught with inequality and difference. What to make of this difference? Is the necessary endpoint of this inquiry a recognition that Miao in China remain subjugated through their third-world status, remain the playful consumption objects of a set of globally traveling Hmong American entrepreneurs tantamount to a leisure class? Or worse, that they can only be consigned to occupying the box of cultural exotica, functioning as emblems of the kind of difference that sells in late capitalist modernity? Or is it possible to also think otherwise, to see this process of what Stuart Hall reluctantly dubbed "diaspora-ization" (1996, 447) as one that productively spans differences, without obliterating them, in a countermove to the globalization that connotes homogeneity? This encompassing of difference has been a key to much minority politics—fought at the site where class meets ethnicity and coalitions may form. Coalitional thinking is what Radhakrishnan (1995, 821) seeks to transpose to the transnational scale through his vision of "eccentric cosmopolitanism." His call is for a radical imagining of a "postrepresentational space where one group will have earned the right to speak for the other in a spirit of equal reciprocity" (p. 821). This speaking for the other is conceivable as oppositional when it is counterposed to the economic pragmatism of capitalism, when it defies the type of capitalist boundarilessness that fractures community.

This kind of ethnic mobilization, then, exemplifies Appadurai's escaped "nationalist genie," one that is out of the bottle of "ideas of spatial boundary and territorial sovereignty" (1993, 413). It is a mobilization that locates its strength precisely in its cosmopolitan character. It is not entirely free of some of the more pernicious features of colonial and nationalist discourses—the objectification of others in exoticizing nostalgia, the battling over women as the putative sites of tradition, the seizing upon cultural traits as essences—but it does replace some of those earlier logics. As an identity production, its inventiveness with regard to social forms and its unfixity with regard to cultural content enable it to transgress disempowering localisms in ways that should not be ignored.

Notes

I am indebted to many local people, scholars, and levels of government within China and the United States for their support of my research. For funding for a research trip to China in 1993 and for ongoing research in 1996–97, I thank the Rutgers University Research Council. I am grateful to the Rutgers-Princeton Interdisciplinary Conference "Placements/Displacements: The Politics of Location" organized by the Rutgers Center for the Critical Analysis of Contemporary Culture and the Princeton Theory of Literature and History Group and to Neil Smith for the first opportunity to present a version of this piece. For inspiration or comments during the development of the article, I would like to thank Michael Moffat and Bruce Robbins. I remain solely responsible for the final result.

1. See Tsing (1993) for a pertinent exploration of the initiative and narratives of Meratus Dayak women in Indonesia in seeking transnational relationships with men from other parts of Asia.

2. See a recent essay by Ong (1997) that interrogates narratives of "Greater China" as articulations of a modern identity wholly identified with the fluidity and global efficacy of late capitalism.

3. Despite its problematic effect of binarizing and overly homogenizing the two "worlds" (and conventionally leaving the "second" world under erasure), I retain the terminology of "first" and "third" worlds here for two reasons. First, it connotes a prestige structure that is very much in place in the transnational strategies of Hmong and Miao. Second, it positions these transnational moves within a larger context of ongoing global asymmetries that substantially condition and resonate with the particularities of this instance.

4. Comments in this section address the following two aspects: (1) social, political, and economic relations enacted in the production of videos and (2) the forms of representation revealed in the contents of the videos. These are components of a larger study of what I call the "China tapes" that will include interviews with video producers and reception studies among Hmong audiences.

5. See Litzinger (1995) for a comparable example among the Yao. He offers a trenchant critique of the overprivileging of hybridity in transnational identity production, emphasizing instead the equally significant impulse toward "cultural protection."

6. This stands in stark contrast to the situation reported by Hammond (1988) in which Tongan immigrants to Salt Lake City used video to create images of themselves. These videos of their lives and special ritual events were often sent back to relatives in their islands of origin as a means of communication and self-representation. To my knowledge this trajectory of communication is rarely found in the Hmong-Miao case, although photographs are often sent to China, especially as part of matchmaking ventures.

7. See Schein (2000) for an extended treatment of this process.

8. The resonance here and below with U.S. minority politics is striking and suggests not only parallels but perhaps also transnational flows influencing the framing of identity political strategies.

9. See my argument (Schein 1987) that Hmong secondary migration to and relatively high dependency on federal cash assistance in the California Central Valley in the 1980s was part and parcel of an enclavement strategy that had everything to do with social and cultural autonomy and with community formation. For an analysis of recent conditions intensifying economic and cultural marginalization of immigrants in California, see Smith and Tarallo (1993).

10. This kind of move also warrants attention for its possible impact on the analytics of the national. As Gupta points out: "The displacement of identity and culture from 'the nation' not only forces us to reevaluate our ideas about culture and identity but also enables us to denaturalize the nation as the hegemonic form of organizing space" (1992, 74).

11. Powerful organizations such as the Minnesota-based Hmong American Partnership dedicated to advancing "self-sufficiency" and economic integration while retaining cultural "pride" epitomize this philosophy in fund-raising statements such as "Your contributions will

provide Hmong American Partnership with critical resources to overcome barriers that restrict Minnesota's Hmong from being *equal partners* in society" (Haus 1995, 5, emphasis added).

12. See my discussion in Schein (1998) of the decision on the part of the Chinese state to deny exit visas to a couple hundred Miao scholars who wished to attend an international Hmong-Miao conference in Minnesota. I hold that the government's attempt to block this burgeoning alliance itself bespeaks the state's recognition of the potential for significant opposition.

References

Appadurai, A. 1993. Patriotism and its futures. *Public Culture* 5(3): 411–29.

Basch, L., N. Glick-Schiller, and C. Szanton Blanc. 1994. *Nations Unbound: Transnational Projects, Postcolonial Predicaments and Deterritorialized Nation-States.* New York: Gordon and Breach.

Bhabha, H. K. 1990. DissemiNation: Time, Narrative and the Margins of the Modern Nation. In *Nation and Narration.* Edited by Homi K. Bhabha. Pp. 291–322. New York: Routledge.

Chow, R. 1993. *Writing Diaspora: Tactics of Intervention in Contemporary Cultural Studies.* Bloomington and Indianapolis: University of Indiana Press.

Clifford, J. 1992. Traveling Cultures. In *Cultural Studies.* Edited by L. Grossberg et al. Pp. 96–116. New York: Routledge.

———. 1994. Diasporas. *Cultural Anthropology* 9(3): 302–38.

Christoffersen, G. 1993. Xinjiang and the great Islamic circle: The impact of transnational forces on Chinese regional economic planning. *China Quarterly* 133 (March): 130–51.

Ginsburg, F. 1991. Indigenous media: Faustian contract or global village? *Cultural Anthropology* 6(1): 92–112.

Gupta, A. 1992. The song of the nonaligned world: Transnational identities and the reinscription of space in late capitalism. *Cultural Anthropology* 7(1): 63–79.

Hall, S. 1989. Cultural identity and cinematic representation. *Framework* 36: 68–81.

———. 1996. New Ethnicities. In *Stuart Hall: Critical Dialogues in Cultural Studies.* Edited by D. Morley and K. Chen. Pp. 441–50. London: Routledge.

Hammond, J. D. 1988. Visualizing themselves: Tongan videography in Utah. *Visual Anthropology* 1: 379–400.

Haus, J. 1995. An invitation to donate to HAP. *The HAP Voice: Hmong American Partnership* 6(1): 5.

Hmong American Partnership. 1996. HAP Visited by Chinese Officials. *HAP Voice* (Fall): 3.

Litzinger, R. A. 1995. Narratives of Identity in Yao "Post-National" Cultural Discourse. Paper presented at the Annual Meetings of the American Anthropological Association.

Mercer, K. 1990. Black Hair/Style Politics. In *Out There: Marginalization and Contemporary Culture.* Edited by R. Ferguson et al. Pp. 247–64. Cambridge, Mass.: MIT Press.

Ong, A. 1994. On the edge of empires: Flexible citizenship among Chinese in diaspora. *Positions* 1(3): 745–78.

———. 1997. Chinese Modernities: Narratives of Nation and of Capitalism. In *Ungrounded Empires: The Cultural Politics of Modern Chinese Transnationalism.* Edited by A. Ong and D. Nonini. Pp. 171–203. New York: Routledge.

Radhakrishnan, R. 1995. Toward an eccentric cosmopolitanism. *Positions* (3): 814–21.

Robbins, B. 1993. Comparative Cosmopolitanisms. In *Secular Vocations: Intellectuals, Professionalism, Culture.* Pp. 180–211. London: Verso.

Schein, L. 1987. Control of Contrast: Lao-Hmong Refugees in American Contexts. In *People in Upheaval*. Edited by S. Morgan and E. Colson. Pp. 88–107. Staten Island, N.Y.: Center for Migration Studies.

———. 1996. The Other Goes to Market: The State, the Nation, and Unruliness in Contemporary China. *Identities* 2(3): 197–222.

———. 1998. Importing Miao Brethren to Hmong America: A Not So Stateless Transnationalism. In *Cosmopolitics*. Edited by Bruce Robbins and Pheng Cheah. Minneapolis: University of Minnesota Press.

———. 2000. Minority Rules: The Miao and the Feminine in China's Cultural Politics. Durham, N.C.: Duke University Press. Forthcoming.

Scott, G. M. 1982. The Hmong refugee community in San Diego: A conceptual framework for the analysis of dislocated people. *Anthropological Quarterly* 55(3): 146–60.

Smith, M. P. 1994. Can you imagine? Transnational migration and the globalization of grass roots politics. *Social Text* 39: 15–33.

———, and B. Tarallo. 1993. California's changing faces: New immigrant survival strategies and state policy. *California Policy Seminar Briefs* 5(15): 1–10.

Spivak, G. 1990. Gayatri Spivak on the politics of the subaltern: Interview with Howard Winant. *Socialist Review* 90(3): 81–97.

Tolentino, R. B. 1996. Bodies, Letters, Catalogues: Filipinas in Transnational Space. *Social Text* 48 (Fall): 49–76.

Tsing, A. L. 1993. *In the Realm of the Diamond Queen*. Pp. 213–29. Princeton: Princeton University Press.

———. 1994. From the Margins. *Cultural Anthropology* 9(3): 279–97.

Villapando, Venny. 1989. The Business of Selling Mail Order Brides. In *Making Waves: An Anthology of Writings by and about Asian-American Women*. Edited by Asian Women United of California. Pp. 318–26. Boston: Beacon Press.

Wilson, Ara. 1988. American Catalogues of Asian Brides. In *Anthropology for the Nineties*. Edited by J. B. Cole. Pp. 114–25. New York: The Free Press.

Timothy Keeyen Choy

11 Cultural Encompass:
Looking for Direction in
The Asian American Comic Book

Introduction: Being There

A throng has gathered on the steps of the Massachusetts state capitol building. People of various ethnicities and political signs in Chinese and English jostle for position, demanding job training and decent housing, decrying anti-Asian violence. The protesters stand tightly packed together, and excitement hangs thick in the air as a rally organizer, clutching her microphone, passionately speaks of unity:

> *We must not let them divide and turn us against each other. We, Asians, all share a common experience in America, and we must work together.*

But not everyone is convinced. In particular, I notice a well-dressed Cambodian American man in the crowd who remarks out loud for all nearby to hear:

> *What does she mean by that? We come from different countries and at different times. How can she say we are all the same?*

He is not the only one who wonders this. "Asian American," though certainly a potentially powerful political identity, is an exceptionally vague term, encompassing a multitude of people who might have little in common. This man's brave comments, I think to myself, must echo the doubts of many people here, especially South Asian Americans and Southeast Asian Americans who frequently voice dissatisfaction at their invisibility in Asian American organizations or literature anthologies, etc.

So begin my field notes, taken during a six-month stint of fieldwork conducted within the pages of *The Asian American Comic Book* (AARW 1991). The comic book tells a story of four people—a Japanese American internee, an immigrant Indian student, a

Cambodian refugee, and a Chinese garment worker—who meet at a political rally, share personal stories, and unite in solidarity in spite of their differences. Although an arguably strange thing to call "fieldwork," the half year I spent in 1996 in this comic book's main story and its four substories moved me deeply nonetheless, and it led me that very year to write this essay. In the following pages, I attempt to demonstrate how reading *The Asian American Comic Book* might allow one to address an issue central to the academic and political project of ethnographizing "Asian America."

Although I take on here just a small piece of the Asian American world, the question of concern to me is fundamental: What counts as "Asian America"? This essay, then, while anthropological and addressing itself to this volume's project of Asian American ethnography, is not strictly ethnographic. Instead, it is an attempt to weave a thread of critical reflection upon the nature of the category "Asian American" into the exciting project of ethnographically exploring different "Asian American" lives. That is, rather than training my eye on how a certain group of people called "Asian American" live and act in the world, I wish to explore how a diverse group of people come to be identified—and to identify themselves—by a single term, "Asian American," in the first place, and to push for an awareness of both the importance and limits of that category.[1]

Comic Book Anthropology?

The Asian American Comic Book, written by Wen-Ti Tsen and the Asian American Resource Workshop, operates in part as an ethnography of Asian America. One of its substories, "The Garment Worker's Story," was based on a team of writers' firsthand experiences working with garment workers. Another, "The Refugee's Story," emerged as a collaborative production through formal and informal interactions between Asian American Resource Workshop (AARW) workers and a number of Southeast Asian refugees. The hands-on methodology of data collection behind *The Asian American Comic Book* thus smells just like ethnographic practice. It is a firsthand "being there"; an ethnographer could not be more proud. The comic book's form might seem a bit unorthodox for anthropologists, but we are all in the business of writing convincing accounts based on experience; a comic book is but one way of doing so. If nothing else, perhaps authors of Asian American ethnography will hear echoes of our own motivations—perhaps even of our writing—in the statement:

> Many experiences of Asian Americans had not often been told *realistically* in this form before. The intent of this book is to tell those stories, and in doing so, to communicate more *truthfully* the lives of those Asian Americans. (AARW 1991, back page, emphasis added)

The Asian American Comic Book's dedication to realism and to truthful accounts of experience shows it to be the product of a desire with a long, though not altogether successful, history in ethnography: the desire to represent. As such, it can be read as a product of anthropological sensibilities.

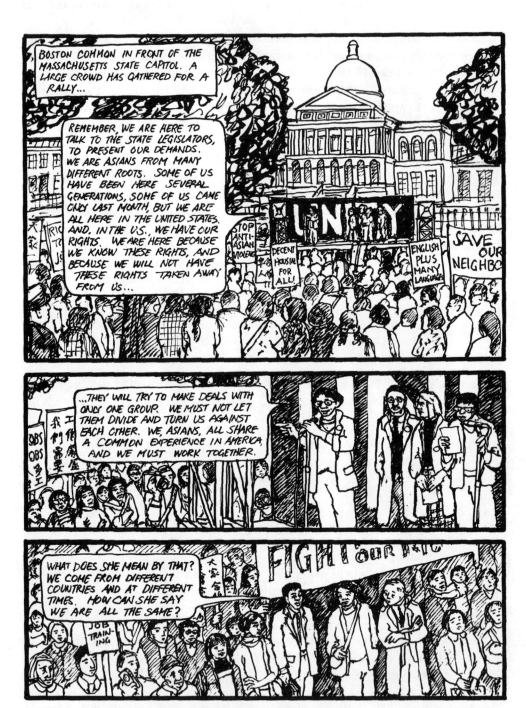

Reprinted by permission of the publisher, Asian American Resource Workshop, and the illustrator, Wen-ti Tsen, from *The Asian American Comic Book*. 1991.

More interesting than merely accepting *The Asian American Comic Book* as an anthropology of Asian America, however, would be to take the text as a cultural artifact, to interpret it, and to thereby derive a story about what life might have been like when it was made and used. A text is an object manipulated, moved, and used within social relations. Just as an archaeologist can investigate what people used to do with a piece of pottery, we can ask how *The Asian American Comic Book* fit into social life. What social function did it serve?

The Asian American Comic Book, it turns out, was published by the Asian American Resource Workshop, a nonprofit educational organization based in Boston whose goals are "uniting the Asian American communities, facilitating Asian American participation in all spheres of society, improving society's understanding of, and empowering Asian Americans" (AARW 1991, back cover). We can get some sense of who the AARW envisioned as the target audience of *The Asian American Comic Book* in their explanation of why they chose the visual comic book form for their message, rather than, say, the pamphlet or traditional life history form.

> [Comic books are] *easily accessible* to people of different ages and language backgrounds. *Pictures can sometimes describe with more immediacy the lives, the surroundings and the emotions of people* and can express their stories more convincingly than just words. (AARW 1991, back cover, emphasis added)

This comic book, then, like an Asian American history book, was developed as a pedagogical tool. It was intended to teach. Note, also, that in this excerpt recurs the desire for unmediated representation, for visual immediacy.

Like all texts, *The Asian American Comic Book* was produced within a moment where certain issues and questions preoccupied the imaginations of its authors and intended audience, and the manner in which the story, or narrative, unfolds depends upon those very issues and questions. I see in *The Asian American Comic Book* four characters from diverse backgrounds coming together for political power, so I ask: What makes a good story concerning Asian American unity and solidarity to the authors and readers of the comic book? What counts in the text as political power?

This doesn't mean taking the book's word for everything; clearly the answers that the comic book proposes to its own political enigmas are not necessarily the "correct" answers. The concern in this way of reading, however, is not to assess whether a text tells its story "truthfully" and "realistically." Instead, it means asking *why* the text says things in the particular way it does, and noticing what answers count as good answers to its authors and social milieu. *The Asian American Comic Book* reflects and speaks to issues and questions that could be called one form of "political unconscious," in this case a political and collective fantasy of "Asian America" and Asian American politics.[2]

When I say "fantasy," I do not mean that Asian American issues and strategies are mere figments of imagination; I mean that on-the-ground, real politics of Asian America are inseparable from the realm of "political imagination," or what is *conceivable* (for now) as social analysis and Asian American political action. These fantasies are split between anxieties (such as the anxiety of not having Asian American unity because we come from so many backgrounds) and their negative inverse, desires (such as the American Dream, or the dream of achieving Asian American unity). Political "fantasies" contain analyses of the present, anxieties and hopes for the future, and criteria for what count as good questions and answers about Asian America. Faced by the comic book, then, I take my task as an anthropologist committed to Asian America to be to search for—and to paint a portrait of—some of those fantasies in action.

Orienting Facts: The Stories and the Players

The story of *The Asian American Comic Book* is relatively simple. As I mentioned earlier, four people meet at an Asian American rally. Lenny is a successful U.S.-born Japanese American man, most likely in his late fifties or sixties. Monica is a young Indian American woman, still in college. Ah Ying is a Chinese American woman of approximately the same age as Lenny. Finally, there is the Cambodian American man I introduced in the beginning of this essay, given no proper name in the text, whose comments spark the initial conversation and eventual story-sharing among the four strangers.

Lenny's personal story deals with his experience as an internee in an internment camp during World War II. Monica tells a story of cultural and generational conflict and of negotiation between Indian and American identity. Then the Cambodian American recounts his arrival in the United States as a refugee and the squalid conditions he had to overcome with his family. Finally, Ah Ying shares her experiences of organizing with her fellow garment workers against unfair labor practices. Through the process of sharing their stories, the four characters recognize that despite their differences, they all share the experience of having overcome hardship as Asian Americans.

While the storyline may be simple, the four main characters are multifaceted in their identities.[3] I've broadly schematized some of these facets in a table, including the roles/titles by which the characters are officially identified in *The Asian American Comic Book*.

Character's Name	Role/Title	Ethnicity	Class	Gender	Sexuality	Age	Immigration
Lenny	Internee	Japanese	Upper-middle	Male	Not given	60s	U.S. born
Monica	Student	Indian	Middle	Female	Heterosexual	Early 20s	immigrant
Not Given	Refugee	Cambodian	Not given	Male	Not given	Late 20s	immigrant
Ah Ying	Garment worker	Chinese	Working class	Female	Heterosexual	60s	long-time immigrant

It is along many axes of comparison, then, that these four characters differ from each other—they come from strikingly different places, both geographically and figuratively. Small wonder, then, that cautious discussions emerge between the four when they meet, questioning whether they all belong in the same place. Small wonder that disagreements erupt, most significantly across age and ethnic differences.

These four characters can be seen as figures of Asian American difference, narrative embodiments of the sheer diversity of people that are today encompassed within the term "Asian America." This heterogeneity of Asian America takes center stage in Lisa Lowe's (1996) cogent work on Asian American identity. Lowe writes:

> In relation to the state and the American national culture implied by that state, Asian Americans have certainly been constructed as different from, and as other than, white Americans of European descent. But from the perspectives of Asian Americans, we are extremely different and diverse among ourselves: as men and women at different distance and generations from our "original" Asian cultures—cultures as different as Chinese, Japanese, Korean, Filipino, Indian, Vietnamese, Thai, or Cambodian—Asian Americans are born in the United States and born in Asia; of exclusively Asian parents and of mixed race; urban and rural; refugee and nonrefugee; fluent in English and non-English speaking; professionally trained and working class.[4] (Lowe 1996, 65–66)

In other words, the differences *within* Asian America might be even more significant than the common ground we create in opposition to what is *outside*. Of course, these differences within potentially threaten the prospect of bringing all Asian Americans together into a solid, unified, politically powerful voice. Thus, underlying the question of whether or how one might craft an Asian American political voice is a tension—a tension between, on the one hand, the reality that Asian Americans differ from and with one another, and, on the other, the goal of Asian American unity.[5] This tension permeates the interactions between the four characters in *The Asian American Comic Book* as well.

Unity and Hope

In *The Asian American Comic Book*, the tension resolves itself on the side of unity. By the end of the book, the four rally-goers see the need to stand together and witness the rally speaker's performance with rapt expressions and joined hands. *The Asian American Comic Book*'s story, then, is a kind of political wish-fulfillment dream of Asian America. It enacts the political unification of Asian America that is so desperately wanted yet so difficult to attain in the face of difference.

Equally hopeful unifying gestures permeate each of the four "personal" narratives as well. In Ah Ying's story, for instance, Ah Ying's husband overcomes his initial disdain and disapproval of Ah Ying's political organizing and joins her in the final protest march. American born college students also come to the aid of Ah Ying and the other garment workers, who speak little English. The Cambodian, in his story, entreats his fellow refugees to "keep the unity" when their landlord attempts to evict them: "If we only stick together, we can win. If we can keep the unity, we can make a difference" (AARW 1991, 44). He also joins forces with a Chinese American lawyer, who helps them win a lawsuit against the landlord. At the end of Lenny's story, Lenny

Reprinted by permission of the publisher, Asian American Resource Workshop, and the illustrator, Wen-ti Tsen, from *The Asian American Comic Book*. 1991, 44.

and his estranged brother reunite to sue the American government for redress for their internment. One is bombarded with successful unifications when reading this comic book. This text produces hope.

I cherish these hopes as well. At the same time, I want to look at what we sometimes have to do, often unwittingly, in our pursuit of the politically exciting and utopian goal of unifying Asian America. For that purpose, *The Asian American Comic Book* is an ideal point of analytic entry. Although this text primarily tells a story about the wonders of unity, close reading also allows one to discern the different stakes and markedly different histories that people carry with them when they come together under the banner of "Asian America."

Through its four characters, *The Asian American Comic Book* acknowledges that Asian American identity is not an easy place for Asian Americans to be as a group and that we often disagree. The juxtaposition of four diverse stories within the framing story of an Asian American unity rally illustrates the important insight that to stand together, we inevitably simplify ourselves to a common denominator and downplay our differences, in the hopes that "if we can keep the unity, we can make a difference."

Read in this light, the four moving stories told in *The Asian American Comic Book* serve as a reminder that while such simplifications make our co-occupation of a politically effective category possible at certain points in time, that category's utility as political "banner" cannot be mistaken for aptness as a descriptive term for those who stand underneath it. Still, I want to push on this comic book a little harder, for even as *The Asian American Comic Book* creates important space for difference, one kind of difference in particular finds itself shortchanged on being resolved in Asian American unity.

The Indian Question

Reprinted by permission of the publisher, Asian American Resource Workshop, and the illustrator, Wen-ti Tsen, from *The Asian American Comic Book.* 1991, 6.

Because Monica articulates one of the book's most pointed and unity-threatening critiques of Asian American identity, I believe it is instructive to look carefully at how her critique is addressed and resolved by the comic book's storytelling strategies.

Monica's irritation with Asian America is a common one, though no less potent for its commonness. She says to Lenny and Ah Ying:

> Why do you always talk of Chinese or Japanese[?] We Indians are Asian too, and sometimes the racism against us can be even stronger. (AARW 1991, 6)

The authors of *The Asian American Comic Book* thus present Monica as South Asian in origin, and as a potential harbinger of ethnic division. She disagrees with Lenny and Ah Ying and does so as a member of "We Indians." But her point is not merely to say that Indians are "Asian"; she gives voice to a pointed critique of exclusionary practices within "Asian America." Monica's statement draws some of its force by resonating with political fantasies located outside the text itself, such as the sentiments and memories of South Asian Americans who have felt like outsiders in Asian American organizations or with the experiences of editors who have been soundly rebuked for omitting South Asian writers in Asian American studies anthologies.

Monica's declaration of "We Indians are Asian too" disturbs; the very necessity of an additive enunciation "We . . . are Asian *too*" illuminates a foundational absence in supposedly-inclusive Asian America. Furthermore, Monica's claim precludes the simple inclusion of "Indian" as something *similar* to the rest of Asian America. It cannot be incorporated into existing structures, for implicit in Monica's assertion that "sometimes the racism can be *even stronger* against *us*" is the dual argument that Indian experience is Asian American and is at the same time *different*.[6] That is, Monica seems to pointedly challenge Ah Ying, if you truly want to mobilize and include South Asians as "Asian Americans"—and we *do* belong, for we are Asian *too*—you're going to have to fundamentally change what being Asian American means.

The anxiety-ridden dilemma that *The Asian American Comic Book* sets out to resolve, then, is this: Will dissatisfied Monica—a figure of both particular Indian American exclusion and of more general fundamental unrest over specifically Chinese and Japanese American preeminence in "Asian" America—be brought into the fold of Asian American unity, and if so, how?

Cultural Direction

In a moment, I will look closely at Monica's narrative, but let me preface that discussion with some comments on the importance of such an analysis. Attention to the ways in which *The Asian American Comic Book* narratively resolves the divisive critique of Asian America is crucial, for this book does not simply reflect and comment on the troubled political context of its production. Instead, like a cultural compass, *The Asian American Comic Book* directs and aligns its readers toward a cultural direction, toward a particular way of thinking about and practicing Asian American identity.[7] The catchy narrative of *The Asian American Comic Book* and its visual form ensure that the reader will stay on for the duration, intrigued by the enigma of uniting diverse constituencies under a common banner.

An allegory, *The Asian American Comic Book* distills large- scale social issues into recognizable and likable characters. Those characters have visually realistic faces, inviting readers to insert themselves easily into the story by identifying with one or another character, or perhaps by identifying with the story of their meeting. The book's visual form lends immediacy; a reader can feel "there"—"there" enough to write field notes—as witness to and participant in the unfolding stories. For instance, after readers scan a series of uncaptioned images portraying the unity rally from a distance, the last panel of the comic (see Figure 2) depicts the rally podium as if from behind the heads and torsos of Monica and the other three main characters, producing a sensation of joining and being among the crowd—among the unity. The changes and the movement *between* images work as much as the individual images themselves so that by the end of the book, the reader's position is firmly planted both visually and narratively in a project of unifying Asian America. My interests center on how a reader progresses from anxiety about the difficulty of unity to hope and optimism; that's the cultural compass work. It is because this text potentially performs such powerful work on its readers—particularly those sympathetic to Asian American politics—that I, as an anthropologist of Asian America, am especially interested in it.

Monica ultimately does, of course, enter the fold. And in enfolding Monica within Asian America, *The Asian American Comic Book* narratively assuages anxieties that South Asians might not fit or might not want to fit into Asian America. Several questions thus arise for me: Through what narrative processes is Monica able to be encompassed by Asian America in *The Asian American Comic Book*? What had to happen to Monica as a character—what kind of character did the comic book's story need her to be in order for this to happen? Finally, what might the use of these narrative strategies suggest about the political imagination available for practicing an Asian American politics of unity and for studying Asian America?

I notice two strategies deployed in *The Asian American Comic Book* in order to resolve the South Asian dilemma. The first strategy involves a ruse whereby Monica is reconciled with Ah Ying and Lenny. This rapprochement produces the appearance of resolving the South Asian question, yet the dilemma that is resolved between the characters actually centers on an issue other than that of South Asian exclusion. The second strategy softens what remains of Monica's diverted critique by revealing that at Monica's core, she is not really as adamantly antagonistic as she comes across in her pointed question. These two strategies make it possible for *The Asian American Comic Book* to tell a story of Asian America that includes Indianness without that Indianness threatening the cohesiveness and unity of Asian America.

Diversions and Snares

Monica's statement at the beginning of the comic book—"Why do you always talk of Chinese or Japanese[?] We Indians are Asian too, and sometimes the racism against us can be even stronger" (AARW 1991, 6)—dramatizes a specific conflict between Indian Americans and Chinese and Japanese Americans. Monica positions herself in her question specifically as Indian with her self-identification, "We Indians."[8]

Who the *"you"* is in Monica's query, on the other hand, could be read a number of ways. Does Monica pose her question to Ah Ying and Lenny? Or to Asian America in general? To leave the ambiguity unresolved leads to the most troubling reading of Monica's critique, because it would mean that for Monica, her interlocutor who "talks" with the mandate of an "Asian" America—her object of address—does not speak with some generalized "Asian" voice, but rather one with specifically Chinese and Japanese accents and inflection. That is, "Asian America" as practiced reflects and speaks to Chinese and Japanese interests, to the exclusion of Indians and other South Asians.

Monica thus effectively voices a disturbing and dangerously disruptive ethnic analysis of Asian American politics. Accordingly, when Ah Ying responds, apparently in answer to the deictic "you" in Monica's query, it is easy to presume that their conversation will continue along the ethnic lines that Monica drew out. But herein lies the danger in reading this comic book allegory with multifaceted characters. For what does Ah Ying say? "Sometimes there is nothing you can do about it and you just have to bear it as best you can" (AARW 1991, 6).

Ah Ying's words of existential advice ring like pearls of wisdom from a weary, experienced veteran. They bring to the fore the "Ah Ying the elder" and the "Ah Ying the longtime immigrant" facets of Ah Ying's identity and in the process hail Monica as a younger and less experienced immigrant. The result: the original context for the exchange between Ah Ying and Monica—that is, Indian exclusion from Asian American identity—finds itself obscured. Through these wise, patient words, Ah Ying as *Chinese* spokesperson for Asian America remains surreptitiously silent, and Monica as *Indian* is ignored. Though Monica speaks, she is not heard.[9]

My point here is not to levy a major critique of the AARW and its important work. They did not silence Monica on purpose. Instead, I point out the narrative slip to draw attention to silencing of a more systemic nature. Simply, the tools available to Asian American studies at large for resolving disagreement and difference are primarily honed on models of generational conflict and cultural assimilation. The writers of

Reprinted by permission of the publisher, Asian American Resource Workshop, and the illustrator, Wen-ti Tsen, from *The Asian American Comic Book.* 1991, 6.

The Asian American Comic Book used the best available tool for the job of dealing with Monica, and the least troublesome fit was a young/old conflict resolution. Yet notice that this tool choice subtly transforms the figure of the critical *Indian* into that of the angry young *student*. And as Monica steps into her new narrative calling as a headstrong youth, the bite of her important ethnic critique fades into the background.

Softening Critique

Any haunting memory of the dropped critique is in turn softened by Monica's narration of her "Student's Story." To recognize how this transpires, we need only turn to her story's beginning. Monica speaks:

> A few months ago, just about the *end of the school year*, my friend *Jung Soon* and I were talking. We worked closely together in the *Pan-Asian student movement* in the college. I was the president of the Indian Student Association and she was with the Korean Student group. (AARW 1991, 25, emphasis added)

The first half of the first sentence—"the end of the school year"—swiftly establishes Monica as a student." The second half tells the reader through the name "Jung Soon" that Monica has a friend of Korean background. A reader's potential anxieties that Monica might be India-centric can be allayed somewhat by the discovery of cross-ethnic friendship. Furthermore, the threat to Asian American unity that Monica embodies at the outset turns out to be a false alarm, for we discover that she works in a Pan-Asian movement herself. The conflict of difference within Asian America is resolved before it ever begins.

The fact that Jung Soon's name so clearly codifies her ethnicity gains even more significance if one considers that in contrast, Monica's name conjures no such associations to Indian identity. In a U.S. context, "Monica" stands as a relatively unmarked moniker, conjuring no associations with diasporic history, at least any related to Asia. The student story of Monica can flow easily, undisturbed by any explicitly Indian personal name that might recall Monica's initial discontent as part of "We Indians."

Thus, although Monica represented a very strong Indian presence initially, Indianness loses specificity quickly in her story. This is evident even from the titles of the four life stories. Consider these pairs of terms, drawn from the titles of the stories and the ethnicities of their narrators:

Garment worker	Chinese
Internee	Japanese
Refugee	Cambodian
Student	Indian

In the first three pairs, strong metonymic associations tie the first term to the second. That is, when you know an Asian American story is a garment worker's story, you understand, more or less, that it is a story of being Chinese in the United States.[10] Similarly, a story told by an internee almost certainly implicates a Japanese narrator. And Asian refugees to the United States have come primarily from Southeast Asia, including Cambodia. The ethnic associations that accrue to the very titles of the substories are rich.

The title of Monica's story—"The Student's Story"—however, does not point toward ethnic specificity at all. "Student" is simply not as loaded a term—it wouldn't make one think, "Oh, Indian." Monica narrates a general story that could be told by a female Asian American character of almost any ethnicity.

Perhaps it overstates the case to say that Monica's tale is completely general. Take, for instance, the dispute in Monica's family whose resolution concludes "The Student's Story." References to India and some Indian specificities do appear. The major dispute occurs between Monica, who wishes to build roots in the United States, and her grandmother, who scolds her, "Your roots are thousands years deep in India. Your birth was there. Sadly you will never know India" (AARW 1991, 33). Their conflict centers on the question of where to construct one's personal commitments.

The issues that Monica's grandmother raises sound specifically Indian. Her concern is that people in the United States "will continue to think India is poor and ugly, with the caste system" (AARW 1991, 32), even though the caste system has been long abolished. She fears that India will fall by the wayside without commitment from Indians abroad. The grandmother's references to India make *The Asian American Comic Book* appear to have performed an invaluable service: it has created Indian voices as integral to a product explicitly called "Asian American."

Here, attention to the resolution of political enigmas assumes striking importance. Certain details in the text make you think the Indian issue has been resolved. But has it?

The word "India" and the loaded term "caste system" in the statement by Monica's grandmother certainly collaborate in creating the sensation that "The Student's Story" is an Indian story. This sensation of specificity is furthered by the nature of Monica's response to her grandmother, where she aligns herself with "the teachings of Gandhiji" and invokes "our Indian teaching . . . to help the less fortunate" (AARW 1991, 33) as a philosophy compatible with life in the United States. The fact that characters are talking about Gandhi and a caste system (as well as the fact that Monica takes a date out for Indian food earlier in the story) puts a big stamp on Monica's story as "Indian."

The Asian American Comic Book's invocations of India and Indian traditions are not, however, enough to make Monica's story seem specifically Indian in the United States. Instead, they serve as embellishments to an already well-worn Asian American *genre*; that is, these references to India add Indian flavor to an oft-told story, but they do no more than that. In other words, the story is perhaps not general, but it *is* generic. The narration of Monica's story is actually dangerous in its gestures toward Indian specificity, for it too easily leads to an undeserved peace of mind for having resolved the burning dilemma that Monica introduced in the very beginning.

Indian specificities (e.g., Gandhi, Indian food, caste system) have been added in *The Asian American Comic Book* within an already existing framework, a story of balancing cultures that has been told countless times already in various forms throughout Asian American literature and scholarship. When Monica was introduced, however, she was discontented with and antagonistic toward the current practice of Asian American identity. She embodied an important call for serious thought about its disagreements, differences, and exclusions. Now, tragically, she has become the narrator of a story where "India" has become just another instance of "Asia" in an Asia/America dilemma. Whereas she spoke dangerously for Asian American difference in the beginning, Monica is now all about sameness.

Thus, the dilemma of difference and disagreement has not been resolved. True, Monica—the differing Indian—has been encompassed within Asian American identity where she previously was excluded. Her critique that we "always talk of Chinese and Japanese" has been answered. But in becoming encompassed, Monica loses her voice of disagreement, which is what had set her apart and what had threatened the political viability of "Asian America" as a unity. She has truly been engulfed and aligned into an appropriate direction in order to be safely contained in Asian America's unified interior.

Uneasy Fits

Monica's story rests uneasily with the other three, even if Monica the character has been encompassed. Notice how each character becomes "Asian American." Lenny opposes racist internment by the American government. Ah Ying stands up against dominating American labor practices. And the Cambodian refugee resists racist housing lords and a position of marginalization created by U.S. imperialism in Southeast Asia. These first three figures narrate themselves as "Asian American" through their stories of the pain inflicted on them by the American "outside" and their subsequent resistance against that force. Monica, on the other hand, looks toward the Indian American "inside"; cultural negotiation and conflict *within* her community comprise her story of being "Asian American."

At first glance, this contrasts my earlier point that *The Asian American Comic Book* renders Indianness generic by resorting to a "student's story." If the story is generically Asian American, then, how can I now call Monica's story an anomaly, an uneasy fit?

This book sets out to tell a convincing story of how four people come to claim a common voice as political actors united against a dominant system—a story of how they claim a voice as Asian Americans. In the process, *The Asian American Comic Book* admirably articulates some internal conflicts, such as Lenny's estrangement from his brother, and Ah Ying's defiance of her husband's demands that she stay home and not make a fuss. However, by and large these internal negotiations are framed within a larger tale of political voice directed outward. In Monica's story, on the other hand, *internal* negotiation and pain are central. Notably absent is any portrayal of the external or publicly political sphere, such as a discussion of what Monica hinted at early on, namely the ways "racism against us [Indians] can be even stronger" (AARW 1991, 6). Thus, although Monica does claim "Asian Americanness" in the end, she does so in a substantially different manner from the other three characters.

But what if we did have that discussion of Monica's as external negotiation? The four stories would then be tied by a thread of "oppression," a narrow line of thinking about Asian Americanness that is dangerous in its seductive simplicity.[11] *The Asian American Comic Book* laudably avoids that easy route, though the transformational conceit—from Monica as Angry Indian who might have articulated a story of racism to Monica as Student who narrates internal negotiation—remains problematic. Still, *The Asian American Comic Book* makes clear through an anomalous representation of Indian Asian Americanness, as well as the numerous mentions throughout the text of internal conflict, that any allegory of Asian American unity will have to be more complicated than one of either "agreement" or "common oppression."

The question, then, is what more textured and rich allegories can we craft to encompass Indian American as Asian American? Can we tell, more generally, a story of Asian American political unity built not necessarily upon tropes of similarity or commonality, but rather on ones of different pains, wild hopes, and momentarily overlapping dreams?

Conclusion: Reinterpreting Asian America

The Asian American Comic Book presents the story of four Asian Americans achieving unity over difference in a political wish-fulfillment fantasy of reconciliation. My purpose in making explicit the narrative treatment of Monica has been to show the work that was necessary for that wish to be fulfilled. Unity does not come easily, nor is it achieved entirely innocently.

The hidden costs and silences that come with Asian American unity—even in optimistic stories of unity such as that in *The Asian American Comic Book*—do not mean that the political project of bringing together Asian Americans should necessarily be abandoned.[12] Those costs do, however, demand that we think about Asian American political unity in a different manner. Thus, I offer here my first attempt at articulating an alternative allegory of Asian America by making one last, short interpretation of Monica's experience in *The Asian American Comic Book*. This interpretation looks to tell a story of what Monica *does*, not merely of what *The Asian American Comic Book* does to her.

Under this new lens, Monica is not a helpless victim, encompassed and swallowed up by a monolithic Asian America. Instead, Monica grudgingly suppresses her difference—that is, her Indian critique of Asian America and her disagreement with Ah Ying and Lenny—in order that she might stand together with her colleagues as "Asian American" at that particular moment. Monica's setting aside of such an important piece of herself for the sake of a temporary political unity is testament to the powerful hopes and dreams she nurtures for a political voice, one that the Asian American political project might offer.

After the rally, however, Monica speaks up again, as do others who are dissatisfied with their exclusion from what counts as truly "Asian" or "Asian American." They must speak, and their issues must be taken seriously without excessive anxiety and defensiveness. Of course, for those people to whom "Asian America" is a kind of "home" space where agreement and sameness nurture a sense of safety, Monica is threatening. Her dissonant critiques and complaints threaten the quiet safety of "home."[13] But I believe that we can move toward thinking about Asian America in a different way.

Perhaps Asian America is more of a *home base* than a *home*, one that is built and rebuilt every day with loving hope by different groups of us who need it. We enter that home base by calling ourselves "Asian American," and we do so both to claim strength and to find a place of refuge where we can regroup and connect with potential colleagues and allies.

Our home base is not perfect, however, and many people find themselves forced to make the difficult decision of leaving other parts of themselves behind or holding back their genuine disagreements in order to enter a temporary unity called "Asian American." These are the Monicas of Asian America, the different and differing Asian Americans. Thus, we construct the important unified appearance that our home base presents to the rest of the world, using as building material some people's oversights and other people's swallowed pride, pain, distrust, ambivalence, and fear. And if our goal is not simply to live in a magically pleasant home of Asian American identity, but rather to create "Asian America" as an organizing "home base" that can shift to suit the needs of the multiplicity of people who use it, then those things that are swallowed need to be heard and addressed.[14]

There are four crucial points here. First, "Asian American" is not a term of identity that captures everybody (or anybody) who claims it. It is a political tool that allows many of us to be counted together. Second, "Asian American" is not a perfect tool; it has historically dealt only marginally with people whose "Asianness" pertains to South or Southeast Asian history, people for whom "America" means Canada or Latin America, queer people, and others. Third, those who point out flaws in this tool, such as Monica in *The Asian American Comic Book*, do not do so merely to be nay sayers, and their critiques should be taken seriously and constructively. They are invested in the political promise that "Asian American" offers and are trying to rework the tool so that it can better reflect their needs. Dissatisfied, peripheral, and yet hopeful Monicas constitute what it means to be "Asian American" as much as anybody else. Fourth, those fortunate enough to be satisfied already with Asian America must be receptive to challenge. Having flaws does not prevent the Asian American home base from being used effectively for some things; the tool does not need to be thrown out wholesale. At the same time, the fact that this flawed tool works does not mean that it should not be open to adjustment when its imperfections are pointed out.[15] We can do better than Ah Ying and Lenny.

Part of the implication of my argument for conceiving of Asian America as an imaginary space where differences come together in temporary unity is that no single ethnography can claim to be an ethnography of Asian America. For better or worse, no single description can capture all of Asian America, no matter how ambitious.

What I have attempted here has not been an objective reporter's ethnographic exploration of Asian America, but rather a staunchly positioned one of "Asian America" the *political* term. I have endeavored to interpret *The Asian American Comic Book* for the hopes, conflicts, and costs that might be entangled in the production of "Asian America" as a collectivity able to encompass divergents and divergence, in a mode that is both critical and committed. And true to the often problematic cartographic impulse of exploration, I have offered through my reflections an alternative map for navigating "Asian America" in the hope that some will find its lines inviting enough to retrace and to walk a different kind of political territory, a different Asian America.

Notes

Warm thanks to Gentle Blythe, Nicholas Brown, Nancy Chen, Margaret Derosia, Jeremy Hermann, Heidi Hess, Taj James, Kim Nies, Michael Omi, Anna Tsing, and Hayden White for the insightful comments and suggestions they have offered upon reading various drafts of this essay. For his invitation to contribute to this volume and his editorial support, I gratefully thank Martin Manalansan, IV. I am grateful also to Tracey Tsugawa, Asian American Resource Workshop, who offered timely encouragement and arranged permission for me to reprint panels from the comic book. Finally, special thanks to Shagufta Bidiwala and Seema Rizvi for critical and inspiring collaborations. Having received all this help, I am responsible for any of this essay's shortcomings.

1. The nature of my questions follows significant precedence in anthropology. In the late 1970s, Michelle Rosaldo (1980) similarly urged feminist ethnographers to pause amidst their proliferation of ethnographies of women to interrogate the category of "woman" that informed their ethnographies and research. More recently, other feminist theorists such as Joan W. Scott (1991) and Judith Butler (1990) have urged the questioning of presumed subject positions in writing history and in constructing unity-based politics. Within Asian American studies, Lisa Lowe's work has most notably sparked reflection on the category of "Asian American."

2. One might recognize in these paragraphs an echo of Fredric Jameson's (1981) call for the historicization of texts in a political moment, and I gratefully appropriate Jameson's related concepts of *political unconscious* and *ideologeme* for my work in this essay, even as I hesitate to follow Jameson in privileging marxism as an interpretive framework over all others. The purpose of my essay is to argue for the anthropological and political utilities of interpreting a text for its ideological work, if "ideology" may be unlinked from its common pejorative connotations of false consciousness.

3. My attention to the ways in which a subject acts through several modes of being rather than a singular identity is informed by linguistic analyses of bilingual code-switching and register-switching (see, for example, Grosjean 1982) as well by feminist work theorizing the

subject as multiply situated (see, for example, Anzaldúa 1987 and Collins 1991). Dorinne Kondo (1990) weaves her theorization of the subject as fragmentary and shifting into the content and form of her ethnography, *Crafting Selves: Power, Gender, and Discourses of Identity in a Japanese Workplace*.

4. The chapter of Lowe's book (1996) from which I draw this quotation is a revised version of Lowe's earlier essay, "Heterogeneity, Hybridity, Multiplicity: Marking Asian American Differences" (1991).

5. The question of how to fashion a political presence in U.S. politics particularly vexed Asian Americans in 1996 during the "John Huang affair," a front-page controversy over the extent of overseas Chinese contributions to the Clinton election campaign. Many Chinese Americans and other Asian Americans found themselves in the uncomfortable position of decrying the racist tenors of the controversy while agreeing on the need to reform election campaign financing practices. The ugliness of the controversy arguably reached its pinnacle on the cover of an issue of the *National Review* (1997), which depicted Bill Clinton, Hillary Clinton, and Al Gore in variously caricatured Asian guises so as to corporeally represent their traitorous duplicities. The *National Review* incident evidences both U.S. xenophobic anxieties over Asian political influence and—more directly related to the purposes in this essay—the necessity for a mobile and strong Asian American political presence to temper and contest such racist figurations, even as we critically consider the differences of "Asian America."

6. Homi K. Bhabha (1994) notices the disturbing power of being additional:

Coming "after" the original, or in "addition to" it, gives the supplementary question the advantage of introducing a sense of "secondariness" or belatedness into the structure of the original demand. The supplementary strategy suggests that adding "to" need not "add up" but may disturb the calculation. (155)

The supplement thus articulates through implication a repressed story, an absence or inadequacy in the apparently whole original. Supplements, and minority discourses like Monica's that deploy supplementary strategy, "are pluses that compensate for a minus in the origin" (Gasché in Bhabha 1994, 155).

7. I pause here to acknowledge gratefully the collaborative work I enjoyed with Shagufta Bidiwala during the incipient stages of this essay's production, particularly our ruminations on the normative applications of cultural compasses. For further anthropological analysis of the power of texts and narratives to invite and interpellate, see Susan Harding (1990). Reading a book ghostwritten for Jerry Falwell on the topic of abortion, Harding deftly explicates the powerful interpellant and transformative technologies at work in its narrative.

8. Roland Barthes's elaboration of the hermeneutic code in *S/Z* (1974) informs my method in this section. Particularly useful has been Barthes's attention to equivocations and snares, narrative tricks that appear to answer an enigma while diverting a reader from the truth, such that the enigma can be truly solved with a flourish at the tale's end.

A useful political supplement to Barthes's work has been Jameson's concept of "ideologeme." Much as phonemes are the minimal unit of phonetic meaning, ideologemes—the minimal unit of class discourse—are a social praxis by which concrete historical situations are symbolically resolved; that is, imaginary resolutions of contradiction (Jameson 1981, 117). I think of ideologemes as akin to Barthesian snares or equivocations, though different in that ideologemes indefinitely defer "true" resolution and enable peace of mind under contradictory conditions; there is no final disclosure of truth at the end.

9. Conversations with Seema Rizvi about subaltern speech usefully directed my attention to the ways Monica's question seems not to be heard—as well as the ways Monica enters dominant discourse transformed. Gayatri Spivak (1988) distinguishes between the existence of a subaltern voice and the completion of a subaltern speech act: there is no subaltern speech if the subaltern speaks but is not heard. Spivak also perceptively notes the ways in which a subaltern is *spoken for*. Thus, the *sati* widow enters dominant discourse either through a Western feminist rendering of her as oppressed by Indian patriarchy, or through the elite nationalist proclamation, "The women actually wanted to die" (Spivak 1988, 297). The subaltern widow's own voice remains absent.

10. In another context "garment worker" could metonymically conjure "Jewish," as Hayden White has reminded me.

11. For a remarkable and considerate analysis of the complications of assuming injury-based identities in political struggle, see Wendy Brown's (1995) *States of Injury: Power and Freedom in Late Modernity*.

12. Kent Ono (1995) comes close to retiring the term "Asian American" in his essay "Re/Signing 'Asian American': Rhetorical Problematics of Nation," though his project is ostensibly to push for a *resignification* rather than a *resignation*. He writes critically:

> The very idea of Asian American, as a collective assignation, is a problematic issue. Indeed, Asian American can only be theorized as an imaginary discursive formation, with no possibility of ever describing, containing, or producing such a community. The fact that such a label, Asian American, never matches the social discursive formation of Asian American subjects (the convergence of discourse produced by and about Asian Americans) produces an acute theoretical "alienation" between signifier and signified. This alienation is itself produced out of a need for terms that fully reflect subjects collectively. Moreover, since it is impossible to envision all Asian Americans in one place or space, the discussion of Asian Americans as an abstract totality needs to be rethought. (Ono 1995, 75)

He also suggests

> "re/signing" the term in favor of constructing relations that prevent such terms from interfering with the material practices that are necessary for social change. . . . I am not calling for "new" terms to take their place, but rather for a reconfiguration of discursive relations that may necessitate the evacuation of the need for such terms in the first place. (76)

Some of Ono's questions about the viability of an all-encompassing Asian American collectivity resonate somewhat with my own, but his relative inattention to theorizing the "reconfiguration" he calls for leaves me dissatisfied. Thus, I endeavor in this essay, post-critique as it were, to reflect upon the possibility of a politics deployed through contingent Asian American unity and collectivity.

13. I will refrain here from a discussion of the abundant literature on "home," including that concerning the suggestive notions of *heimlich* "home-like" and *unheimlich* "unhome-like/uncanny." For this essay's purposes, I need only follow Elaine Kim's (1993) lead. Kim writes thoughtfully about her own search for an Asian American "home," its comforts, and its limitations.

> For the most part, I [used to] read Asian American literature as a literature of protest and exile, a literature about place and displacement, *a literature concerned with psychic and phys-*

ical "home"—searching for and claiming a "home" or longing for a final "homecoming." I looked for unifying thematic threads and tidy resolutions that might ease the pain of displacement and heal the exile, heedless of what might be missing from this homogenizing approach and oblivious to the parallels between what I was doing and dominant culture attempts to reduce Asian American experiences to developmental narratives about the movement from "primitive," "Eastern," and "foreign immigrant" to "civilized," Western, and "Americanized" loyal citizen. (Kim 1993, ix, emphasis added)

Yet, Kim changes her outlook:

No matter what we wish for, things do not necessarily come to a harmonious resolution. *Perhaps after all there is no "home," except for a place of contestation that negates as well as affirms. And identity, like "home," is ever in process, less a refuge than the site of contending multiple meanings.* Inevitably, the Asian American identify offered by cultural nationalism could not but produce conflicts that portended its own undoing; what was excluded and rendered invisible—the unruly, the transgressive, and the disruptive—began to seep out from under the grids and appear from between the cracks. Eventually, the seams burst and were exposed. In the case of Asian America, this unruliness has come from women who never stop being both Asian and female, as well as from others rendered marginal by the essentializing aspects of Asian American cultural nationalism. (xii—xii, emphasis added)

14. My arguments here are not incompatible with those made in Yen Le Espiritu's (1992) important book, *Asian American Panethnicity: Bridging Institutions and Identities*. Well aware of differences within "Asian America," Espiritu argues that pan-Asian group identification has nevertheless been an important political identity for members of different ethnic subgroups. In addition to analyzing how pan-Asian identification has been required to secure social service funding and to increase electoral power, Espiritu directs attention to the importance of pan-Asian solidarities in countering racial prejudice and violence in which perpetrators fail to differentiate between types of Asian ethnicity.

While convinced of the political importance of pan-Asian solidarities, Espiritu also recognizes that Asian Americans need "to take seriously the heterogeneities among their ranks and overcome the narrow dominance of one class or that of the two oldest Asian American groups" (1992, 176) and she calls for efforts "to bridge the class, ethnic, and generational chasms dividing Asians in the United States" (p. 175). I follow the spirit of Espiritu's arguments here but hope to interrogate somewhat the idea of "bridging." If we consider *The Asian American Comic Book* a bridging effort—or as a narrative toolkit for hopeful bridge makers—it appears that the conjunctive techniques available to us do not simply join disparate elements, but must in fact reshape some elements so that they will be connectable. Mindfulness of the hazards of reshaping or encompassing might yield more sturdy bridges.

I thank Michael Omi for pushing me to clarify this position.

15. Asian American Studies must be receptive to challenge from its "Monicas" as well. What immediately comes to mind here is anthropologist Sylvia Yanagisako's (1992) examination of Asian American history course syllabi, offered in the spirit of constructive criticism and collaboration. However, Yanagisako's critical edge was greeted in Asian American studies with suspicion, and Yanagisako found herself estranged.

Similarly, when a recent issue of *Amerasia Journal* edited by Michael Omi and Dana Takagi (1995) sought to reflect upon the value of different types of theoretical approaches to

Asian American studies, it was quickly dismissed as nonactivist, as intellectual, and therefore of little import to a community-based, activist Asian American studies. Such easy dis-
missals of arguments as "merely theoretical"—not to mention facile binarisms of "theory"
versus "practice"—must surely impede potentially fruitful dialogues in Asian American studies, including ones where new kinds of political and pedagogical "practices" might be
conceived.

References

Anzaldúa, Gloria. 1987. *Borderlands/La Frontera: The New Mestiza.* San Francisco: Spinsters/Aunt
Lute Book Company.
Asian American Resource Workshop (AARW). 1991. *The Asian American Comic Book.* Designed
and illustrated by Wen-Ti Tsen. Boston, Mass.: Asian American Resource Workshop.
Barthes, Roland. 1974. *S/Z.* Translated by Richard Miller. New York: Hill and Wang.
Bhabha, Homi K. 1994. DissemiNation: Time, Narrative, and the Modern Nation. In *The Location
of Culture.* Pp. 139–70. New York: Routledge.
Brown, Wendy. 1995. *States of Injury: Power and Freedom in Late Modernity.* Princeton: Princeton
University Press.
Butler, Judith. 1990. *Gender Trouble: Feminism and the Subversion of Identity.* New York: Routledge.
Collins, Patricia Hill. 1991. *Black Feminist Thought: Knowledge, Consciousness, and the Politics of
Empowerment.* New York: Routledge.
Ebron, Paulla, and Anna Lowenhaupt Tsing. 1995. In Dialogue? Reading across Minority
Discourses. In *Women Writing Culture.* Edited by Ruth Behar and Deborah A. Gordon.
Berkeley: University of California Press.
Espiritu, Yen Le. 1992. *Asian American Panethnicity: Bridging Institutions and Identities.* Philadel-
phia: Temple University Press
Grosjean, François. 1982. *Life with Two Languages: An Introduction to Bilingualism.* Cambridge,
Mass.: Harvard University Press.
Harding, Susan. 1990. If I Should Die Before I Wake: Jerry Falwell's Pro-Life Gospel. In
Uncertain Terms: Negotiating Gender in American Culture. Edited by Faye Ginsburg and Anna
Lowenhaupt Tsing. Pp. 76–97. Boston: Beacon Press.
Jameson, Fredric. 1981. *The Political Unconscious: Narrative as a Socially Symbolic Act.* Ithaca:
Cornell.
Kim, Elaine. 1993. Introduction to *Charlie Chan is Dead: An Anthology of Contemporary Asian
American Fiction.* Pp. xxi–xxx. Edited by Jessica Hagedorn. New York and London: Penguin
Books.
Kondo, Dorinne. 1990. *Crafting Selves: Power, Gender, and Discourses of Identity in a Japanese
Workplace.* Chicago: University of Chicago Press.
Lowe, Lisa. 1991. Heterogeneity, hybridity, multiplicity: Marking Asian American differences.
Diaspora 1(1): 24–44.
———. 1996. *Immigrant Acts: On Asian American Cultural Politics.* Durham, N.C.: Duke Univer-
sity Press.
National Review. 1997. Vol. 24, no. 5 (March 24).
Omi, Michael, and Dana Takagi, eds. 1995. "Thinking Theory in Asian American Studies."
Amerasia Journal 21(1&2).

Ono, Kent. 1995. Re/signing "Asian American": Rhetorical problematics of nation. *Amerasia Journal* 21(1&2): 67–78.

Rosaldo, Michelle Z. 1980. The use and abuse of anthropology: Reflections on feminism and cross-cultural understanding. *Signs* 5(3): 389–417.

Scott, Joan W. 1991. The evidence of experience. *Critical Inquiry* 17 (Summer): 773–97.

Spivak, Gayatri Chakravorty. 1988. Can the Subaltern Speak? In *Marxism and the Interpretation of Culture*. Edited by Cary Nelson and Lawrence Grossberg. Pp. 271–313. Urbana: University of Illinois Press.

Yanagisako, Sylvia. 1992. Transforming Orientalism: Gender, Nationality, and Class in Asian American Studies. In *Naturalizing Power: Essays in Feminist Cultural Analysis*. Edited by Sylvia Yanagisako and Carol Delaney. Pp. 275–98. New York: Routledge.

Contributors

RICK BONUS obtained his Ph.D. in communication from the University of California, San Diego. His forthcoming book, *Locating Filipino Americans: Ethnicity and the Cultural Politics of Space*, will be published by Temple University Press. His research interests are in Asian American studies, Filipino American studies, cultural studies, and race and ethnicity. He is currently an assistant professor at the Department of American Ethnic Studies at the University of Washington.

TIMOTHY KEEYEN CHOY is a Ph.D. student in the Anthropology Board of Studies at the University of California, Santa Cruz. His dissertation research in Hong Kong focuses on legacies of colonialism, capital, and scientific expertise and their articulations in contemporary environmental practice.

MILIANN KANG is a Ph.D. candidate in sociology at New York University. She is finishing her dissertation on the construction of race, class, and gender in Korean nail salons. She has served as a board member for the Committee Against Asian American Violence (CAAAV) and as a consultant to KIWA (Korean Immigrant Workers Advocacy) of Southern California. She helped found APASS (Asian Pacific American Support Program) at New York University.

KAREN LEONARD is a professor with the Anthropology Department at the University of California, Irvine. She is author of *Making Ethnic Choices: California's Punjabi Mexican Americans* (Temple). Her work focuses on caste and ethnicity, family and life history. Currently, she is looking at the construction of identity in the diaspora by emigrants of Hyderabad, India, who are settling in Pakistan, Britain, Canada, the United States, Australia, and the Gulf States of the Middle East.

ANDREA LOUIE is Assistant Professor of Anthropology at Michigan State University. She received her Ph.D. from the University of California, Berkeley. She is currently working on a book that examines issues of diaspora and transnationalism in relation to

American-born Chinese Americans, within the context of mainland China's reopening to the outside world.

MARTIN F. MANALANSAN IV is Assistant Professor of Anthropology at the University of Illinois, Urbana-Champaign. He worked in AIDS prevention education and research for ten years and received his Ph.D. degree in social anthropology from the University of Rochester. His book *Global Divas: Filipino Gay Men in New York City* is forthcoming. He is presently completing a manuscript on death narratives, modernity, and the Filipino diaspora.

GINA MASEQUESMAY is a queer Vietnamese American graduate student in sociology at the University of California, Los Angeles. Her interest is in the intersection of race/ethnicity, gender, class, and sexuality. She is working on her dissertation proposal on multiple identities.

AIHWA ONG is Professor of Anthropology at the University of California, Berkeley. She is the author of *Spirits of Resistance and Capitalist Discipline: Factory Women in Malaysia* (1987) and *Flexible Citizenship: The Cultural Logic of Transnationality* (1999). Her edited volumes include *Bewitching Women, Pious Men: Gender and Body Politics in Southeast Asia* (1995), and *Ungrounded Empires: The Cultural Politics of Modern Chinese Transnationalism* (1997).

KYEYOUNG PARK is an Assistant Professor of Anthropology and Asian American Studies at UCLA. Her book, *The Korean American Dream: Immigrants and Small Business in New York City* (1997), is the winner of the 1998 Outstanding Book Award in History and Social Science from the Association for Asian American Studies.

LOUISA SCHEIN teaches anthropology at Rutgers University and specializes in ethnicity, gender, sexuality, and transnational processes. Her book *Minority Rules: The Miao and the Feminine in China's Cultural Politics* (2000) on China's post-Mao era is based on fieldwork in China since 1982. Her ongoing research includes a multisite study of Hmong-Miao transnationality for a book on cultural politics in the Hmong/Miao diaspora.

BENITO M. VERGARA JR. grew up in Los Banos, Laguna, Philippines. He is the author of *Displaying Filipinos: Photography and Colonialism in the Early Twentieth Century Philippines* (1995), nominated for the Manila Critics Circle National Book Award in 1996. He is currently finishing his dissertation on the Filipino community in Daly City, California, for a doctoral degree in anthropology at Cornell University.

LINDA TRINH VÕ is an assistant professor in the Comparative American Cultures Department, Washington State University. She is completing her manuscript on Asian American mobilization in the San Diego community. Her work has received support from the University of California Humanities Research Institutes Fellowship and from the University of California Berkeley Chancellor's Postdoctoral Fellowship. She teaches Asian American studies, race and ethnic relations, gender, and ethnography courses.